C000154758

Juliet Fisher is a mother of four boys, one daughter and her trusted Labrador, Hope. Her time is spent busily juggling the demands of working, feeding the family (not always Pizza for breakfast), cleaning, driving to various sports matches and generally running a busy household. Juliet enjoys swimming, meditation, running, drawing and writing. When time allows, she loves nothing better than to share a good bottle of wine and delicious food with friends and family.

I would like to dedicate this book to my wonderful children who are my absolute world, my amazing family and all the friends that have made my life so exciting thus far. I would especially like to dedicate this to my mother, father, siblings and my grandmothers Elizabeth-Ann and Jean for their unwavering love, guidance and support throughout my life. Also, to my late auntie P, who inspired the title 'Growing Wings'.

Juliet Fisher

GROWING WINGS

The Honest and Unabridged Diaries of a
Businesswoman, Wife and Mother

*To Brian
Enjoy the book.
Always,
Juliet*

AUSTIN MACAULEY PUBLISHERS™
LONDON • CAMBRIDGE • NEW YORK • SHARJAH

Copyright © Juliet Fisher 2023

The right of Juliet Fisher to be identified as author of this work has been asserted by the author in accordance with sections 77 and 78 of the Copyright, Designs and Patents Act 1988.

All rights reserved. No part of this publication may be reproduced, stored in a retrieval system, or transmitted in any form or by any means, electronic, mechanical, photocopying, recording, or otherwise, without the prior permission of the publishers.

Any person who commits any unauthorised act in relation to this publication may be liable to criminal prosecution and civil claims for damages.

All of the events in this memoir are true to the best of the author's memory. The views expressed in this memoir are solely those of the author.

A CIP catalogue record for this title is available from the British Library.

ISBN 9781528999243 (Paperback)
ISBN 9781528999250 (ePub e-book)

Front Cover Artwork
Sarah Elder
http://www.sarahelderart.com/

www.austinmacauley.com

First Published 2023
Austin Macauley Publishers Ltd®
1 Canada Square
Canary Wharf
London
E14 5AA

A big thank you to my creative writing lecturer for encouraging me to publish my diaries and believe in myself, to teachers throughout my educational journey that inspired me, to work colleagues past and present for your leadership and camaraderie and to my Grow Group for their unwavering support and friendship.

Hello, my name is Juliet and this is my story.

'Growing Wings' is a collection of my diary entries covering an 18-year time span from 1998 to 2016…

It follows the ups and downs of my life: university, work, career, travel, relationships and the ebbs and flows of finances.

This journey sees marriage, becoming a mother, divorce, suicide and surviving parenting the 'famous five'. It sees me being a student, an employee, a business owner, an employer.

Like so many, I have experienced my fair share of love, laughter, and heartbreak. And in both the happiest and saddest moments of those times, my diary was my constant. It was my confidante, my therapy, my friend.

I started my first diary in 1990 aged 11 and, 33 years on, I am still writing today. Back then it seemed like a small experiment, but somehow it evolved into a journey that I never expected. I soon realised the more I wrote and expressed, the more I was cracking the foundations and experiences of life. It was a first clue in discovering me.

The 'Growing Wings' journey starts in Switzerland, with me being an enthusiastic18 year old university student who is embracing all that life has to offer and more. I am at the start of my Business Management Degree; and ready to take on the world!

This book ends with me as a busy 37-year-old mumtrepeneur, still on that journey of discovering who I really am...

These moments of contemplation, musings, doodles, lists and slightly incoherent ramblings are lifted directly from the diaries. This book is not a novel with fictional characters and perfectly scripted story lines. It is a real and honest and authentic account of a period of my life – warts and all! The only editing of the diary entries has been the removal of names and some physical places.

I am Juliet. I am a mother, sister, daughter, grand-daughter, godmother, friend, auntie, niece, cousin and so much more. Thank you for choosing to read this book. I hope it brings you both great enjoyment and comfort and I look forward to sharing with you further, the twists and turns of my life's journey in the sequel…God willing.

This is my journey. This is my story.

Love,
Juliet x

"My dreams are my wings, I am learning to fly."

- Purvi Raniga

www.julietfishercreatives.com

CHAPTER 1

Swiss Injection

"A woman who walks in purpose doesn't have to chase people or opportunities. Her light causes people and opportunities to pursue her." —Anon

Wednesday, 28th January 1998

I woke up this morning in an excellent frame of mind. I decided to finish the section of my diary that I didn't complete last night because I fell asleep. It's awful; I've decided I don't share enough with my book. I don't go deep into how I want to express myself. I don't think my hand can convey the messages.

Anyway I received a letter from Auntie today – it was lovely to hear from her. It was such a relief to hear an English person. The gossip going on back home!

Lunch was particularly dull today. I was put on a table with 5 girls who only spoke French. I really did not enjoy their company. I could tell they were engrossed about blokes and painting nails. Not my cup of tea. Blokes yes!! But fingernails…

I reckon some people were looking and thinking weird thoughts. Why do I always have such a complex? On Sunday I think I'm going to go to Montreux with my letters and work and possibly go to the cinema. Relax and do my own thing. That's what I love!

Good night, sleep tight.

Thursday, 29th January 1998

I want to get good work experience, probably in London. Must go and organize the skiing trip tomorrow. Exhale any negative emotion I'm carrying today.

Friday, 30th January 1998

Grabbed my swimming stuff and headed on my bike off to the swimming pool. The air was chilly and refreshing. Swam for about 45 minutes and cycled leisurely back along the pier. It was pretty to view the mountain, lake and ambiance of the town. People all doing their separate tasks, leading their lives.

I really enjoy my own company; I can do whatever I feel like. No one will look, view or judge me. And if they do, they will not remember it and it won't affect my life in any way!

Saturday, 31st January 1998

My dear Lord, there is a meaning for each one of us to have a place to live on this planet, but are we designed to be loved and cherished by the ones we like? The freedom of the slopes, speed, adrenaline, excitement, weather unbelievable…

I loved it! I had such an enjoyable and memorable day.

EXCELLENT!!

The afternoon went by radically quickly. I did worry about what I looked like in my ski suit, and I did feel quite like a robot, but hey, I shouldn't care. I'm just me. I know within myself here I am not me. Everyone else seems to be having a great time; I just do not want to join in. I am happy in my own company.

I keep asking myself I am too young to get involved deeply? I mean what shall I do? Write him a letter, phone call? I plan all the time; the future is always laid out in my sensible fashion.

1st February 1998

It's the start of a new month. I finally woke this morning, not in a rush. Just to take life at my own pace. The morning was peaceful– no one was about. I had a marvellous view of the lake and mountain. I felt totally at ease.

2nd February 1998

Such an amazing evening, with stunning views overlooking the lights of Montreux and the lake. The rich deep night... Breathing in my thoughts.

3rd February 1998

Another lesson on Tourism today which certainly dragged on! I really lost interest. I never normally do. Anyway, classes finished and I managed to sign myself in for an early supper, so my dear friend and I munched happily and then headed to the pool. I love our little gossips. We do try and build confidence inside each other. We both know what we like and don't like and also what we miss.

We are both great home lovers and I don't think we have quite let go of the past. My reckoning anyway! We are both free and open with each other. We chatted about our days. How we were feeling. I imagine all the negativities expiring away replaced with purity and calmness. Succeed and pleasure.

I tried to call him tonight, but sadly he had gone out. The first time in a long time apparently. I wondered what has happened to him. I miss him with a great passion. I want to be with him, share my life, stories and heart. But I reckon he is out partying, drinking, chatting up the ladies, making me jealous over here. Then again, we are still very young.

4th February 1998

I had French all day today. The entirety of it all…

I ventured down to classes and I was actually the first one there – I needed to be for goodness sake. I need to make a professional appearance in my professional life! The day continued French, French and more French.

The party was fun though. I must admit, I got very tiddly. Not be sick and very ill drunk, but a lot. I was happy knowing that there were people to chat to, who I could dance with, not that the dancing was extremely lively, but hey you cannot have it all. Lots of friendly faces and wine to drink. I was content. I got chatted up, naturally. I also naturally flirted but for god's sake we only live once.

Please wake up tomorrow young lady...

VERY IMPORTANT. NEW TIMES.

Love yourself and live for the present!

5th February 1998

What was I writing last night?? I reckon I was a little drunk…

I woke this morning feeling very composed. I was actually looking forward to seeing how everyone was. The morning after the night before... In their own words, recovering!

I must admit my mind did drift when we were talking about hoovers! I thought it might be nice to get into drawing while I am here; it's an artist's opportunity.

I needed fresh air so headed down for a swim. When I finished I cycled along the pier, absorbing the rays from the sun, and looking at the passers-by in my world. I got very involved and forgot about all my worries. It's my life here.

I spoke to him today and he sounded in good form and was actually beginning to do something with his life. How marvellous. I still feel very strongly for him and because there is no one that knows him here it is so difficult to talk about him, because they will be bored.

I am enjoying myself here. It is a wonderful opportunity to meet all these new people and to study and do things with my life. I just cannot wait to travel around, venture into the unknown and live there, have my babies, and bring them up to be strong and healthy individuals. Sleep well.

6th February 1998

My dearest diary, I am really beginning to love it here. The people. The place. I don't need to get attached; I can survive alone and enjoy the company of others. I basically rose and thought about who I had to write letters to back in England. I cycled back into Montreux along the lakefront, it was beautiful – the sun was setting. It was a special end to a special week. I loved it. If life carries on like this (which I pray it will), I am extremely fortunate. Pray that it will be, that it does. I miss everyone back home of course, but at this moment in time everything dawned upon me, this life is mine. I am adapting to my new situation and I am going to make the most of it.

Saturday, 7th February 1998

I had a wonderful day. I thoroughly enjoyed myself. All happening and I am still breathing. Anyhow, take care and live for the present Juliet.

Sunday, 8th February 1998

Cycled along the pier admiring the stunning scenery.
I am going to get back into my art while I am here. There is so much beautiful hidden architecture.

Monday, 9th February 1998

I cycled along the promenade; it was such a beautiful morning, fresh and calm. The air was new and still untouched, but it was still early when I caught the Fini up.
Supper was okay. I was with a group of chaps from Lebanon. They are a funny crowd. All such fun. After supper I worked really hard revising. It was actually a great system, be organised. Then I headed up to bed and organised everything for tomorrow. Good luck Juliet.

10th February 1998

Food and Beverage exam. It was all right, only my mark will tell me. See what happens. Anyway gave us an extended lunch break. We sat on the terrace, very calming admiring the stunning scenery. I must admit we are so fortunate with the view here. It is incredible, never ever looks the same.

Tourism test followed in the afternoon. I tried to answer everything but I reckon I made up a lot of bullshit. No one appeared very happy to be truthful.

Wednesday, 11th February 1998

We had a group trip to Geneva and visited two hotels. The Ramada a five-star hotel in downtown Montréal close to the lake though, and the Movenpick, which is an airport hotel.

I trekked off to the lake. It was such a beautifully sunny day and warm as well for February – I could not miss the opportunity. I ventured off not knowing where I was until I recognised the train station. I looked and viewed the various people on my travels, again in different directions, backpackers, men and women shoppers, young and old mothers with their babies and grown-up children, the odd roller skater and dog walker. It was a random occasion, but I just breathed in the fresh air, absorbed how lucky I was and how grateful to my parents I am. It was a truly memorable experience. Geneva is such a lovely beautiful clean city; a mixture of old and new, all very exciting.

Saturday, 14th February 1998

HAPPY VALENTINE'S DAY!

The sunrise this morning was so calming. The colours over Lake Geneva were pure and pastel. I saw the birds flying low over the surface; it was picturesque. I breathed, didn't say a word – just saved it for future moments. The journey lasted half an hour. I was anxious to get on the slopes, feel the adrenaline; the excitement was uncontrollable. I managed to keep my calm.

When we got back I cycled along the promenade. It was dark and peaceful. I felt as if I was the only person around – that was until I cycled into the heart of Montreux. There must have been a concert on because a lot of groups and individuals were dressed up for an occasion.

I am choosing my destiny. God has created it for me. I had a wonderful day today.

Many options to choose from... I could have gone to France, I could have flown home, and I could have even gone to see Spain. I chose to go skiing... I lost my ski trousers and I broke my bindings, but hey, shit happens! I enjoyed myself, not enough that my heart was fluttering, but enough that I could give a smile to every random person I met.

I cannot stand people asking me what is wrong with time, even if this is the evening of Valentine's Day. I am 19 years old and sitting in a local self-service restaurant viewing what is happening around me. Just people watching: couples out eating, children with grandparents, lonely men with beer and fags, and an overworked manageress! I very much doubt I would be any happier. I don't belong to anyone, I don't have much to say to anyone, I believe that I am here to succeed, and work hard. I plan my input and output in everything I do!

Monday, 16th February 1998

I called home to see what was happening back there. Quite a lot it seems. I am actually going to have to call home tomorrow and tell mum to call Easy Jet! I hope she does. I had better depart off to bed. I am absolutely knackered. This evening was excellent fun, we all got thoroughly drunk. Had fondue etc. It was great fun. It was splendid! It will be fun tomorrow too. Sure of it. Sleep well.

Saturday, 21st February 1998

I drew for a while. Breathing in the air, contemplating life. Communing with nature. Enjoying the essence of my whereabouts. It was warm; the sun was shining. I was perfectly content. I cycled back up to Glion and went to the club. We caught the train down and chatted and chatted. Supper at the Grand Cafe. The crème of crème.

Sunday, 22nd February 1998

Rain was tipping outside this morning. I felt I could just curl up all day. But no, it was not to be. I changed into my comfy clothes, and cycled in the rain. I felt as if I was back in my old ways. Through rain or shine, I was doing what I set out to do.

I telephoned him this evening. He seemed on good form. I didn't really know what to say to him, just wittered fascinating conversation, but we spoke for about an hour. He decided that he will have to come out soon. I cannot wait, although I don't really mind if I see him or not because I am focusing myself to this course here, which is a lot more necessary.

Monday, 23rd February 1998

My dearest diary, what happens today?

Well, I stupidly fell off my bike, and I have the evidence to tell me so! Oh, well. It felt rather like a dream. I cycled back along the promenade in the pouring rain. I could see the snow line. It was as if I was giving myself a geography lesson. Called home. I certainly am looking forward to seeing them all and hugging my special mother, my heroine. I spoke to JC. He sounded on good form. I really miss him and he said he was coming home especially for the weekend to see me. I was touched.

Thursday, 26th February 1998

My dearest friend, I don't know what happened in the aura of everyone today, but it certainly was strange. Do my work most importantly and in some strange fashion care about the people around me. I miss getting into people's inner hearts and I reckon this is annoying. I don't want to interpret or be nosy, just share an ear and not a mouth.

I didn't feel quite in the mood for partying, too many discussions going on. I wish everyone would live in peace and harmony.

Sleep well, Juliet.

Friday, 27th February 1998

I am flying home today; it seems unusual, and I have no butterflies and excitement. Of course, naturally, I am dying to see everyone.

Saturday, 28th February 1998

I woke in my bed this morning; it did feel rather strange. Like normal, I told myself it was my day; I am going to make the most of it. Enjoy it and enjoy the company of people within it. Anyhow I went through my usual jog, when I'm at home that is, and I took the dogs with me. It felt good to release the endorphins.

Sunday, 1st March 1998

It is March already, my goodness where is the year running away to? I do hope that I am making a success of it. I found myself on the floor of the family room. I was slightly confused. I didn't know the time. I must have been on another planet. I certainly felt as if I was. I went out for a jog around the fields, Tinker and Freckles came too. It was such a pleasure inhaling English countryside air.

Tuesday, 3rd March 1998

Very exciting, I received letters today. I love to get letters. It makes me feel wanted.

Wednesday, 4th March 1998

I woke early this morning. I immediately jumped out of bed and jogged into Montreux. It was calm and tranquil. The day was going to prove nothing to be of great remembrance on the weather front; however, it was nice to get some fresh air before the programme of the working day began. I arrived back in time to do some last-minute revision and get back in time to prepare my room and dress. Organised plans to go to Milan in a few weekends. Should be excellent. Take care. Keep the spirit up.

Friday, 6th March 1998

I woke up this morning in a most positive frame of mind. I felt tired yesterday; I just needed to have a good day. The morning started before lessons of room divisions, I got slightly side-tracked, got into artist mood, and I drew a picture. It was a change of scenery from normal people. We had a lovely meal in a rather crappy restaurant although I did have some delicious pasta. We chatted about languages, Russia, drugs, people. It was pleasant. Don't judge a book by its cover. Once dinner had finished, we wandered around to various clubs, cafes, bars, etc. I didn't drink very much, but hey, I had better disappear to my bed before I???

Sunday, 8th March 1998

My body clock was not me! My swimming was good, very productive.

Wednesday, 11th March 1998

My goodness, I have the whole day of French today. I dressed and gathered everything together, and ventured down to the dining room at 8.15. I saw the notice board for jobs in London, one at The Four Seasons, I would like to do it; gave me something to think about all day.

I realised we were organising details about the Milan trip. Should be cool spending the weekend in a hotel in Milan. I do pray that I will do well in the test tomorrow. I 'will' and must succeed! Good luck!

Thursday, 12th March 1998

This morning I woke immediately, and in my regular robot mode, I dressed and went to finance; an exam first thing – excellent. It put my mind seriously into mathematical focus for the remaining day. The exam took me just over an hour. Lunch was nouveau cuisine style; extremely small portions but very tasty.
He drove me down to the pool...he is so kind. He even offered me a trip to Paris this next weekend. I wasn't sure.

Friday, 13th March 1998

Friday the 13th and the end of the week again, my goodness, doesn't time fly. The whole week of exams is over now. Excellent. I woke this morning in a pretty good frame of mind.
We got our passports checked, it was unreal seeing so many different passports all at once, English, Mexican, Greek, Norwegian, Brazilian, French, Italian, it was cool. All different stamps visas, etc. We arrived in Milan at 11.20 and caught a taxi to the hotel. There were many sexy men around. Seriously watchable. I could be a people watcher if I had more time here. Everyone travelling in their directions, even me on mine!

Saturday, 14th March 1998

I had the worst night's sleep last night.
The tube was quite eventful none of us knew anything; however, we managed to find some good shops. The morning progressed away. Milan's first impressions were smoggy, unclean, old people. All the people look similar especially la fillies. There were a lot of Italian stallions. Milan certainly, 'Is the only city where men dress better than women'.
We wandered around admiring garments that were way above my bank balance and others that satisfied and others that I would never even consider. We went to the great Cathedral in the centre of Milan. The enormity of it was incredible. The

structure and architecture were out of this world. We ventured off to eat lunch in a typical Italian restaurant. Pasta and ice cream.

I am writing all this now outside a café, 'Bar-Da-del Corso', for lunch on Sunday 15th March. It is lovely; we are admiring men and giving them gazes of perfection. It was such fun.

Sunday, 15th March 1998

What a day, I don't know where it went to; everything was rather a daze.

Caught the metro into the centre of Milan, to where the cathedral was. We were all shattered and wandered off to find a café. We managed to get a place on the street, serious people watching, yummy baguettes. We wandered up and down the street, window shopping and admiring guys, which seriously were TOO sexy for their own good!

The afternoon was peaceful, I enjoyed my time, and we sat in the middle of the square in front of the cathedral. I got out my pencil and started drawing. It caught quite a lot of attention; I was surprised. Lots of guys came up and stayed for ages, talking, trying to communicate in Spanish, Italian, French, German, and English, it was quite a laugh.

We caught the metro to the train station, got drinks and food for the journey home. Jumped on the train at 6 o'clock and travelled and travelled until we arrived back at Glion. Many people personalities to see, arts to be drawn, postcards to be written.

CHAPTER 2

WHAT THE HELL

I have had some confusing moments lately.

I'm Gonna Wing It...

"—me, about something I most definitely should not wing." —Anon

Tuesday, 17th March 1998

What a day. It started early with finance. I stupidly did not do very well in my test, I was actually quite depressed but hey, you know shit happens my life still goes on.

See what is happening on the home front. Not much by the sounds of it. But hey! Shit, I love doing nothing at home. Mummy sounded really well. I really do miss her and of course Papa!!!

Thursday, 19th March 1998

Karaoke night started early for us guys, 7.00 with dinner *et beau coup de barrions*. It was immense fun, the whole evening, lots of laughs, which was great. Brilliant laugh! Far too much drinking, smoking, snogging, but hey, I am living it all plus enjoying it a lot! Keep it up.

Friday, 20th March 1998

My dearest diary I don't really know what I did to deserve today. I was totally gifted with the attitude, of making it to my classes, being happy and participating. Everyone was feeling particularly hung over. The morning after the night before... We all had a great time though!

Saturday, 21st March 1998

I have been naughty. I am writing this on Sunday evening, it is just I didn't sleep in school last night and I couldn't lug my diary around with me everywhere. Anyway, Saturday morning, I was tired, but I managed to go for my regular swim, followed by a touch of necessary shopping shampoo etc. It was such a glorious day; I didn't think anyone would be in a bad mood (apart from of course, the train drivers in Montreux, Glion and Caux). I went for lunch. I just love to sit and observe the people. It is fascinating, the young, middle, and old; everyone in their own separate lives. I just find it interesting, seeing adaptation.

Sunday, 22nd March 1998

What a lovely day. I woke up early, to just appreciate the silence and peacefulness of the morning. I was content and didn't feel as if I was imposing at all. I LOVED IT. A Sunday morning to remember...

I pottered around, made the beds, tidied up slightly, left a note, and got on with my morning activity. Swimming was next on my agenda.

Wednesday, 25ᵗʰ March 1998

What is tomorrow going to portray?

Well, I was extremely impressed with what I had accomplished today. I thought spontaneously a lot. I enjoyed the moments and felt many different emotions. But hey, that's what the day must consist of I reckon!

Helping all mankind. Why generations can succeed. We had a Venezuelan talk, which was fascinating. My heart was touched so deeply that it made me feel that one, I repeat, one person can do much and next semester I am going to do it! I love it here and I always must read back on this when I am feeling low. There is much greatness in the world and I will be one to produce it. I must do this. I reckon it is my destiny. My lord, it must be! Please tell me it is no regrets and no questions not answered. Great enlightenment.

Thursday, 26ᵗʰ March 1998

I know that this time a month ago I was sitting under a tree in the darkness in a hotel garden, admiring the immensely touching view of Montreux and the deep contemplation of my positioning here on this planet. I really would love to express my deepest inner passions and for everyone around me to realise that I am an individual. I expect a few do already. I must admit I must give more of myself. I am incredibly fortunate to have been given the opportunity, seriously, of a lifetime. I will make the utmost of my stay here. Attend every course with enthusiasm and heart.

I watched Romeo and Juliet this evening. Again, my soul was touched. I adore love stories. I felt quite lost. I had no one to turn to and express my feelings, but hey, I believe now that this is my key to success, freedom. I know one day I am going to marry and have lots of little me's! Horror story, I expect!!! I would just love a piece of me to love the world more and for the world to love them more also.

Anyway, today was different. I did feel slightly isolated, alone.

Friday, 27th March 1998

I know this night that I am not going to be able to express everything I feel on paper.

I just would like to commence by saying that I am immensely fortunate to have been placed here on this planet. And I hope for the ultimate drive and will to make everyone around me appreciate who I am and what good I want to portray to my environment.

The day started with red wine tasting. First thing on a Friday morning at 8 o'clock, it was quite a hurdle to climb, considering I have always told myself never to touch alcohol when I first wake up in the morning!

Saturday, 28th March 1998

I cannot believe that the twins are now two years old today. The time has flown fast, where has it gone?

I got on a bus up to Verbier. I found the chalet easily. I went on a random wander and looked at the shops, the individuals, families, groups, children coming back from their day skiing, the roaring drinkers and the calmer passers-by.

Sunday, 29th March 1998

An excellent day skiing, new parabolic skis were great for perfect turning. It was super! Perfect sunny conditions. Almost shorts on the slopes!

Monday, 30th March 1998

I worked a shift at the Garmin. It was hard work standing on my feet all day.

Tuesday, 31 March 1998

I do not have a great deal to enter into my diary today. Not much actually happened. I unfortunately didn't receive any post but hey I can't all the time. I was actually more worried about the job applications.

Thursday, 2nd April 1998

I got an interview with the London Hilton, and this made me radically excited. I will calm down a lot though. I certainly do not want to jump the gun or count the chickens before they hatch. Organised the flight home.

Friday, 3rd April 1998

Had a pleasant walk by the lake, a refreshing dip in the pool, and a warming and cleansing shower, followed by the afternoon events. It was good fun although I knew nothing that was going on in my academic world. I WILL start paying more attention.

Saturday, 4th April 1998

Cold, windy, no view and sleet. Oh well. I have had a great season though.

Sunday, 5th April 1998

The day looked glorious and ended up being very special. Lots of wonderfully touching moments occurred. I love everyone. Everyone is unique and has some meaning in my heart.
I adore and cherish my family and thank my God for creating me and allowing me to live.

Wednesday, 8th April 1998

The touch and tingle, I miss the smiles and flirting moods. I had a special day. I drove up to Caux, it was tranquil and astounding to admire the lake in its splendour and beauty; I love my life, I seriously do! I hope and I know that I will endeavour each of my new tasks with effort and I will enjoy each passing moment. That is my quest. Success!!!

Thursday, 9th April 1998

Today started with finance...which was rather confusing with a slight hangover. I managed to give everyone an Easter egg to wish them a Merry Easter. Traditional Easter eggs. Then R&D which I must admit was particularly dull. Didn't interest me in the slightest. I contributed though.
Lunch was delicious, yummy chicken. I phoned home to make sure someone was picking me up and I spoke briefly to my honey bunny. He sounded well. Computers completed my schoolwork before Easter. We were doing excel, it was interesting, even managed to organise the photocopied stuff for the Hotel Project. Drove up to Caux while listening to gorgeous music; it was beautiful, the full moon, etc., perfect situation!

Friday, 10th April 1998

The flight was easy; I slept all of it. Perfect – just what I needed.

16th April 1998

What an especially lovely Easter break. I cannot believe how radically fast it went. I was rather busy, but it was excellent: airport pick up, lunches, work, birthdays, shopping, interview, swimming, return flight.

Monday, 20th April 1998

Finished off the project. I even got my swimming in and read down by the lake for a while. The day progressed. I tried to squeeze in as much work as possible, recorded some tapes and went shopping.

Tuesday, 21st April 1998

Bordeaux wines. I really would like to become a wine entrepreneur. Oh, well, see what life must offer first.

I drove to the swimming pool afterward instead of lunch, which was an excellent break. I tried to wash the car, proved quite impossible and we went for a drink at the Mayfair, checked out sexy dark men! Admiring the sunset... It was gorgeous, stunning, astounding colours. Met for fondue, good gossip, etc. It was lovely, everyone got back into the swing of things. Loved it. The whole evening was splendid. I very much enjoyed it, plenty of giggling, partying, enjoying a happy and very content mood.

Wednesday, 22nd April 1998

Jumped in the lake; took a few pictures. I felt refreshed and ready afterwards. I am pleased I can manage to do these kinds of abnormal activities. It adds to individuality. I drove up to Caux, and took a random little alley and discovered a very peaceful spot. It was lovely, I am going to just do work, be alone, appreciate Ma vie!

Thursday, 23rd April 1998

Dear Father, what is my destiny here, which road am I meant to choose, which door should be wide open? I love everywhere I am and at present I believe that I am focussed, but no one is telling me.

Am I lying to myself?

What am I doing?

I believe that I am confused. I say what I say and do what I do. All the time I am occupied. I love it.

Do you think that the Hilton is going to accept me? I really do enjoy the London life, the scene.

I then had an interview with the Hyatt in Orlando. It was all right, I was rather chatty. I wish I had spoken like that in London, but hey, it is different and it's over.

Friday, 24th April 1998

Headed off to France, we firstly stopped at McDonald's, and I drove for four hours. It was pretty when we left at dusk heading towards midnight, it was darkness nearly all the way, rather irritating and kept me focussed on driving. Also, the guys were funny, but they had beer on the mind. Incredible! We eventually reached Dijon at 12.00 and found our hotel and the nightlife. Chaps, we were sorted.

I got carried away dancing. I eventually hit the sack in at about 5.00 knowing that I must wake up in three hours…

Saturday, 25th April 1998

What an immensely marvellous day! It started extremely early. I had a shower and woke the guys, who did nothing but fire abuse at me. I just told them – if you are not ready by nine, then I will leave without you. Naturally, they fired more crap in my face; I just took it with no relevence to my life whatsoever. Fortunately, they were prepared, and we set off through the Burgundy region. Dijon all through the Cote des nuits, Cote St George, Cote de Beaune, Cote Chalondis, Lermarsanne and the Beaujolais. It was staggering admiring the vines, the vineyards, and especially the châteaus; we stopped at various suppliers and chatted. It was great fun, always a new laugh,

Sunday, 26th April 1998

I tried and tried to learn the wines from the Bordeaux, Burgundy, Cotes de Rhône, Switzerland wines. It was interesting, however a lot of hard work.

I reckon to finish it with him is the best thing to do. I will remember him forever, but this chapter of the book in my apartment department is over. I love my independence and I am just going to keep that for the time being, succeed on my level.

The chaps were really understanding, I felt secure and trustworthy with them. It was strange there being three blokes to talk to instead of four girlies. I have no physical feelings with them, purely friendship. No more! I know that this is the correct solution. My future holds pleasing and positive surprises. I love my life. CONVINCING???

Tuesday, 28th April 1998

Dearest diary
What a day…

Thursday, 30th April 1998

I won the computer prize – a lovely pen, which I am writing with now and the gorgeous Glion bags. Splendid.

Saturday, 2nd May 1998

Interview, swimming, eating relaxing, chatting, supper, group discussions, etc. Wonderful stuff.

Monday, 4th May 1998

MY LORD, WHAT A DAY!

Please may I just love myself for who I am? I am having an amazingly fortunate life. I love it immensely and I just wish for one moment that I have the confidence for everyone to love me. I know that no one is perfect, and I am far from it. Please can you send me some sign that I am making a success of my life. Please?

Tuesday, 5ᵗʰ May 1998

My goodness, I really didn't feel like scribbling in my diary this evening; basically because I didn't know what to write. I just don't know how I feel. How I even want to feel.

What am I meant to do with my life God? Perhaps I'm taking the easy option by asking you and making you decide when the decisions are my own. Whether I will get out of bed tomorrow, it is me who chooses.

Well the day was pretty excellent fun I had a wickedly excellent time.

It was the first day in the kitchen, lots of joking around.

Wednesday, 6ᵗʰ May 1998

Are we going through a strange moon sign now? I have been feeling dreadfully strange all week and I just don't comprehend!

I want to make a success of my life, a leader converting my companions from nastiness to the pureness of everyone. Bad to good.

What is my life, my destiny, my choice? How can I make decisions?

I know it's for me to decide when I'm meant to do. I tried to be perfect and please each person I meet throughout my life, but is it seriously necessary? Perhaps I must be able to stand my ground. Respect the person inside of me for a change.

I mean, why should I care what I write in here? No one is ever going to read it anyway. I don't need to impress people and neither myself in the words and sentences I collect and scatter on paper.

Remember always to care for individuals; we all have hearts and souls that easily damage. Seriously, I don't know what I have written, but I just want to add that I have had a smashing day.

Thursday, 7ᵗʰ May 1998

What is happening in my life?

I don't know. I feel as if I have a front on the whole time.

Am I lying to myself or my friends?

Everything I pretty much say it's the truth, my problems, my life, what I have done. Just what I say I think is being judged or perhaps I'm judging myself Lord, I don't know anymore...

The day started early in the kitchen; I was in the pantry. It was fun, tiring, and frustrating.

Friday 8th May 1998

I again was in rather a strange mood, perhaps it was because I was so focused on my book, I couldn't snap out of it.

Saturday, 9th May 1998

The kitchen was slightly annoying; our teacher spoke no English. I mean okay, my French is improving, but he was mean, horrible.

Everyone was being gentle, relaxed, and calm. I don't know and analysing this is not even helping. I did feel very deeply about it. Engrossed at moments throughout the evening. I love the intensity, the slight-know how you feel but not the new company again; it was interesting to settle back and watch it on occasions and to participate sometimes. Then possibly the feeling that they were analysing you from what you had just said. Then they think of life in the same manner. At times, we agree and have a good giggle, or possibly sometimes, we don't know fuck.

Perhaps I just read into things too deeply?

Sunday, 10th May 1998

It was lovely dawning this morning. The sun was bright, I knew I was going to have a peaceful day: relax, think, read, do the things I enjoy. Swimming, my interaction with other people. I love to think, never drawing the lines with the thoughts that are buried inside my mind.

No one must grab these moments, these thoughts. You prefer keeping them to yourself. Then knowing what you are going to do in the next few moments, minutes and it works. I reckon it's incredible how other people operate. The way that each of us has been put here 'I reckon by God's creation' but then because there are many people that do not believe in God.

So, I mean what is our guide?

Probably each other... The communication with one another is immense. I think it staggering how many different cultures in such a unit interact, mix; I love it. The intensity of each passing day and what occurs. The meals, the moments in the club, everyone manages to be here. They know there is togetherness. The people whose names I don't know and haven't bothered finding to know then again, I would like to! What's going to come of it I think? Might it be an asset or liability you never know! No one knows what the future is going to hold.

Getting onto what I did today – my swim, brunch, washing, reading, sunbathing, swimming, driving, spliff, bedtime, sorted things out for tomorrow!

Monday, 11th May 1998

Allow me to entwine myself with today's events. The monotonous day of facing the teacher, being taught, wanting to just achieve, I must struggle through it until the end!

The completion of my lifetime here at Glion, what am I to do? Am I choosing my destiny here?

I know that I am too focussed on my thoughts and feelings and expression of needing to find myself. I read and act too deep.

What is my outside emotion, what aura do I portray? Am I seriously unlikeable? Just uncommunicative? Possibly I have nothing to convey to the exterior world?

I dream that I am going to achieve. Innocence will overcome one day. Perhaps I am always going to be a scared little mouse, unsure whether I will get caught out in my actions? Who knows!

I miss my companions at home, but my life is here now.

What am I expected to do? How am I expected to do it?

There are many random people in the universe. How am I meant to know their perception of life? The people who think they know it all get to a level of pure extravagance. My mind was blown up, caught in a crossroads.

DIRECTIONS! WHAT IS MY DIRECTION?

Which door is open? Which door has opportunities or mishaps behind it…? Always stay interested and keen. Love everyone, even your enemies. Who are my enemies???

I must sleep. Shed some excess energy and wake bright and sparkly for tomorrow.

Tuesday, 12th May 1998

What a day in the life of me, I love my thoughts and feelings, and the motivation I have in writing each evening. It's a shame that I don't find the time to convey more messages. I had to wake early this morning because I was in the kitchen all day. I was rather shut off from the outside world as well. There are people everywhere on the planet who don't communicate with others. I have been fortunate enough to enjoy and participate in many moments. It is different from being alone and striving for yourself. A challenge I reckon.

I wish I was able to be loved by everyone. Be perfect. Naturally, finding happiness is not an art, it is a gift I am perfecting; it is a success, an achievement. I never know what I write in my diary each evening but who cares. No one. Because no one cares what I do, who I really am. It's only when their lives are affected. It's only natural.

Christ, I had a super day today in comparison to last week. I don't know what happened. I felt entwined with pity. I needed help. Not big help, just a chance to express. I wanted to be peaceful, and I was, fortunately. But I was alone. Alone in my own anger which I couldn't convey! No politics or religion. You can say that about many different cultures or races; they're black they're white, Lebanese, Italian, French, Spanish, American, Indonesian, Japanese, Chinese, African, German, Norwegian, Indian, Australian, Dutch, Ecuadorian, Kenyan, Tanzanian, Moroccan, English, Scottish, Danish, Irish, Portuguese, Brazilian, Mexican, Cuban.

I don't know but everyone's been brought up differently, obviously, we all react differently in certain situations...

But being stubborn, when it affects others is just ignorant and relies on the person being self-centred and full of self-pity! It's not for me to judge, hey, such is life, and the sphere is continuing to rotate!

I love meeting new and exciting people. Some I never have anything in common with; we just talk. DEEP! People analyse and conclude.

Be natural for yourself...

No one is ever, ever, I REPEAT, EVER going to change that. Even the person you end up with. Your sexual companion! Your physical and mental human being. There is nothing wanting to stop me. It just must be done to capitulate a grasp on tomorrow.

Sleep is proving to be an important aspect of my day...

Wednesday, 13ᵗʰ May 1998

I just got offered a place at the Hyatt Orlando in Florida! It might just be excellent if I take it. I expect I might like it!

But naturally, I will miss everyone of course, but you know I must get on with my life. America is a wonderfully enormous place.

I finished languages and had to set up for dinner.

Thursday, 14th May 1998

I was excited with the prospect of going to Orlando Florida, for my internship. I travelled through the day making the most of each passing moment. I received my fax contracts, which I will sign tomorrow. You never know what's going to happen tomorrow, whenever it is always a mission of suspense.

Saturday, 16th May 1998

The orgasmic feeling of falling into bed this night will not be forgotten.
I woke up early this morning – had to be done!
I think the travelling motions are satisfactory, understanding, seeing, watching the others work. How the school is divided, how we separate into our directions. I think often about what others are doing! Reading, TV, eating, doing sport, working, singing, drinking, smoking, dancing, having sex, driving, art gallery, sailing water-skiing, camping, swimming, writing, communicating, telephone, fax, email, paragliding, hiking, flying, scuba diving, sleeping, smoking, showing off, impressing, dieting, chatting, informing, gossiping, meeting. I don't know what others are doing, but I pray that they are having as stunningly wonderful a life as I am.
I appreciate the bad moments; I can feel how much I must appreciate the good ones. Fucking excellent my survey says.
People are strange. Why do I think that they're strange? Not even the way they act, but in the things they say. Perhaps others think I am weird? I possibly could be. Who else do I know who goes swimming every day, writes letters and read books at any spare moment of the day?
PREOCCUPIED

Monday, 18th May 1998

My lord, what a day!
Had to wake up extremely early this morning to be in the kitchen. I was in the pastry department which is a huge mistake as I didn't stop eating, oh well, shit happens.

Wednesday, 20th May 1998

I couldn't believe how normal I felt this morning. It must have been the swim in the lake that got my enzymes moving.

Thursday, 21st May 1998

Swiss national day today and I must work I didn't mind; we had a lecture about fish all morning, particularly fascinating.

Monday, 25th May 1998

The first day in service, I managed to get my swim in first and the day progressed from thereon. Had to serve lunch and dinner, all good fun but hard work, the lessons are quite tedious and finished at 8.00 in the evening. We went out for our committee supper, which was satisfying. Everyone joined in and what was discussed was productive.

Tuesday, 26th May 1998

Love can touch us one time and last for a lifetime
Confusion is my word of today, I am unsure of the person I'm turning into.
Perhaps, I'm two different people; I am a different kind of person, the adaption.
I feel unmotivated now. It is unlike me, what am I to do with the person I am?
What is my destiny as a person? I know at 19 years old, I shouldn't be asking myself this question, but perhaps for myself, I need a focus. What kind of person or people am I going to share my life with?
What has happened to my three p's?
POSITIVE, PERSONNEL, PRESENT! It is necessary I respect everyone who has got themselves involved in my life.
I am not an easy person, diverse, as one would say. Perhaps satisfaction within each person's heart is what is necessary? Making them feel good, worth it even?
I mean this is a little example of something in my life that I cannot understand.

Wednesday, 27th May 1998

I can't explain what happened today, but it felt like that I wanted to get in touch with another guy. I don't know whether it was through looks, but whatever it was, I felt some attraction for goodness' sake, I don't even know his name, but he is damn lovely.
I mean am I unattractive? Sometimes I just think it must be. I have no contact, my smile is childish and what I say sometimes gets me depressed and back in my mood swings. I am just another random person on this planet, I want people to love and appreciate me. Offer me attention, love, a giggle, or passing

comment. I perhaps think too much, but hey, shit happens. It bought me much courage even to say goodbye to this guy. And when I did, I rushed it and didn't even kiss him. I might just be unusual, subtle...

I might subconsciously be doing it to be different.

Thursday, 28th May 1998

I mean what am I meant to do here? I just want to be noticed/loved for who I am. I love my life so much. I have been given many chances to succeed and perhaps in my subtle ways, I am and not everyone is going to accept me for it. I have energy, it is my exhausting support for others, but hey, I am still me. I'm an individual here on the planet. Perhaps when I am 25/27, God knows what my life is going to be like. I know that God my creator is going to choose it for me, but of course, I am not going to use this. It is my fall back; it is my succession, my achievement, my love home. I vow to thee my entire country and all creation above, it's entire and united and perfect. Service and love I offer.

Saturday, 30th May 1998

My life, the intensity of each passing moment... I love the adaption to be a person in certain environments. Good deeds are always important, interaction and communication of everyone.

What am I personally chosen to do today?

What is my destiny?

Who am I going to be with and why?

What I might be doing professionally wise?

The thoughts that go through your brain – honestly! Engrossed and compact. Precise and you always have answers. I am not going to write anything that happened today, because it is unnecessary.

ADAPTION IS MY WORD...

Sunday, 31st May 1998

Jumped in my car and headed off to the swimming pool. I was relaxed and calm. I just watched people, observed the fathers taking their babies for paddles, the synchronised swimmers, and the regulars. The morning was warm and fresh, but by the time I was down in the club for brunch thunder and lightning crashed and rolled over Lac Leman. It was an incredible change. Everyone was focussed in their individual ways: girlfriends and boyfriends together, the popular guys wanting a break from their studies, knowing that they are wonderful individuals, friends working in kitchen and service enjoying and communicating. It was a break and escape; we chatted and listened to rhythms and beats.

Monday, 1st June 1998

I did the breakfast shift this morning, which was okay. I, fortunately, had the best time to do it. It meant I was off at 10 and then had the whole day to choose what I wanted to do. I still opted for my swim. It was refreshing, gorgeous, and cleared my head.

I could ask him out for supper or something? Get to know him, and he might find out that I'm a regular normal person. Not comparing because everyone here on this planet has a right and notion to be here. And I'm no more special than anyone; I am just me! I suppose I'm succeeding a life in other ways. Motivation. Determination.

I will just be forgotten about. Personally, diary, do you think people are going to know and remember me, or am I just another feather floating in the wind? I love my life immensely, sometimes just too much and I'm beginning to discover my happiness, my life and love, my passion, and understanding. It is steadily taking time. I do however have my eternity in front, who knows what I am going to do and what I'm going to learn from it?

Success? Belief? Mainly believe in you, no one else is going to!

The sun was shining, people relaxing due to the bank holiday, water splashing, watching myself enhancing my life with more freedom to think and the pleasure of my will and motivation.

Tuesday, 2nd June 1998

An aggressive thunderstorm over the lake, enlightening lightning, electric blues, pinks, yellows were seen.

Perhaps I want a man who is going to get me out of myself? I don't have many paranoid and bad feelings, they distress me. What are these negative vibes I portray?

I'm a nervous wreck!

Everyone has nerves; they puncture you, sending pulses arisen through your senses. The movement, the feel...adrenaline, the fighting, and endorphin creating ecstatic emotions. The intense presence of everyone, are we all we have?

And fights to conquer. I love myself and all the people I meet, the passers-by even; they are all stored in my brain somewhere representing my life, feelings, thoughts, comments, suggestions.

Take care Juliet. You must always remember that health is the most important. Be strong always J! Sleep well.

Wednesday, 3rd June 1998

I must die to my fantasies. Nothing is impossible I am me, human and real. Feelings of realisation.

How is it not a dream? What is dreaming?

The unconsciousness of reality? Who knows?

Who explores and defines? Is the truth certain?

The feelings of the real me... confusion within myself! It is far out between you, the outside, and me.

BE CONFIDENT IN YOURSELF. Challenge is your only friend. It is instant and now you show yourself, portray and give what you learn.

Why do I suffer this! I just need to be loved and know. My face wants to grab and attach. I am asking everyone why I am a depressive call, an irritated individual.

Too blind to see the world. Remember and attach.

Destiny is a strange thing, are these the emotions that I should be feeling now? Utter hopelessness and confusion.

WHY AM I NOT SPECIAL, UNIQUE?

I have the character to love and to give everything I have (to an extent).

Fantasies are my reality, why can I not involve others? Because they are not true. Perhaps if you work on it longer, who knows? Then again, why would it happen? Stop asking questions and get some shuteye! You need to be serving at 6.50 tomorrow. Important. It is like a new day at work. Show enthusiasm and motivation, the leadership of perfection.

Thursday, 4th June 1998

I couldn't believe how awful I felt this morning. I dreamt badly and felt like absolute shit. I could not start work; I think perhaps my body had completely packed up and I desperately needed to catch up on some shuteye. I told myself to pull my act together and do the afternoon classes, which I did. I will wake up tomorrow for the kitchen; show that you're motivated, willing and enthusiastic. Tres necessary if you want to pass this part of the course.

I was irritated I think. A lot of it had to do with the heat and I felt as if I had let my enthusiastic side down this morning. Listen to your heart, no one else is going to do it for you. I don't need anyone and I'm strong enough to succeed. I have friends; I have my family, my car, good education, a roof over my head.

Friday, 5th June 1998

Christ, my living, my human self. I had such a great day!! Full of drive, motivation, charisma. I do enjoy my time. My heart is willing to succeed but my brain is trying to confuse such courses. Tonight was incredible, I saw everyone necessary.

It was strange; I knew nothing intimate was going to happen because I would allow my extrovert aura to expand. The sad thing is, he is lovely, dying to be happy, settled, comfortable, but he must realise who he is and what he is doing. Enjoy other such events in life. What about myself? There is nothing I can do to make myself extravagantly happy. Why my wheel will continue to turn, I must have some good here. What is it I am doing to discover it? I hate this moment of jealousy that occurs. It's not jealousy, it is pure analysing. I adore it. It's my conversation in my head. Cruise off in every and any direction. And just love and adore yourself, keep smiling and don't take things for granted.

Sunday, 29th June 1998

It's been a long time since I added anything to this. I have had a rather hectic few weeks but all excellent fun.

The last party at Glion 1998. With the third semesters partying in the Montreux Palace followed by backstage. Everyone had an excellent evening... END OF AN ERA.

Had lunch with friends, all nice but with rather strange attitudes. Couldn't handle the negative minds. I'm content in my little world. It is great to catch up with people again though.

30th June 1998

I am working in a counselling place now. It is interesting, I really am fascinated. I could not work like this all my life though!

All people have problems; it is how you deal with it. I find these people all lovely: alcoholics, drug addicts, etc., but they must find that there is a real life out there. I must admit they do know it, and a lot just want to get away from it. The escape of reality... Back to life! It is a big number if all you have had for the last 20/30 years is pollutant injected into you. And then other people telling you that you're useless.

I love my home life. I am just confused about it all, I haven't been able to relax and calm down. I seem to be the slave. It is making me angry. Why me? There is no right or wrong that is not the answer I reckon. We are all here for ourselves, we involve ourselves in other's lives, but yet they are only additions. We are the only one person who is really going to change the way we think and feel. Others have an influence over this, but people feel isolated by this; they know that they are the only ones that put their heads to rest each night and sum up the day, their life, and the past what can be changed for the better in the future.

I strongly believe that it is good here, he is listening, watching, and guiding my path, this means that I am never lonely, I am always happy in my own company because I natter to myself about life: the scenery, the scenarios that occur. I do love to treasure the passing moments, inhaling and trying never to let go. But if I didn't ever let go that would then be the end, the conclusion of my days. I certainly don't want that to happen yet.

I HAVE MY LIFE TO LIVE, LOVE, AND ADAPT TO!

I want to marry, to succeed in a career. I want to work and be productive and excel in everything I do. I want children. I want to show my breeding with another human that I love passionately. I want them to appreciate the child and accept that he is a father, alone that has to take some responsibility for another person's life for a while. To live in happiness, to entertain, and take pride in my living. It is strange, all our lives.

I am unsure of the future. I think it's a lie. I am focussed; I just am not sure what I want to do quite yet. I want money though; I want a nice car that drives fast. I want a house and I want to travel. I possibly don't want to live in England, I want friends and I want a husband. I want to marry around 25, but I want to analyse situations and always at the end of them sum up what I have seen and whether I agree or not with the outcome.

WHAT IS IT, WHAT IS MY LIFE ALL ABOUT?

I need no one, but I need everyone.

I can live alone but I can live with other people.

I need focus and attention, but I can strive without it.

I really don't know where I go from here; America is the first, then back out to Switzerland again. I am looking forward to seeing everyone out there, I love the people, and they are genuine friends that I have made. I appreciate the company, some of them anyway. I want to chat and go out for supper with random punters, I was happy. I still am happy; it is variably happiness. I love my friends, my colleagues, my desired future, and friends. I love to talk and act and be me.

4th July 1998

A hectic, however, incredibly educational evening. Went to go and see friend's art. Her pieces are of exquisite quality. I have started working at a counselling clinic, where they deal with drug addicts, alcoholics, people with serious problems that they are not able to overcome their fears and anxieties. It is fascinating I am really enjoying it.

10th July 1998

I had this incredible urge to write this evening.

The totality of my unique character. We are all actors and actresses on this planet. The earth will continue to rotate into uncaring of each creative present. We pick and choose for our pallet others as just unable to select.

I loved Buckingham Palace yesterday. I was invited; I was immeasurably touched by such a moment of pure ecstasy! In certain scenarios, it's all different. The adaption of people, the counselling if you want to succeed sometimes, sit back, and listen to people who have other experiences and know something in-depth!

I don't know about my love life either. We had a few memorable nights and days. The times we spent time together, have been a giggle. He is someone with who I could spend some of my life with.

With the power of my person, I can express and dedicate time to others. I believe that I respect others; we are all sheep on the fields being nourished with information being fed back into the ground again. Death a frightening but truthful word, it happens to everyone. That is what each of us all has in common, birth and death; it appears and touches. That's what makes us individuals, are open characters, mind some people don't get that until the gap years. Conservatives and politically minded characters just must keep and live by the books. Rules and regulations, just I think the respect and do it always. Even often, indulge in knightly deeds. It adds spice and amusement and just another occasion, another day completed. Satisfaction. Let's awake tomorrow, with spirit, strength, creation, and success on the mind I rise through and more importantly enjoy!

11th July 1998

Why does my mind wander in that direction? Of course, I have immensely powerful feelings to express in that area! I would love to know whether we are destined to hold one another together through the good and bad.

The one chap who I have really missed...
I don't know how honest I should be with you. I believe that I want to tell you everything (you wouldn't) want to know, just like I wouldn't want to know about you. I naturally want to know that you have been having fun and keep yourself ready (physically fit) but male honesty is the key, you must be truthful with your partner, someone that won't judge you in that department. I think that I am always going to keep you in my mind. I doubt I will have much to say in changing it!

I love my life this far. I am waiting in anticipation of more travel, seeing new people, meeting old friends, focussing on the next step, which is what I am doing at present, but I want to entirely be engrossed.

It will never be the same because no one can remember, although the story will be good, emotional, powerful, entertaining, and always have a memorable conclusion. (Hey, we never remember.)

12th July 1998

I want to go into a higher state of realism.

My life: I live, I hope, I dream, I participate, and I adapt.

I kind of jump to the extremes though. I find that I do have some very magic and memorable moments. Yet I mostly feel failure. Although I really can't be.

I had a lovely day today though. We had lunch at the Jockey Club, a family gathering.

A prediction on my life? Success is my hope. One thing I know is my primary goal is to never be stuck in concrete. Respect one another and honour everyone.

CHAPTER 3

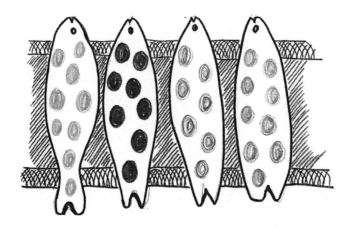

Living the American Dream

"Your Success and Happiness Lies in You."
— Helen Keller

Monday,13th July 1998

My Visa arrived today. What a day. I am moving forward in the best possible way. The American dream for a while. My small amount of success. I want to be a person, be a leader of my rights, my willingness. I would like to be perfect in every perfect way, but it's just not possible.

We all are that is the story. I am no more special than a checkout person in Tesco's or an artist, or a barmaid, or a shop assistant. I am special to some people, some only choose others. If I am selected it's like saying you choose your friends you have your family – at this moment in time.

15th July 1998

I hit quite a depression in my body today. I don't know why, but I kind of knew that I would – very frustrating. I thought it might be a good plan if I wrote a few of my qualities and weaknesses down. Only by being honest to myself I can realise I am not perfect. I want to be perfect, but no one is perfect. Sometimes getting embarrassed, get annoyed with people when they make you look small, sometimes out of control.

What you must do is play the game, fight the battle, and win the wars. I want to be successful. Perhaps I am thinking too much or perhaps I don't have the confidence yet? FEEL ALIVE.

Friday, 17th July 1998

The flight was pleasant. I sat next to a lady who had four children; they must have been quite wealthy. Long stay on the island sounded gorgeous. It was warm when I arrived.

I made love to him passionately; it felt brief and rushed the entire weekend. I miss him incredibly while I've been back in England. How can we get attached over just one weekend? It wasn't perfect, it was unique, and I will treasure it in my heart and soul forever.

Tuesday, 21st July 1998

What an immensely strange day. I had a very special weekend.
I will write about it in a little while...Perhaps another moment in my random life.

I do know the good things always appear in a handshake. I will be happy tomorrow as it is another day.

Thursday, 23rd July 1998

I cannot believe I was meant to be leaving to go to America today.
Dipping occasionally into my other dimension, I opened my heart.

Friday, 24th July 1998

I am enjoying being young!
The freedom of individuality!
The creation of one's passion!
The options and opportunities arising! Taking for our use, our well-being an entirety, the addition to our lives!
I love interaction, movement, unique persons.
We have all lived differently. I enjoy understanding and listening. The pureness and direction are simply heartening.

Saturday, 25th July 1998

Sex, men, ambition, hope, positive attitudes, people, success, girlfriends, food, sport, dinner, parties.
It was nice just to feel one to one and we hardly know each other as intense friends although after today I think differently.
Off to London for housewarming party. The hosts and hostesses are very eccentric.

Sunday, 26th July 1998

King's Road – so interesting to watch the random punters around us: some having been up for hours, others having a coffee and croissant, and reading the Sunday news, others who had just been dragged out of bed.

Monday, 27th July 1998

I always receive tears in my eyes when I part from my mother. I am unable to look her in the eyes and express my love and admiration for her! I love everything that brings happiness to my life.

Thursday, 30th July 1998

Another day on my travels, this time to Florida, and the journey wasn't too dramatic. I plugged into movies to distract me from the exterior world. I remember the time we flew out as a family – a long time ago now.

Friday, 31st July 1998

Another day in the random life of Juliet... It was certainly interesting! I don't even know where to begin. Very out of the blue – the moments that arose...

I cannot describe the events: the swim, gym this morning, letter writing, the walk to the supermarket. Chat, chat, the weather was excruciatingly hot. Music, talking, utter relief.

Tuesday, 4th August 1998

I'm really looking forward to starting work. I am enjoying my relaxation, but I know that it must end someday and soon I will have a routine and regulation. I am looking at it with much determination and motivation, adaption.

Drove to Orlando today, serious tourists! It was lovely, we gossiped, relaxed, walked for miles, had lunch, shopped and I bought a bike. It was charming.

Orlando was pleasant, everyone leading their separate lives, individual characters, and styles: cowboy lookalikes, schoolteachers, bankers, lawyers, librarians, policemen/women, runners, children enjoying ducks and ice cream. We walked through an area of gorgeously hidden houses, beautiful plants, and hidden lives behind closed doors. I was in the pool for a long time this evening. Flirting, giggling, chatting, sunbathing, and absorbing the children's attitude and moment of the day.

I will have children one day; I cannot wait to bring my unique creation into the world with the one I love or not as the case maybe.

Wednesday, 5th August 1998

My final day of freedom for the time being; I had a wonderful time. I woke early to do the gym session. I was particularly fortunate. Who knows the lights will guide the direction one day.

Just good luck tomorrow, appear interested; it is all a learning experience, and this moment tomorrow is the very first impression, make sure it's worthwhile and they think that you are important, unique, and successful, hard-working, determined, individual.

6ᵗʰ August 1998

My induction course today. I reckon it went well. I kind of observed everyone in their different departments how they spend their day and whether they are enjoying themselves in their given tasks that have arisen. The day proceeded steadily! Lots of conference room meetings, people information, uniform fittings, and new employers. I met some nice people. Some were down to earth, some over the top, everyone living there on their levels.

I swam and exercised, watched friends and went to Pleasure Island. I thought about how much this place must make. I must start getting into the moneymaking theme. I want to make a success of my life, money is an object, but I really would like to create something that others enjoy, where I can observe their pleasure and happiness. Maybe a club, a bar, a pub, a restaurant or a resort complex where people can relax?

What a perfect way to start as of today. In the Hyatt induction course, I cannot believe that I am meeting many random people through my days. I mustn't take anything for granted; there are individuals that I can be led astray by. I must focus on my own life, my interpretation, my smile, and contentment. I am unique. And here, so is everyone!

7ᵗʰ August 1998

Gym and swim woke me early this morning. I arrived at my job in good time and ready to face the tasks given. First job was to stock the caddy with sheets, towels, pillowcases, etc.; it was unbelievable the amount of the stuff that was on the trolley and how heavy it was! The heat of the day made me rather frustrated, but I learned to adapt, and I spoke to other trainers who had been doing the job for 20 years plus, commitment or what – I was fed up within half an hour! I simply got on with the situation, listened, and followed instructions. Hopefully, I will be all right doing this. Lunch was a BBQ, was quite surprised, it was the employees' lunch; people were awarded prizes for their achievements. It was great to see and it gave me ideas, but most importantly it made me feel good about the place I was going to be working for the next few months.

Won four cinema tickets. Unreal!

Saturday, 8th August 1998

I do miss everyone back home, but I have managed to adjust and settle out here. I am enjoying it; my first day working properly was long and interesting. Another evolution... I have worked in a variety of establishments and mais wee; I am enjoying the diversity. The life I am leading – making beds and welcoming guests is not the most riveting; however I am earning money from my work. LOOK, LEARN, LISTEN – TRAVEL, EXPERIENCE, GRASP.

13th August 1998

Dearest diary, I haven't been in touch for a wee while, but I've been incredibly busy, living, being in touch with the person whose destiny and achievement I am experiencing.

I had a couple of days off this week, Monday night until Thursday morning; extremely fortunate I might add, what a life God has given me!

I hope it stays like this forever, I know life goes up and down; we experience good and bad times. This adds spice to the days we lead!

I love the pleasure of meeting people, through many different environments but smoking, relaxing the body and the mental exterior – pure involvement in one's day. I wish I could write what's inside my head, how I feel when I listen to music how it affects my emotions; hitting areas of my brain, relating to the atmosphere and adaption.

14th August 1998

Making my parents proud and happy. That's one of my most important goals before I die; they must be pleased.

I will prove to them that I can create the human being of enjoyment, character, charm, individuality, heart, ambition. My ambition is to go a long way in this life. Make people love and trust one another. People to be equal, always unique in their ways, their thoughts, and living. A gift given to me by God. I believe that God is out there, listening, watching, constructing all our people, like the characters in a book.

August 1998

God, I know, is choosing my destiny for me. My life is just travelling. I do however, feel stationary. It must be my housekeeping. People have done this for years. Yes, it is interesting but how do people cope, stay committed, I know money is a big factor, but I am not here for the money. I am here for the experience, learning, observation, what's happening, where, when, why, because, etc. I will get it on a plate soon and present it to the boss. What I'm doing helps.

Identity – within each of us is a loving magical power for being… A real self, cocooning us from our worries enabling that hidden self to emerge.

Christ, I adore your creativity. Individuality. I am going to capture and achieve. I am going to capture and achieve my adventure. The risk is fabulous. The friends you make along the way, the understanding of passing companions.

The intense beauty of my entirety. I love my creation. Myself – the unique, formalised lifestyle. I ponder my life…probably to make sure that I can organise and adapt to my surroundings however exclude such a moment.

The immensity of the moment.

Analysing the situations. The people around us…

Arising. I offer an adventure.

Different people's lifestyles.

The next moment. The anticipation. Adrenaline runs through your anatomy, pulsing every millisecond. What is it? Travel?

Programmed its eternity (living forever), treasure, recall, remember appreciation, friendship, respect events.

'My' experience and learn through life. The people you meet, places you go, learn, listen. Is this what creates characters, enabling them to develop into unique species?

The inner movement, quenching the cells of my body.

Deeply, I feel I cannot write. I am scared and nervous.

I desire to express feelings. Cherish every passing moment. Ritual passing, pure pleasure.

The life, the torment of everyone, captured by the fear, the escape.

What escape? The problem will not disappear if you don't hold onto survival.

– Scared of words and expressions placing.

– Enjoying the moments, second minutes, hours, days, weeks, months, years, decades, centuries…

The smiling faces of the innocent gifts of creation bring want and tenderness to me and deep love to my heart.

The Beauteous Treasuring Moments

The clouds drift yet to protect me from the squalors of the outside
Secure and warm

Trust

Trust. Trust who? Who to rely on? The soul in the world. I am individual, capable, and unique.

Unique

Individuality. Creativity.
Alone and responsible.
Controlling and powerful.

Monday, 17th August 1998

Another day in the life of the Hyatt. I think that many of my prayers were answered today.

     i. Tips $147, what a surprise that is like a day's work
    ii. I spoke to a lady in the sales department; she said that I could work there for a wee while. A few days' good experience.
   iii. Spoke to head of security. I could also work in that department before I leave. I must however get my feet wet in housekeeping.
   iv. Did some shopping. Bought a few necessary items to keep me going until…
    v. Was deeply involved in my book. Excellent.

19th August 1998

Relaxing day today, it was my day off; we were planning to go to the beach. We were all a bit naughty drinking, not the best combination. However, I did feel fine, with no effect! Today, I did my usual swim and was back in the apartment, we planned to have lunch and go to the bank. Had a midnight swim, perfect day, ready and jet set to tackle tomorrow?

27th August 1998

Cannot believe it's been a week since I decided to drop my expressions and thoughts down, I think I have been unbelievably busy, running around working and having fun. I am enjoying myself out here in the states, it is a shame that I am not 21 yet, I really would enjoy going out seriously partying. I think it's quite a good thing that I am not!

Confusion. An understatement perhaps?

Love, pure and tranquil hurt and desire.

Afraid and alone

Understanding and the hope of success and independence

The true being of oneself. Through each passing moment of the day is their guidance, special lifestyle, I wish that I was perfect. I know that everyone does. I wish I had the confidence to smile all the time. It is however an impossibility.

What am I to do with the person I am?

Do I bring contentment to the surroundings?

I feel not to everyone. I wish to write, have immediate ideas, spontaneous and super.

Intimate, poetic moments

Unfold gently thoughtfully,

Subtle

Direct

Embellishment

Pure

Beautifully

Emotionally

Rich

I don't think I have yet found my place. Does anyone, who knows? Tonight, I wish I could talk pleasantly about everyone and everything, but God has made us all people of individual characters, we all strive differently.

The Canyon de Chelly, there simply were no words, pictures, photographs, and statements to measure such a creation.

As I walked through the deep forest, dense greenery was lost, and yet adventurous.

I need inspiration. Perhaps I should meet someone natural and pure, different, nothing I've experienced before? Change my lifestyle, my image, my human person? Become someone new, change total identity, and discover a new world experience, a new being. I am however content with the life I have. I do get anxious, cautious, guilty and jealous. It is necessary though in my life, running away from me, out of my control. Adaption, the totality of the image I portray to the exterior.

A lifestyle

A style for oneself

To live in what, who wakes up at what time?

Who does what and what time?

Are we all separate?

Individuals, randomly passing in directions of completion

Who knows?

Who's taking care and what moments?

Who's happy and when?

Who knows love and when?

Feelings of eternity, the head on the pillow, the paper, cardboard box. Are we all fortunate and believe that we should be someone others don't judge?

Who am I going to meet tomorrow, become acquainted with, and talk to? Fall in love, suffer from hatred?

I am only 19, what else am I going to learn? Running on questions, control born leader, a naturalist, freedom for all, places everywhere in every town, country, city, village, hamlet.

Who is interested in me…?

Who loves me…?

Who uses me…?

Who judges me…?

Who laughs with me…?

Who understands me…?

Who hurts me…?

Who experiences my presence…?

Who's taking care of me…?

Who's listened to me…?

Who agrees with me…?

Who repels me…?

Who operates like me…?

Who enjoys my company…?

Take life every day as if it is the most important one in your life; strive for the ultimate. Operate with satisfaction. Live for yourself and share with others.

Confidence

Is it an expression or a desire?

When do you have confidence, who promotes it?

A small child learning to swim?

An old man living after his wife died?

The clothes we wear in a shop?

A dress at a party?

Once we have had our line of Coke?

After a few drinks?

Making love?

What goes through our minds?

Some people I know are overconfident; this annoys me so. Perhaps I am slightly jealous, is that true?

Is it possession or projection?

Get up, rise, enabling you to do something

Stand up for your rights – your belief in yourself. You know what's right and wrong. Don't allow others to judge you on your contentment.

DON'T GIVE UP THE FIGHT – always strive, live for the ultimate achievement.

31st August 1998

My god, life has its ups and downs but to experience them all in the space of a few seconds is just too much! Not necessarily too much because I am still living. It is that through life, we are going to be judged and categorised on the wants and needs we possess. I thought that I was a free spirit and individual able to aim high and to improve, succeed. This is all a learning experience now.

The gym – pleasure

The swim – awakening

Work – satisfying

The swim – relaxing

The cinema – amazing

Drinking – progressing

2ⁿᵈ September 1998

Spread my wings, look brightly into the future. I noticed today that I was one of these people, never able to stay in one place. I must keep moving. Keep my mind occupied, otherwise my brain voices take over, telling me I'm being lazy, do something. Things just pass through, as people in my life.

My heart is living in separate worlds now in England, Spain, Switzerland, and America. I am living in unison now with people from all over the world. I love it, the diversity.

People back at home, those who don't travel, who are content just to move to the end of their street, not venture on, see new horizons, everyone's lives have such opportunity, we surely must as individuals, seek, take, hold.

Life is short, before I know I am going to be old. Do I hold onto my past? Should I let go of my playground?

My home... I can run home whenever I need. I don't regret anything, there are things I shouldn't have done, but I believe it adds to the spice of life. My pride, joy is my smile, a smile tells a million words, understand, deep inside. Fly. Helpless...

Miami

We set off to Miami, technically after a day's work in the Hyatt, scrubbing the shit out of the bathroom, making beds, etc. The entire occasion was immense fun watching, absorbing, appreciating, and seeing America in a different light.

My future is with a thousand words. The future is captured by my experience, when I am bounding down the river, wild water rafting, absorbing the fresh wake of the Atlantic, and inhaling the pure crisp air of the mountaintops in Vermont.

Words, words, words, what words can I use to describe how my emotions feel and when, when in my individual being. Naturally, I care, feel for other beings, but their minds are not mine, I cannot think and allow others to be affected by me. Their questions are their own.

I walked into a masterpiece. Chinese art, deep, peaceful, meaningful. With the thought determination and motivation behind their creators, I will never know what possessed them to develop and portray such exquisite skills.

15ᵗʰ September 1998

Thank you – that's what sums up the entirety of my life. I am happy that I have been given this planet to live on for a few hundred years. I am positive that I am going to be able to experience other adventures entirely.

Words just arrive in my head, and I just wish that I was able to express myself on paper. Who knows where my adventures arrive at?

It is my mother, my dearest mother, my heroine, my greatest person, that I admire in the ecstasy.

I would love to express now aged 20 years, now I have experienced the teenage years! It was seven years ago now. It was the beginning of an era. Devotion, lifestyle, achieve, succeed always…

I stayed in the Sheraton Bal Harbour, absorbing the intensity of my surroundings. Noticing how the operation occurs. In which department, where, when why. I was lucky to appreciate being the guest for a while with serious VIP treatment. I was treated to a delicious breakfast on Sunday morning. The sun shone through the morning room, glistening on the freshly polished glasses, lighting happy faces from the previous Saturday night. The light capturing the waterfall. The Atlantic, the enormity. The old moon is beautifully situated. Beams like a lantern lighting a room. The moon was the only light where I am. Miami, South Beach happening and hectic in my past behind me, I was able to think, breathe, capture the moments. They are rare and few, but I always managed to do something memorable with a full moon.

The discovery no matter where I go, I will find if it takes a long, long time. No matter where I go, I will find you even if it takes 1000 years.

I gave blood, and I pray to save someone's life; another beauteous creation, who can feel alive again. I am healthy now. Perhaps I'm useless. I am not a human being, beautiful, flamboyant, glare of attraction.

The presence. The importance now, what am I doing. How can I act? People think that I am wonderful. I want to experience others, discover the uniqueness of each creation. Destiny will take its toll. God is listening to me up above and knows what I need and want; we will make things generate in the direction of my life.

Don't defer anyone. Even yourself!

Do it for yourself. Look into your heart. You will find, don't hide!

Thank you.

Please, can you allow me my destiny? You know what will be my right and wrong. Love is too broad.

Spontaneous: what arrives at everyone's thoughts? The morals and attitudes that people accomplish?

The thoughts, moments, seconds, planning achievement.

The action playing a game of tennis... the moment I hit a special shot.

Who knows?

What do others believe?

Do I love everyone I infatuate?

What is right?

What do you mean?

Objection!

Allow each moment to happen!

Kiss me, a kiss of security.

What has happened in the past few days? I have been busy. Running around indulging in work, physical activities, people randomly have come and gone. I organised a party for my birthday, plenty of underage drinking, but hey, you know where I come from, it's legal! I enjoyed it. Part of my childhood, doing things you shouldn't do. The eleventh commandment, I shalt not to get found out. I didn't, luckily.

I received some special cards and gorgeous presents. I am a very gifted individual.

The waiter and waitress offered our meal in commercial style. The food was great; I enjoyed a succulent piece of salmon, washed down with a few glasses of Chardonnay, buttery, and light. Interesting chitchat occurred, all relevant to the situation, I personally enjoyed everyone being present. I had a lovely birthday. I did work, but perhaps that is my destiny just to work, succeed, and be earning my own loaf of bread. Who knows who can foresee the future?

On 16th September, I treated myself to a day off. I organised an aromatherapy birthday massage, it was seriously gorgeous, relaxed all my organs, and recaptured my mind, my thoughts, and well-being.

I NEED JULIET.

Do I need to change? I have learned up until now we cannot get on with everyone. You can be a sheepdog. Not everyone is going to be a sheep. Focus on your own life. Individual creation. Think of pure happiness, joys, and moments of your life.

Sunday, 21ˢᵗ September 1998

Emotional analysis, the cycle of my entirety here – laid here on this planet. I am placed here. I am of course, oh, we all are unique species, all with different diverse upbringings, experiences, habits, feelings.

Yet I am truly happy with mine. I am. I believe I am. What is it that makes me rise every day? Is it the weather that provokes my outgoing, my mentality?

I wish I was able to start such a masterpiece that everyone: children, adolescents, young, old would appreciate; music, words, pictures, business, a charity. But not everyone will like it. My smiley face sometimes is my only positive emotion. How do I know, I thought I could explain everything on paper but some moments it is so?

Who has an interest in me? Perhaps I seriously must start opening up to others, letting go of the past, absorbing each present occasion? Live my life to the fullest? Which I believe I am.

There are however always limitations. I wish that I was able to express happiness and fun, that people could relate it to me. I wish I could relate to me and could understand what my life is all about. Then if I had an answer to it, there would be no questions, nothing. I need something, a challenge, I need to be hit with immense disappointment, and then I can appreciate how fortunate I am. God has my destiny taken care of.

Monday, 22ⁿᵈ September 1998

I must get my life in control. Let me open. Who knows? Am I perhaps trying to find too much? My expectations are too high. Perhaps I am too critical? Do I hate my parents? Who the hell am I? I know that I am loved, I cannot relate to my inner human being. I must pull myself together and enhance my strengths. I wish for everyone to remember me as a positive, content individual. Do I think they will, what is in my head, what do I want to express? I wish to know the world, explore. Exterior.

There will be words to make me smile

There will be words to make me marry

There will be places, situations that make me on fighting form

Who knows?

Saying I love you

Help me decide,

Who is going to help me, get on my unique level?

I am confused. I have finally really admitted it to myself. I AM LOSING CONTROL. Control of what though? I have turned my illness around. That however gave me another form of confidence. Nothing lasts forever, I know that. When am I going to truly gain my happiness? I am unsure of myself. But I am me all the time.

I cannot open to him, even though he seemed open sometimes. How do I just let everything go, no worries, thoughts of departing in two months, who knows? I will probably walk away from the situation, and no one will remember me. Seriously, I am going to be another feather blown in the wind. Please say you will remember me!

Democracy

Let me look into my father's eyes. What will I find there, wisdom, my creation? What he has seen?

The poor guys, sitting in front of me! No way! Bed right now. I have nothing else inside of me to place on the paper! What am I supposed to do here! In this situation?

Thursday, 25ᵗʰ September 1998

I was quite a cheerful bunny today, I worked, had the Hyatt in turn meeting. Had lunch. Got a sweet letter from him… I was so rude to him yesterday that things have to come to an end at some point. I must progress with my life. I sent some letters, had a swim, watched a glimpse of television and went off to Pleasure Island and partied.

Wednesday, 30ᵗʰ September 1998

Hello again, another day here in glorious Florida.

Destiny will take its path and arrived at doors that shall be closed, ajar, wide, or wide-open. It's my choice and decision for success in my time. It was now the interaction of everyone else that consumes some moment in your day that adds to the diversity of your days. I am doing it constantly here with many different, different kinds of people from such extreme backgrounds. I am again lucky to see and observe, judge and analyse for my personal assumption. I was thinking today about how the life I have led has turned on and on. It is like a conveyor belt at the airport

I reckon that I am sometimes funny, a little fragile, but very real.

It's up to man to respect the laws of nature.

It is just a little crush; there is a little amount of direction now.

I am going to write a few things down about what I should have achieved by the time of departure home in December…

Successful training at the Hyatt, but also, I am 20 now, I am going to change into a new person, new clothes, new complexion, new appearance, more sophisticated, more forward, more knowledgeable. I will accomplish my goals and face the fact that I am leaving my childhood and adolescence as memories, and face forward with power into my prospects. This is the beginning. I am going to travel with ambition. I am going to become confident with myself. Being, accept who I am, what I can change.

Yesterday

I am only a human soul placed on planet Earth. Gifted by God or special powers – I can do many things. What will people say about me once I'm gone? Just another leaf blown from a tree, blossomed, nurtured, breed, then lost, flown free, landing in a far-off place. Allowed to then rest, decay, and add new food, nutrients for the new leaves to follow. Beauteous creation.

6th October 1998

Hello again.

I have been rushed off my feet over the last few days, playing working, resting. I have, however, really enjoyed myself. I have concluded that in my life now it's time to: make a change, act, react and grow up. I am fortunate to have money at present. It's finally my adulthood, I am now 20. It's just the next few years that I must capture and seriously enjoy because in time, work, family, child, bills, cars, taxis, mortgages, holidays will dominate my mind and I am young, so I will treasure each moment and convert it into pure happiness.

Thursday, 8th October 1998

Day off today. Hurrah! Finally! I woke up, went for a run, read my book. While in the gym I went for a swim. Changed my air flight ticket, went to the Hyatt's to get my pay – bought stamps, postcards, etc. posted letters, had lunch, phoned airline companies for New York flight, came home, relaxed and wrote a diary.

Life is a strange thing. I reckon I must use other options for the word strange. It is blunt and uneventful and describes nothing. I miss sex, I miss a man to hold and for the holdback, making me secure; an animal being taken care of, like a lion protects his lioness, I need certain support. I was analysing the characters of the chapter of my life at present, far off in the clouds somewhere. What an accomplished day. I achieved everything I set out to do. I wish I could share this with someone!

Tuesday, 20th October 1998

What happened to my time? So much in the last few days...
I cannot capture everything in my brain and lay it out upon this paper. The engrossed mind operating at a rate of a hundred miles per day. My percentage of the eternity is summoned up upon and you pass over what you need for that time and the forgetfulness and neutrality of souls on the planet.
1) lots of tennis
2) lots of swimming, hundred lengths today
3) finished my book, Cold Mountain.
4) had intense thoughts
5) been working, housekeeping
6) been babysitting
7) cinema
8) grouped with people
9) changed to working of the shift
10)Working on the new nightshift now. It feels like a slight promotion.
I am moving, making changes, hopefully going up in the world. Let me bring some warmth, happiness, and pure honesty to my brain. My organ of understanding, knowledge, wisdom, and appreciateon that exposed to the outside is ultimate ecstasy.

Thursday, 22nd October 1998

Last night I organised a little gathering of all the interns. It was quite good fun. Everyone, I think, particularly enjoyed themselves.

Saturday, 24th October 1998

Cigar tea – the universal name of the tea in the house. (Ha-ha!)
I am fortunate with my life up to now. I am ecstatic with my attitude. I respect everyone around me. There is no greater power than the true love I spread

throughout the individuals I randomly get into an acquaintance with in my short life on this planet, there is nothing left… Hide, seek, saying goodbye. My time is certainly not through yet, I have yet much to learn on this planet; the excitement of living the next day, month, year. Years onwards, what's going to happen, to occur?

26th October 1998

Analysing of individual characters, the repetition of the robot housekeeper: programmed to rise, relax, walk, read, swim, shower and cycle to work – quite an event before the beginning of the day. Who would be interested in that? Other people just sleep. I believe I have the world captured in my hands at this moment.

Wednesday, 28th October 1998

Prospects, what I feel I want to achieve now?
-    My education
-    Get a career underway
-    Married
-    Get a Dalmatian doggy, a sweet new Freckles for myself, as a puppy, I feel its needs, wants, and desires as it grows
-    Dinner parties, social gatherings

I would also love to be able to dance properly. What I think I might do when I go back to Switzerland is get in touch with a dancing school. Learn a few steps and then when I go out in the future, I will be able to express myself as a partner, a union.

Who knows which path I will take? But I am positive everything is going to be an immense learning experience, and I will contradict everything that occurs. I will live happily. Enjoy the company of others and live as a content human being. I know though that everyone has their slow moments. One of my main ambitions is to be successful and produce wonderfully unique and able offspring. What generation will I grow and educate them into? A world of peace, in my dreams.

Friday, 30th October 1998

What a working day, I am immensely fortunate with my training position. It's not too difficult, I sometimes feel that I am doing things wrong, but what is wrong? Perhaps I am just trying to look for a negative point in my life. I know I do.

However, I believe there is a God above me and I am choosing my life. How can I tell people not to take what I am enjoying? I love doing certain things, learn things, perform things, and excel in things and its things I enjoy. How do you tell others not to appreciate such things? I suppose it boils down to the situation. For my personal feelings it is firstly part of a section of my life.

I am meeting new people. Getting acquainted with unique individuals, reading, and being active and also, working. I am performing all my skills; I would like to lose weight before I leave here. And I know I need to. I can sense and feel it again.

Week – 31ˢᵗ October to 6ᵗʰ November 1998

The aggression and anxious behaviour in me…

Everyone I am subjecting myself to. Am I just kidding? The activities I partake in, the analysing of what goes through my mind. Capturing the correct message of hopefully positive!

My intimate relationship with others and I have always felt too deeply involved. I need to capture your advice and lead my life to my extreme happiness, success.

Who analyses everyone?

Am I leading my life correctly?

Abiding by rules and regulations in life?

Who is going to answer this question?

I have worked, earned my money, done the shifts, even turndown service, shadowing in the separate departments. Shopping for suits. Hopefully, I will maintain to capture a nice figure by the time I leave here! I want to be beautiful, attractive, and have the confidence to express the strength within and not allow it to become a cover-up.

We are all the next generation that is going to focus and dominate society. What is going to be accomplished, more rockets firing into the universe to discover and mission achieved?

Monday, 9ᵗʰ November 1998

Worked as per usual, organised myself to rooms divisions manager and collected the Christmas decorations. The commitment is that we must be involved.

Had eight checkouts. We will both keep travelling. We both want to explore, adventure, accomplish and overcome new territories. I love to immerse myself in other cultures; it is always new, exciting, and completely fascinating. Life is one big learning experience. Voyage.

MOMENT – looks like a long instant! Don't even think about suicide. Look back on the satisfaction, I am achieving with my life. I believe this, which is most important. I strongly agree with the belief that I am living my life to its maximum, I cannot experience everything all in one day, and it takes an entire lifetime.

Wednesday, 11th November 1998

REMEMBRANCE DAY.

The soldiers: fighting for their beliefs, their standards, their next step forward; were enhancing the future for us as we now travel through our lives.

I thank my dear great grandpa; he was a successful and immensely significant man in the logical future. Nowadays what can I do? What people will think is wonderful, move on, move on, and always fight for what's right, experience the emotions, feel the pain for struggling individuals, but maintain a warm and strengthening smile.

I cherish the life I have been offered so far, I have chosen the doors or roads to take. I have been helped by the love and respect of my parents; they have treasured me and given me such a special life. I can challenge all new experiences with determination, motivation, and the originality of achieving everything expected in a day. I have others' thoughts, I have felt, I have moved and captured what I am doing as well. Are others all over the world recording moments of adventure, the expression of their lives? I am lucky people allow me to experience the moments of total turmoil, so I can learn and look with anticipation to the next pieces of time?

The pieces of pleasurable enjoyment: sex, eating, running, working, swimming, physically challenging expertise, snowboarding, socialising, drinking, dancing, travelling in airplanes and cars, new destinations, recapturing, talking, writing, phoning, intimate conversations, wine tasting, cycling, exploring, regarding, analysing, the future moments, sleeping.

I cannot remember now what I have written, but surely, life is here for the given moments? God has created his abundance for the exploration and understanding, the future moments of achievement, altar.

I am pleased; I have got back into writing, reading, grabbing and capturing specialisations in our own life!

I am writing in green just to express that I do feel moods, sensitive situations and subconsciously, the simple. Yet however complex mind we possess, we can portray it to the exterior being.

I have done a lot recently: organised to go down to Miami, been to the SOP classes, found out about the intern meeting Friday and set me up for PBX and the front desk tomorrow, called the bank, thought about buying a computer. Prioritising things, what is the correct way? I will discover for myself, I reckon. I am lucky now. Perfect training, work, learning, and understanding the career paths of others. Analysing ages. Sunbathing, delicious food, swimming, shopping, cinema, tennis, cycling, organising, shadowing finally. Arranging and scheduling time. Living with my dear fellow apartment buddies. They are lovely creations. I am fortunate.

The SOP classes were quite interesting, I participated, I hope that I didn't make too much of a fool of myself. I was able to understand and eventually with more study in the next few years convey and express to others, knowledge, wisdom, expression of individualism and how people all must work together to achieve overwhelming goals.

Everyone is leading a life separately, we acknowledge, register, communicate with others after the day; it's one person who closes their eyes, shuts the world out, and indulges in quiet, peaceful solitary moments.

I have been reading quite a lot lately and I am enjoying it. A book is a friend. Language always experienced more vividly, words scattered and chosen together, stringing sentences, creating meaning, live another achievement for an author or authoress. Lord, I adore travel, adventure, new cultures, expectations, and ways of living.

12th – 18th November 1998

My God where do I start?

What a week in the life of Juliet. From my last moments of expression, flowing, experiencing, I will jot down briefly and when I can feel the moments enhance greater.

Do you know I wake every morning with the anticipation of achieving my highest goal? I cannot even begin to express what has happened to me. I am living in my present, my reality, my creation and exterior each inflection on life.

I like to relate to people on certain levels. I must admit I sometimes get captured on the adaption level. There is such a mixture of individuals in my life, and I am immensely fortunate that I can relate. I have met people throughout my life and what I enjoyed doing is keeping in touch, adding spice to the present when you have reactions of a blast from the past.

Miami, the main purpose of my Miami trip was to attend the meeting.

23rd November 1998

It is nearing the end of November already, my lord what an achievement of a year, over the last few days, a lot of changes. I always live in the present and dream and get lost in ideas and opportunities of the future. I think that I always focus on the future with much ambition, this is positive.

However, I feel that my life is running away too fast!

I am still a young, innocent 12-year-old just before starting secondary school. I was apprehensive, scared more to the point; I don't know whether I achieved anything in those two years, when I got extremely ill. I look back at myself; I am a new person now. I used to be caring and with my Virgo star sign, very perfect. Everything had its right place.

Thank God I have calmed down slightly, certainly no way as pushy now.

I can live life spontaneously, be flexible to people's ideas and emotions, as well as my own. It is important to take care of number one, others around are caring, friendly, offer ideas, but at the end of the day, it is only myself in control, me who closes my eyes at night and decides when to open them in the morning. I am pleased I can enjoy, live, treasure, experience every day to its most maximum.

Beauty for my mind, anxiety, brainstorming, concentration, delegates, exercise, fear, goals, happiness, luck, music, negative thinking, procrastination, relaxation, stop, time management, visualisation, wonderment, stop strengths, reach, opportunities, potential positives.

28th November 1998

A romantic dinner in celebration... It was gorgeous; we shared an exquisite bottle of rare Italian white wine, specially chosen with splendid seafood, continually chatting.

He is a good friend, and I will miss him terribly, he is totally lovely and even though he may not be the one that I will marry or end up with, he is making me learn things and settling points inside my head, which certainly need addressing.

I am having a special time and it's completing my training. PERFECT CELEBRATION.

Full of happy holiday people who realise these things happen out of their kitchens and the way from their televisions. When we arrive back, the house was overloaded with people again.

HAPPY GATHERINGS.

I can imagine myself when I am their age, escaping real life, just hiding away for the week occasionally. I would especially love to jump on an airplane to Spain, anywhere in Europe, just adventure, classical arts, music and culture, natural beauty of lakes and mountains. Canada has immense appeal for living; I would love to go there again.

What am I talking about? I am going up there in about two weeks! That reminds me, I must start organising my trip up there, and who I will see. I must pick up all my art and photography.

Monday, 30th November 1998

Now we must prepare to live only by the guide of our faith and character. Direct us to know and care about what is right and wrong that we will be victorious in this life and rewarded in the next.

1st December 1998

Twelve months just like that, what a learning experience year. I have enjoyed it and I reckon I still have the best to come.

Christmas time, hoorah!

It's going to be such immense fun. I was working today. Doing renovations wing, had a nice time, and went out for supper in Point Orlando.

2nd/3rd December 1998

I analyse to such an immense degree. I know who I am, what I want. Perhaps it will come. What questions does my future hold anyway, career-wise, familywise, relationship, activities, enjoyments?

Things settled down when we went to the Dali exhibition. It was particularly interesting; I was fascinated by the mind and hidden approaches to the life of the artist. Certainly, Dali is unique, what an experience.

12th December 1998

I have had a hectic few days, mainly revolved around packing, finishing work, saying goodbye to made friends, partying, and spending quality time with the new love in my life.

I am however, believing through everything that I am participating in at present, that I am such an insignificant person on this planet.

I keep reminding myself now. I want to become known, well known, proud, and a respected human being; of course.

I have heroes, it's important I believe, to have important people to respect for their hard work and natural powers. I admire people who can bring up a family, work, remain unselfish and kind after all the horrific thing's life can throw at you!

I have now finished my internship at the Hyatt Orlando, and I seriously have learnt an immense amount, perhaps nothing in the theory department. But human lives, the days of individual communication, an immense achievement I think is to behave, everyone in their everyday lives needs to know how to behave, otherwise…it's logic to think what happens.

I am in New York now, with many diverse personalities, languages, origins, race, education. What is the ultimate makeup? I ate a delicious lunch that will certainly keep me going, then sat and watched the travellers, the workers, holidaymakers, business participants. I am now waiting to catch an air flight up to Canada.

14th December 1998

I am observing changes in characters, which I am finding very interesting. Caught up with Canada friends, it was a delicious supper, and everyone was friendly. Looked after the kids and borrowed a car.

15th December 1998

Finally, Canada has come to an end.

So, this is who I am this year. I will stand by others, a symbol of my face and I must follow all the paths ahead…feel your destiny. I have found that will come true. I will find my way.

18th December 1998

Kind sweetheart that he is dropped me at the airport. I was lucky; I didn't pay for excess baggage. What a lucky, jammy person I am sometimes!

My plane was delayed, which gave us an extra hour together, we chatted, contemplating life and had an extremely romantic embracing kiss goodbye. What a gentleman.

Chapter 4

Internship Interlude...

"I was in the middle before I knew that I had begun."—
Jane Austen

19th December 1998

Gatwick, London, England. The whole morning I felt so terribly anxious and really excited about the entire occasion. I managed to get through passport control and customs no problem and my darling sweet friend picked me up. I could not believe that we have not seen each other for a whole year.

We have both gone off experiencing our complete directions and we get back together and gossip and gossip! I love her, such a dear friend.

England for once actually had blue skies. It was rather chilly though. I arrived back home at about 12.30, mum was the first person I saw. She was in great form and shed a tear as I walked in.

Great 21st birthday party followed later on, glass of champagne in one hand, fag in the other and I just gossiped. Caught up with everyone it was great fun. I sat next to friends and they both got me incredibly drunk, conversation flowed...

21st December 1998

Saw friends at the pub for supper. We caught up on news and told each other about our new experiences. It dawned upon me that I have moved on. I am a changed person now.

I popped in for a wee while then realised jet lag was kicking in and it was time for home.

22nd December 1998

We all gathered in the evening to celebrate Mum's birthday. Dad got an Indian and we all pigged out till our stomachs were content! Captured moments on camera, and chatted like one big happy family, shared a lot of champagne and had a lovely day.

Wednesday, 23rd December 1998

It dawned upon me – it's time to seriously move on. I am 20 years old now and have determination and motivation in mind and I feel like he's holding me back. Life will evolve. I will enjoy and destiny will take its path.

Thursday, 24th December 1998

All in great spirits ready for Christmas, consuming large quantities of alcohol. Went to Midnight Mass. It was very rushed, but it was lovely to catch up with God. I rarely go to church and there can be no excuse in finding the time, but this year I have been working my Sundays, but I relate to him in my way. He offers support and calms my nerves down about questions that revolve around my head all the time.

Christmas Day, 25th December 1998

I found my stocking loaded with goodies; Father Christmas had come. I was touched by many of the spoiling gifts, I am lucky. I dressed and took the dogs out on my run, a bit of exercise. We all had drinks in the smart sitting room. It was such fun. The lunch was delicious, served up on silver platters: turkey, goose, and all the trimmings. It was great. Crackers, champagne, Christmas pud and lots of gifts. The afternoon was taken up with opening more presents and organised games. It was such fun. We couldn't go out for a traditional walk because gale force winds and strong driving rain put us all off. So, we cuddled up in front of the fire with tangerines, Quality Streets, turkey sandwiches and the television. It was warming and I really enjoyed Christmas this year.

26th December 1998

I basically did my regular home routine; I cannot believe that I have been back here a week now. Christmas was quite an event this year. I completed all my thank you letters and spoke to him. He really is a self-centred shit at the moment. Anyway I expressed all of my thoughts on paper and constructed a letter, sent it feeling immensely relieved.

We also had a power cut, which meant family involvement, we ran around the house sparking candles, all rather dramatic. We managed to play a traditional family game of Scrabble! All rather good fun. We actually finished it without any arguments. The lights came on before Men Behaving Badly and French and Saunders. I quietly passed out on the sofa.

29th December 1998

I arrived back at home at 7.00 this morning after really a strange night. It was bizarre what happened to me! I woke after about an hour and a half and just let the day take its toll. I drove to Granny's around 12.30.

31st December 1998

Happy New Year 1999

Sleep, for now, eyrie domain alrighty! What a day, the morning was routine swimming, run, shower, changing. We drove down to London, chatting, listening to music, and anticipation towards the whole evening.
Juliet's in Kensington. I had a high a New Year!

Dear Juliet,

As I promised you… My theory about life! The prisoners of war. Dreams have been abandoned. We belong nowhere. The sail is unchartered on troubled seas. We may never be allowed ashore. Our sorrows may never be sad enough. Our joy never happy enough. Our dreams never big enough. Our lives never important enough to matter.
I think by now you know me enough to know how to take these lines
Yours always,
????

January 1999

The year 1999 is going to be fun, work-filled, with plenty of determination and an immense amount of success and happiness shall be achieved.

5th January 1999

I realise that it is time to let my wings fly, taking me away to my pad.

8th January 1999

I got on with my regular schedule, morning activities, running, swimming, reading the newspaper, sorting the twins out. Around 10.30, I drove off to London. I listened to 'Talk, Think and Grow Rich; it was quite interesting and certainly passed the journey by pretty quickly. I arrived in London just after

12.00 and did some shopping; I just window-shopped and then went to Lloyds. Then caught a tube to Bank, I haven't been on one for a long time, it was people-watching time. Analysis of characters. I went to a meeting with at 2.00 in the Après Midi. The meeting was two hours long and opened my eyes fortunately to the stocks and shares portfolio. Thank God. Living the city life, I don't think I would like that very much; it might have something to do with the depressive rain. The meeting finished at 4.00 and I caught the tube back to Knightsbridge, where I did plenty of shopping. I bought a lovely new coat and new shoes as well. Perfect for Glion. I left London around 6.30, it was appalling driving conditions, traffic jams and awful weather.

Chapter 5

Destiny Decisions and Moët Moments...

"It's in your moments of decision that your destiny is shaped." – Tony Robbins

14th January 1999

My break has finally come to an end. It is all over; family life and I don't know when I'm coming back into it.

I know that next term will go well. I'm however slightly apprehensive about the whole ordeal, fortunately, this time, I know what to expect, not in all departments though. Destiny takes its path, I love it, won't get back to my reassuring notes, sayings, phrases, etc. I know these holidays have been slightly up and down. I'm immensely lucky though how everything has gone, what I have received to help progress to the next stage. Good luck driving tomorrow, wake early, swim, bathe and leave, drive to Dover, stay awake, and don't forget tickets and passports. Thank your lucky soul for the warmth and security of home and remember that it is always open here. You are never allowed to shove away the love.

15th January 1999

Said goodbye to mum and dad and simply burst into tears. It felt good to cry, let everything all out: confusion, stress, anxiousness, excitement everything plus the long, lonely drive ahead of me... The whole drive through France was particularly continuous, ongoing, straight motorway, not much pretty scenery due to the weather, strong winds. I told myself to get to Montreux and see what will happen. I arrived at 8.00 and checked straight into the Swiss Majestic.

16th January 1999

We do provoke the moments, hey! It's great to be back, an immense change from last year. Dramatic. I cannot believe it. The world turns in mysterious ways and I reckon that I must accept every moment that occurs. My God, life is short. Everything happens and then disappears to the past. We can hold onto and cherish the marvellous moments and learn from our mistakes. Hoping not to make them again.

18th January 1999

Destiny is in my hands, and I perfectly knew this drama would arise, but hey, I'm still living and enjoying it. I love being back. I believe that if I stay positive, focussed, and determined then life will be brilliant. I work, I play, I just enjoy myself wherever I am and I hope I know that it will? Always the contradiction, hey! I had many immensely different thoughts this evening. We will see/decide/give it time. Life is short. Why? Why? Why worry about it? Kitchen joys of everyone, the entirety of the day, welcoming, treasuring, hating, and caring more/a lot, etc. goodness, I appreciate life? Analyse on!

19th January 1999

We have chosen separate directions and I for once, the right one!

23rd January 1999

My goodness, I have been emotionally drained over the last few days; I hardly know how to stand on my own two feet. Yesterday, I was even unable to write in here. I conducted a letter and gave it to him first thing; I mean how was I able to! I cannot stand this; it hurts and drains me incredibly. My life, however, must progress.

26th January 1999

We are all striving on our little planets, covered with our bubbles! I had better sleep, but I'm tired. It would be lovely to get at least one decent night's sleep.

28th January 1999

I worked all day, in the kitchen. We then had the tutors' party in the club. Sorted – we had a Moet Chandon to begin.

4th February 1999

I got 3X mastered brilliant in kitchen. Service is shit; I hate the hawks, the analyst gods, what bullshit. I really cannot stand the way they treat people. I must just get into my sweet bubble and continue happily on my level. Life is my oyster.

24th February 1999

Wine presentation & meeting with finance.

27th February 1999

Saturday morning, I was up with the larks, squeezed in my finance and economics work, even read through tourism again. I had an excellent day in the end. I love to just live my life.

Appreciate what I have! Stop searching and wasting precious energy.

28th February 1999

Today, I woke up in a marvellous mood. The sun was shining, perfect blue skies. I drove to the swimming pool, relaxed and calm, everything was peaceful; people were gardening, walking, going to church, it was too late for the partygoers and too early for regular people. The pool was empty, I got on with my exercise, pounded up and down; it was particularly perfect. Brunch followed – with plenty of exquisite cheeses and deliciously tempting desserts, it was just wonderful.

Monday, 8th March 1999

I believe that an entry into my diary this evening is necessary. I do wish things would start to go right for me. For goodness' sake, I'm in exam week; I try to be unbelievably perfect. Live my life to such a beautiful, beautiful extreme, and now, it isn't working. I'm in such an unbelievably tricky situation.

11th March 1999

Things began to get much better today. I started to think straight. Take one task at a time and calm down. I have been living at 200% and now, well, the last few days, I began to feel it. Yet today, I rose in a fresh frame of mind and just didn't think too much about the next step, more like I just took it when it came. I found out I'm working in the club all weekend I'm not going to have any time off.
I received all my stuff for the Australian Visa application. My goodness, I have numbers flowing around my ears. I wish you incredible luck tomorrow; we shall see and just take one step at a time. Relax and concentrate. Empower your mind. Stay/remain in control. Succeed.

16th March 1999

Monday, I was emotional today… Even the teachers said they were disappointed, but what am I to do? I studied.

17th March 1999

I just got a positive answer from Park Hyatt Sydney; however, I must organise my Visa!

19th March 1999

Friday, I haven't been able to put words properly on paper for quite some time. The pace of life is running fast. I'm now at Geneva airport waiting for a flight back to England. I am quite unsure if I want to go back. I know that I'll have a lovely time. I however think now I'm being quite weak. I'm running away from my problems here at Glion. They are not problems just tasks that I have had to overcome. One thing I really cannot stand in life is to wait around. I take pleasure in living in the present moment and I'm being to realise now that I never am... What I am doing is looking deeply into my future, analysing, praying to succeed and live, but when the future comes, I am always looking into the next task and never fully taking experience and pride in what is happening right now. I have an immense amount to express to you. Thank you firstly for all your letters, they are all very meaningful and reach my heart deeply. I know that I have needed to take some time to contemplate our relationship. The more and more I'm with you, the more I feel that you should be searching for deeper love. I know that I'm terrible at expressing my feelings; I think it is probably because I'm very unsure of them. I really will cherish our relationship that developed in America; it was unique, free, and perfect. I don't know why we cannot carry it on here, but both of us are great worriers. We both search for perfection within ourselves, and I know I spent a lot of time thinking about perfection without living it.

21st March 1999

I have just spent the weekend at home; I flew on Friday night. Mum and Dad welcomed me with open arms. It was gorgeous. Traditional roast, a good glass of red wine and special company.
He was completely on another planet. I think he has lost the plot slightly. I had an early morning jog this morning and swam for ages.

Tuesday, 23rd March 1999

I love the Swiss mountain air first thing in the morning – it is pure and opens my heart for the coming, facing the day. I received all my exam results and passed, it's all good and positive! We shall see what will happen with life.
I cannot determine my happiness now. Why? Why? Why? Application, adaption, experience, spontaneity, love. What words can I think of to scribble down about what I have learnt? Destiny will travel and take its toll; we must see what will

happen! Where I will end up, what will happen to me, who I will be with? The who, what, why, when, where, and how! Plus, I'm young.

Friday, 2nd April 1999

I am now at home after all my plans of going away travelling for a few days and I decided spontaneously to just go home and be with my family. Hardly am I doing that… I'm off running around, contemplating deeply and I need to just stop. Stop everything. Take the passenger seat for a while.

Supper in Geneva, it was seriously delicious – excellent Saint-Emilion wine and seriously splendid food. Lovely company. Tiny restaurant with Geriodon service. Lucky girl. Very delicious.

Ickworth Park and took some photographs of the splendour. It was calm and pleasing to return to my family's 'origin'; it is a shame that we are unable to live there because it is a magnificent place. I constantly had such an immense amount of stuff for my mind.

Pick some tulips for Freckles' grave. I feel that she would have appreciated them from there because that's where she and I spent most of our life together. I went home quite tearful, it was such a beautiful spring evening, the sun reflected off the greenery, sparkled into the car, and the daffodils blew in the wind. I really appreciate spring in England.

JC seriously flipped out over dinner, swearing, throwing things, it was scary!

Sunday

Easter day, I went to church with Mum. It was calm and rather achieving, just relating myself to God again. Just to thank him for everything and ask him for some guidance now, which I just really need. I think that I do. I'm the only person that can listen to my heart and mind!

Tuesday, 6th April 1999

Back in Switzerland.

He is not in a good way, there is not a lot I can do about it, just be supportive. I cannot stand Mum and Dad being so incredibly hurt. I cannot comprehend what is happening. It all used to be so lovely, childhood memories. We will have them again and it will be next time with my generation. Our future – now take control. Listen to your heart!

I spent a great majority of the weekend studying, oh, well, shit happens, it is in the past and there is nothing much I can do to change it!

We went out to Château Gruyere for supper; it was a very delicious fondue! Yummy, I was quite high and flying. I was content just travelling my path unwinding.

My feelings have been total and complete. I just let myself live. I thought last week, it would be nice if all the girlies went out for supper, drink, etc. and we all managed to get together. Absolute perfection. I think that we all had a nice time. I rather enjoyed it. Serious control freak! We will see what path destiny takes.

Saturday

Class finished at 3.25 on Friday and my weekend has been happening ever since. Lots of lovely times. I'm staying in the Excelsior hotel, it is gorgeous, beautiful lake view, and the mountains are stunning first thing. The world is incredibly peaceful. I have a lot on my plate this weekend, revision along with serious relaxation and taking care of myself, which I haven't done for a very long time.

Monday

I want to get all my exams over and done with. I really need to. I cannot stand the stress and nervousness.

Tuesday, 20th April 1999

Whose ever will is the strongest will take over, either we do our training together and seriously invest in each other's company or we keep it as it is now. The apprehension of what the future holds. This exciting feature should be looked upon with serious enthusiasm.

Wednesday, 21st April 1999

Life is incredibly confusing sometimes!

Sunday

I must shed some of my thoughts from my brain. Disillusion. Discomfort. Why do I feel alone?

Monday

Who knows what the future holds? Destiny will travel with its own words and happenings. My mind captured in such incredible and diverse activities my moods and feelings all swing, enhanced and gorgeous! My life can take many directions and aspects. I really am unsure what I want and desire, but I know certain feelings and thoughts, what am I able to do!

I will tell you a little story! He gave me a watch; a classic Jaguar one, very touched, he said it was for his son, I said it still can be! Little subtle comments touch my heart. Then he said he was lending me the watch, which means I must give it back. Who knows what will happen? Dreams may come alive. Let's hope! I really would like a focus and direction. I want to work, live, enough of studying, stress, filling my mind with the knowledge that I don't care about anymore.

Tuesday, 27th April 1999

I have decided that if Egypt takes me, I will go there, if not, then I go to Australia. I do not want to go back to London! Not yet. I love to travel, explore, and experience!

Firstly – go to Australia. Love my life, work, enjoy life, go through the ups and downs, possibly apply to a university, Australia Sydney University, complete a management course, public relations in a year or two.

I could imagine opening a bar, little restaurant, and party place, near the beach, on the beach, sun, sea, stars, waves, places to dream, dolphins to fly, fish to swim, people to entertain, money to make, a place to be content, allow my children to be raised strong-minded, individual, and healthy. Swimming, running, riding, building sandcastles, dancing, working hard, observing life, loving my husband, giving him everything I have apart from my ability to move and love my life.

What an achievement, a discovery, a place of pure and utter peacefulness.

We got stoned by the lake; it was a real giggle!

Went for a coffee when we had finished our tour around Bern. It was very pleasant. Read the newspaper, I didn't want to be with anyone. I went off to a wee cafe and wrote some postcards. It was great! Then I met up with everyone else, which was awful. I didn't want to be with anyone.

The bird's twitter in the sky, the air around is pure and fresh, the creation of each day. What a pure true righteous world we live in today. The war and turmoil. How come I'm excluded and those around me also? These poor people specimens that are involving themselves with this. It cannot be their fault surely;

they were born who they are. One day something might happen to me just because I'm born where I was born.

I cannot find my pure happiness, what is it? I'm unsure, but hey, I'm going to keep living life. I'm sure sometimes that I just want to jump off the planet. Float into heaven and be with creatures. What's it going to be like there? Is it going to be better than the place I'm in now?

Thursday

I haven't written in my diary in ages. Expressed thoughts and feelings I believe now is the time, as I'm not doing anything right now!

I had a great time in the UK – a perfect time to reflect on my life, my being, and my survival. I've replenished my lost energy, slept plenty.

I have finally decided that I am going to Australia. I believe that now is the time. Is what I have always dreamed, and life is too short not to live, and be happy.

Saw JC in the clinic. It was very strange, too emotional. I burst into tears when I left. I think the whole day was hectic! I didn't know what to expect and when I arrived, I seriously didn't want to leave. He is a human being; my brother and he is locked up unable to enter mainstream society. And there is absolutely nothing I can do apart from love him. I do love him so much. He is my brother; we have shared our whole lives.

I remember when I was a wee young lady completely not unconfident with life. It was around about the time Granny died. Exactly 10 years ago. Sometimes, I wish I could join everyone in heaven I really miss. I miss Freckles immensely. I will search for a friend that close and that perfect – perhaps that friend will save me.

The excursion to Bern was an emotional nightmare. He is a confused individual, and he is making me feel unsure and ridiculous.

Sunday, 8th May 1999

I believe now times are not going to change. I'm going to go to Australia as a new person. Individual. No way of forgetting my past, but searching and looking for my goal and achievement and for someone to find me to be the queen of their hearts.

10th April 1999

I'm beginning to understand life. The way people operate and perceive direction. I must just continue my level of happiness and understanding. I'm out of here in three weeks. I have my exams, my work, my direction, my perception.

In 5 years!

Five years… anything and everything can happen within that time, which again will influence and change my mind.

I had a dream when I was about 12 to go to Australia and work at the Olympic Games. I kept the belief that it was going to come true and now it is. I have decided to finish Glion and not go to Bulle quite yet. The year 2000 beckons and I will be heading out to Australia to work for the Park Hyatt Sydney for six months; I will then be working for the Olympic Games (2000). My dream and belief are coming true.

I'm a person that takes each day at a time; I work hard, and play hard and have an immense amount of enthusiasm and determination to succeed. For the very near future, I will be heading back to England for a couple of months to regenerate and prepare myself for the next stage of my life. I find that it is very important for individuals to take time and reflect, contemplate the future and life. I know in my capabilities and myself that I'm a people person, I adore to work and make the most out of each passing day. I love to capture new ideas, visit new places. I know I am a sales and marketing person. What I would personally love to do is get into public relations. One day I dream to have my own company, however for now, what I need is experience and knowledge.

Education is extremely important, but personally for me, experience, spontaneity, and adaption are more. I'm 20 years old now. I will never stop educating myself, I love to learn, but I know that it is time for me to make money and live-in working life.

Sunday, 16th March 1999

Organised my flight back to the UK. Went to the BBQ, it was lovely. Lots of people, perfect weather, I'm extremely lucky. I played football, ate plenty, watched the Grand Prix, relaxed, listened to music, danced with the Brazilians.

Sunday, 23rd May 1999

What shall I choose? Egypt will be an amazing experience! I know I do not have the most amount of weight on my plate, but now, I don't know where to start. My witch in Canada told me when I was feeling low like this to write down my talents, qualities, and weaknesses.

Monday

I feel in a more positive mood to express some thoughts on paper now. Goodness, my life is incredible, what choices do I take! It's my life, and I must follow my dream, my life and enjoyment; let's see what productivity comes from all this! Working for the Ritz being in London… I really wasn't completely sure. Confidence and control, we will see!

Tuesday

Well, I woke from a beautiful sleep and the sun glistened through the window. Rays enlightened my heart to face the day ahead.
Go to Egypt, see what it is like.

Wednesday, 26th May 1999

I have decided now to go to Egypt, the new opportunity, country, life. That's the decision. It is going to be new and unique. I cannot wait, seriously! I spoke to Egypt today, they seemed rather relaxed, but I reckon the new, unique life and experience is going to be a real eye-opener
We decided spontaneously to play tennis. It was such an ecstatic decision – the sun was setting, lovely cool breeze. The most perfect time!

Thursday, 8th May 1999

Another glorious day. I believe I'm on a roll! It's great; just hold onto this until the end of the semester, for as long as possible. I had work and a little to eat in the Jaman and settled my debts. Absorbed the last sunrays until huge thunderstorms. My choices will come true!

1st June 1999

Oh, my goodness, all these exams are over, and I cannot believe my mood! I'm happy and I just cannot wait to be out of here. I know that everyone gets analytical, but I don't seriously want this anymore. I want to go freely to Egypt and live my life. Seriously, unbearably. If he comes with me that is great.

8th June 1999

Paris was incredibly romantic and an eye-opener for us both. We spent a lot of precious unique time together, fondling, enjoying, talking, and believing in one another.

Tomorrow is a big day. I will call the Ritz and decline their offer. I must call Egypt. Go to the travel agencies and arrange a flight! My goodness. Life can be complicated.

Buddha-bar! Great fun!

It was sordid and dark, very relaxing, two delicious cocktails. We walked along with the Champs-Élysées. Beautiful sunset and we ate in Chez Clement and walked to the Eiffel Tower!

Vitelli – in France where we stayed for a couple of days on the way home. It was very calm and relaxing.

I went to see JC. It was incredibly emotional. I do miss him lot. What has happened to him? I hope he realises and lands back on earth again.

Wednesday, 16th June 1999

Well, today was full of adventures. My goodness, life is incredibly strange. I drove to London, to the Egyptian embassy. Saw friends for lunch. I picked up my visa; then had dinner, in a rather relaxing restaurant, far from country life.

Tuesday

London at morning rush hour! Drove down to Ascot, looking frightfully glamorous, drinking plenty of champagne. Betting, winning and losing.

Friday

I sat reading the newspaper regarding the morning Kings Road traffic! We left for Sloane Square tube station to meet my dad as he was taking us out for lunch. We went to an exquisite Spanish restaurant. Fine wine, rich and unique food –

serious treat. Dad and I then went to see an art gallery. Staggering pieces, but sadly no way do I have enough money to buy any of them!

Wednesday

I'm tired and I don't feel like writing today. I'm in an extremely bad mood. Everything it seems is pissing me off and annoying me.

> 1.) I have my period, sore tummy.
> 2) weather is miserable, what's happened to the English summer.
> 3) He didn't call.

Anyway, shit happens. Let's hope life picks up tomorrow.
Went to the cinema. Watched Cruel Intentions.

Thursday

JC threw a complete mental, went ape shit and hit and broke all the windows in the family room, what a complete nightmare. This guy needs help. Serious aid! It's his call though!

Monday, 28th June 1999

My lord, personally today was great. The day was extremely temperamental weather-wise, which disrupts the mood of the person. I had things to focus on, I managed to maintain on my level! I had a lovely weekend seeing friends in London. It was unbelievable. I'm a very fortunate person to live my life and enjoy everything. I feel awful about JC, my goodness. The only thing I can say is I have given up worrying, it is not getting me anywhere. I'm incredibly fortunate that I have found myself able to express the way I feel and think on paper and still maintain a real life! It is important to realise, to take care of number one. Things change when you have children, but hey, we are here for ourselves! Dear God, I do believe this. Is there a god?
After swimming, I read the newspaper, watched the tennis, had lunch, and then went to the dentist. Spoke with Mummy, a lot; she is desperately concerned, we went to the video rental.
A day of regulation, I loved it. I spoke with quite a few people. Chilled out. I have given up writing lists; however, I'm not sure I will maintain it!

Tuesday

Today was a huge learning curve. He does so incredibly well; father of seven special children, he maintains to love us all individually. It's an immense learning curve for each one of us, decisions decided in the family.

It is devastating to believe what is happening. I really don't know and cannot believe to comprehend, we shall see, hey! Life is operating for him just as it is for every other human being on this planet, he is lucky! JC must realise that people are helping him.

I wait patiently for him; however, I do live my own life. I am not in his shoes, his life, I really don't know how he feels about me, we shall totally see, hey? No matter where he goes now, I must maintain to live my own life. I have my own dreams and eternity; we will totally discover each other! I will find him and if he feels the same, he will find me. Even if it takes an eternity! Who knows? A relationship needs work and commitment. I love him at present. He is my man, my dreams, and my focus in sharing?

Wednesday

Off to Egypt next week, a completely new and unique experience! We shall see what happens. Everyone has their fair share of excitements and anticipations; this is another one of mine.

A hundred feelings rushing through my head at present. I would love to express them all; it's just spontaneity and reality! I cannot wait to get out and work, mainly lead my existence, afford my travel, destiny, engagements, and pleasure!

Thursday, 1st July 1999

I felt quite hung over when I woke up this morning, probably too much German sweet wine and lack of sleep. Anyhow, I managed to gather the strength to get out bed and organised myself for the adventurous day ahead. Drove to Wimbledon, it took a good three hours, but we chatted as great sisters do. It was rather annoying, our day at the tennis, because it was scattered showers the entire day. We managed to catch a few games of tennis; it was good, just very frustrating probably more for the players.

Chapter 6

Egyptian Externship Extract...

"A whole lifetime was too short to bring out the full flavour; to extract every ounce of pleasure, every shade of meaning." – Virginia Woolf

Wednesday / Thursday Night

I am at Cairo airport, ready to travel to Sharm, and what an absolute adventure I am having. I left London around 4.00 this afternoon. Flew to Amsterdam, stopped off briefly, and caught another airplane to Cairo. The flight wasn't bad. I had a good meal, watched a good film, and fell asleep. Arriving at Cairo airport was quite an enormous eye-opener! People from anywhere and everywhere are here. It was particularly scary, enormous and smelly; men staring left, right and centre. I felt incredibly watched and everyone trying to help. My goodness, unbelievable! I was quite a focus of attention, which I disliked. No one was going where I was going so I had to manage and calculate my direction and destination. Fortunately, the heat is not overwhelming.

I've just looked at the clock. I have another three hours to wait, what the hell am I going to do for that length of time? Write? Read? I am too scared to sleep because of all the unknowns around me! Money, etc, is all rather nerve-wracking. Oh, well, before I know it, I will be on my travels again.

Thoughts are thrown from angle to angle, and I love to deal with it all. I would like us to be more physical, in love, but I am positive with time, reflection, space, and work on each other; we will have a great time. Time is the essence!

I can see already life here is particularly relaxed and laid back. I rather like it. I have a beautiful piece of artwork on the wall next door to me of three people giving gifts. Whatever I want to believe. I heard a few people before doing/performing their prayers. Rather authentic.

The clock is ticking slowly, 'but surely' I must add I will get there. Relax, take time. I am doing much reflection!

I have had enough, let's go!

Friday Morning

He picked me up from the airport.

Slept most of the day; I was tired. I went to the beach in the afternoon; it was boiling, boiling. We wandered down. I couldn't believe how enormous the entire hotel was. The beach was wonderful, with loads of multicoloured fish in the sea, snorkelling heaven.

I had a little induction course and was shown around the hotel, really it is huge! I love it; I cannot believe it!

As I was saying, completely new environment, mentality, everything. I am so fortunate. It is bloody hot but I reckon I will just have to adapt to the heat. It shouldn't take long and surely when I am in the rhythm my body clock will change and become regulated!! Time / time.

Its' great at this very moment, I am lucky; I cannot wait to be here and make the absolute most of what's to offer!!

Friday, 9ᵗʰ July 1999

My first day at work, 9.30 start. It wasn't too bad. I didn't really have very much to do.

Saturday

Work is beginning to get underway; I arrived at 9.00, this morning. It was slow, but at around 11.30 there was a management meeting I could attend.

Sunday

I worked the whole morning; they are giving me much more to do now, which I prefer because it keeps me very busy.

Tuesday

My dearest JC, where are you? I know there is absolutely no point in writing to you now! Perhaps my soul will transmit the message to you because I believe your soul is lost somewhere and mine may find yours. What has happened to the chap full of life, hope, the one I used to imagine, create, and play with? Have you chosen Devil's Road? Please tell me! I had a vision of you in that room. Alone. Always alone. Why? Portray, express the soul and meaning of your life! Can I help you at all? Can anyone?

Wednesday

Sunsets are soft, light pinks, purples, and blues. Greys, yellows as the night falls, rich purples, dark blues, and the sky is coated with gold sparkles. It's totally clear from any clouds. I am recalling the giant mountains and reflection in Switzerland, the calm and pure atmosphere in the Laurentians, and the views that I captured in the states. Too many to encounter! Absolutely staggering!

Boy where shall I start today, my goodness I am so upset, so desperately upset. I miss my family so much. I so want them with me now. Right now I don't know what to think!

Friday

Do you think / imagine what the future holds just to make you feel better hey? What road is chosen for each individual?

I know that I am not doing the right thing. It will take a little time for me to build up some courage to be free Juliet. I know that's what I need to do! Someone will find me for a correct person, it's just not now! I know!

Time is the essence of everything. I don't care anymore really what people think and feel about me. I love life too much. I really have too many dreams and achievements too.

Sunday, 18th July 1999

Thank goodness I was able to have a little lie-in, what a relief. Six days, seven days, eight days to weeks, three weeks' work, work, work…

Ras Mohammed. It took us rather a while to sort out the car details. It was all under control in the end. What an incredibly warm day. I was hot – swimming in the deep blue. What an incredible astounding experience. Day off, thank the Lord! We played tennis.

Monday, 19th July 1999

I have had some confusing moments lately. I am enjoying myself, but I can feel that I am not happy. I miss my family so much I even miss him enormously.

Tuesday

I was absolutely too messed up and mushed to write last night. The whole day was pretty strange. There is absolutely nothing that I can do that is right. I really am getting particularly depressed.

Wednesday

Unreal scenery, delicious food, camel riding, selective company. I had a lovely evening!

Tuesday

Good lord, I haven't written in here in ages.

All is going well, I am enjoying things. The day seems to fly by. It is all going good though. I haven't really felt inspired to write and my mood seems to be jumping from left to right all the time.

I am overdrawn in my bank. I have had a lot of trouble getting in contact with my bank. Oh well.

My manager is kind of annoying me but hey I just have to get on with things. Enjoy life, be happy and positive. It is sometimes difficult. I often think about what is happening back at home. And while there is not much I can do about what's happening back there I miss it plenty! I had a lovely chat with mummy last night.

I will write in my diary properly soon. I have this thought that I might be pregnant. I have missed my period; what would I do? What an enormous decision. What would I do? I wouldn't, I couldn't have an abortion. My parents, I know, would simply kill me. I know they would. I will take a pregnancy test.

I cannot jump any guns and rush away with strange wild thoughts. Just keep it for the imagination.

Thursday, 29th July 1999

I went to a wild party last night in the desert. It was seriously brilliant. There was a full moon, which bought such life and excitement to the air/sky and the whole environment!

What else has happened? Just more work. I helped in the general manager's office. Also, I have been working in reservations. The food and beverage department are quite messed up. I have been sunbathing, writing long letters, swimming, snorkelling, and smoking up, driving, relaxing, eating delicious food! Simply wonderful. I have been giving my future serious thought…

I am contemplating going to Australia to finish the course.

Friday, 30th July 1999

What a week and it isn't even over yet. Can you believe it? I had such a brilliant night last night. We were cruising on a boat for birthday celebrations; it was a great surprise. Brilliant – cruising with a pure full moon. Chatting, listening to music, dancing, jumping off boats, meeting new people, learning their party moves and their enjoyment of life.

Monday, 2nd August 1999

I know that I am going to make another big decision and go away, leave this place and flyaway. I have been here for a month now. What can I say? I came out here with completely different hopes and expectations. I am not enjoying myself. I am given too many other choices. I need time alone to contemplate and discover the truth of who I am; I just need time. I cannot have time here.

I have decided now that I am going to leave, go travelling, and see Africa and what the continent must offer! Leaving behind what is not helping me, which is making me angry and frustrated. I am seriously out of here.

I love adventure, the unexpected and I am going to go out and find it. It is not going to come at once; it could take years and years. I am out of here; please Juliet, just have the courage to do this. Be strong, sophisticated, and explore. Discover!

Thursday, 5th September 1999

I am going to pack my bags and leave. Not to run away but gather enough courage to part. Leave this guy alone, he is perfectly capable of living life, and most importantly, I can live my life without him, but not here. I find the day is particularly repetitious. I miss proper communication plus deep and meaningful, truly from the heart.

Tuesday, 10th August 1999

I have decided to go back to England; it is no easy access, it is just another adventure and experience in my life. I have travelled halfway across the world and still think about this gentleman.

My lord, what a life I have! I am incredibly lucky to be home and enjoying my family. I have my entire future ahead of me. I need to gather my pride together and get on. The past has happened. I have to be able to continue. I am going to maintain my strength and except what has happened. I am capable of happiness. Let me sleep and experience this solar eclipse at home!

Thursday

I went to the Aldeburgh ball last night with friends, which was great fun. I need to get my feet back on the planet…

Friday

Looking back to Egypt, I had a good time, but I was lonely and couldn't open to anyone. My heart is broken, but I know it is getting sewn back together!

I have just been out to the pub with some friends. I have come to some decisions now; I must focus on my future and live my life. I am thinking of calling the Ritz again. What do I have to lose?

I have things to do and places to go if it doesn't work and right now I have been thinking the world is my oyster, everything seriously just takes time. I believe that there is someone helping me and looking after me. I am incredibly fortunate to have such supportive parents and very special home friends who are really wonderful. I shall call the Ritz when I wake tomorrow and see what will happen. Just we will see hey. Relax, take time. Think. Sleep and just get into recovery mode.

I had a great day today; I saw auntie and spoke with her for some time about everything.

Sunday, 15th August 1999

I am now in a little cottage on the Norfolk coast, bustling with hyperactivity and excitement.

Monday, 16th August 1999

Well, I have had two nights of incredibly vivid dreams. It is quite incredible.

Tuesday, 17th August 1999

Dreams: Wednesday night – Cross-country swim, swimming to little houses, cottages, etc. through the Canadian wilderness. All very odd!

Sunday

Written on Monday

I cannot remember my dream last night.

I went to the V99 Festival. It was brilliant fun. I have had such a jam-packed weekend. It was brilliant. We saw the Doctors, Lyden Marc Hall, The Cardigans, Orbital, The Stereophonics, Gomez, Massive Attack; it was excellent. I did however get a dreadful headache.

Monday Night

Scottish country dancing – I was wearing one of Mum's garments. Lots of travelling around on a bicycle, through small villages – meeting people en route. Now is a new beginning for me, myself, and I. Off to Australia, the Cornell in America. I love my life! Thank you, God!

Tuesday

I sense within myself I am beginning to change into a strong, unique human being; the Juliet who was proud of herself, who loved arts and reading, loved passion and intimacy who loved control and determination.

The future is in my hands and I am going to create myself into a wonderful and happy person again. Love and appreciate each radical passing moment, inhale the beauty and love of life and everything it has to offer.

I woke early today, usual jog and swim. I love the morning freshness. The still awaiting the breaking sun, by the power of the instrument I wish to create, the impossible is possible, believe and strive for hope.

Fuck the buggers in the world, who don't and never will appreciate. One million moments, one hundred dreams, the entirety for creation, believe in yourself Juliet, you are a capable and successful human being, allow no one to put you down. Run for the present. Believe in your future and capture the memories.

When you return to Egypt:

Art, reading writing, photography.

Work, train, learn, explore, question, answer.

Scuba dive, have fun, laugh, share, talk, open.

Discover the unknown uncertainty.

I have my reasons, my desires, my needs, you were, you are, my future is a success, belief!

Wednesday

Another day in this glorious life! I just hope that this happiness continues in Egypt. It was a big deal today because I called to reserve a ticket.

Pray that you remain to hold onto the belief of yourself. Be Juliet most important, write a novel or something, a play of confusion, frustration, happiness, belief, trust, love, and hatred, understanding and misunderstanding.

I do have such a beautiful future ahead of me. I cannot wait to just live it. Rather like what I'm doing at present. It is all good fun; I am lucky. I have had a great weekend in London.

I am at the stage when many wonderful things are happening and I do not have enough special words to write. I have realised many things that happened in the past! Opportunity to use it – for good or evil. Some things are just beyond our control. Beautiful! Success is a road that is always under construction.

Monday

Let them burn for all eternity in the flames of hell
Consult, cease to plead.
Nothing short of a miracle.
I agree with his grace.
If it would please you, sir.
Remember who you are! Be afraid of nothing.
I am a true and faithful subject.
I do not need your pity.
I shall not forget this kindness.
I have committed none.
I promised to act as my conscience dictates.
Perhaps there is nothing apart from us and our thoughts.
Innocence is the most precious gift to…
Encounter security!
And it is marvellous in our eyes.
Consider proposals.
War is a sin but sometimes a necessary one.

Thursday

I am here now; I'm in Sardinia after one hell of a trip! We made it! We did it! True achievement.

Sunday, 5th September 1999

I said that I would write in my diary refreshed. Three days have flown past and much has happened. I have sailed, read, swam, walked, chatted, drank, scuba dived.

Monday, 6th September 1999

Perched on the balcony! It is very peaceful, distant bar, waves gently crashing onto the beach. I have been sailing the whole day, peaceful, relaxing. It's certainly such an intense amount of sun.

Tuesday, 7th September 1999

Well, what atmosphere am I observing, living, contracting, abstracting this evening?
Today – sailing, wakeboarding, skiing, swimming, eating, walking, socialising, drinking, contemplation.

17th September 1999

Well, I am back in Egypt now.
I actually had a great birthday. It was brilliant fun. Lots of people turned up and it was great to see who really my true friends are. It was a shame there wasn't more people from Canada or Switzerland but hey shit happens. I just won't bother with them, actually that's bullshit of course I will. Well the whole evening of the 15th ran pretty smoothly.
Things are seriously beginning to change now. Who knows what's going to happen in the future? Just believe in yourself Juliet, now and forever. You have had the space, you are back just please enjoy life. Take one easy step at a time. If it gets you down, it is all-natural; all our nature is to take its course.

18th September 1999

Good people are my only stepping-stones. Mountains of thanks. Keep all my enemies at bay!

19th September 1999

Hey Juliet please accept to be happy and enjoy life. It is difficult sometimes but just really live life and be happy please. You are an important person. You may not be the most wonderful looking person or the person with the best heart but just be Juliet. Be happy all right.

21ˢᵗ September 1999

This lover's stuff…

24ᵗʰ September 1999

I think tonight has been a big turning point. I don't want any more of this. I feel pathetic and stupid. I must maintain my pride and self-esteem.

26ᵗʰ September 1999

Making the most of my spontaneity… My goodness in two days, I decided to leave Coral Bay hotel and I am now in Cairo having had met an American family and Egyptian man!

I have to find myself. I am away from everything. I am doing exactly what I want to do and no one, I repeat no one, is involved in this. It is me and only me, I am content, not stressed. I'm just taking one step in front of the other. My lord where is this direction going?

I am off to Africa, travelling. I am excited and content, growing up and becoming Juliet. Thank you! Thank you!

Tuesday

Alexandria. I woke early in the morning and went for a nice long walk along the seafront. Swam in the sea. I am on my own, away from home and people I know. I saw the museum caught up on culture, went to the Roman theatre – it was special. Unique and unbelievable. Statues, mummies, sites. I am extremely fortunate.

Alexandria, Cairo – 12ᵗʰ October.

Tanzania

Malawi.

Wednesday, 29ᵗʰ September 1999

Forte! An incredible castle lying on the Mediterranean. Has an amazing view of Alexandria. Saw fishermen, locals, tourists. I hardly blended in, but hey, I had a real exploration. It was a calm day. Went to the market, astounding jewellery, people, and material. The evening again was filled with events. It was great fun, children, babies, adults, and a whole spectrum of generations. I was able to eat excellent food, good conversations.

Sunday

Another day in the life of a young girl, travelling, exploring, and adventuring new and unique places! Everywhere has its heart and everyone has their home, whether it's a mansion guarded or cardboard boxes. I must come back to Alexandria in a few years to see what happens after the reconstruction. I am off again on another adventure!

Thursday

Coach from Alexandria to Sharm el-Sheikh. I arrived at 5.00 in the morning. I am staying at the Pigeon House, which is a little hotel. I have got residency of one of the huts. It is very cosy and sweet. Small, but I managed to squeeze in. All is going well now. I have even been offered a job by the diving company! Life is good.

Friday

Today I was in Ras Mohammed, beautifully calm, tranquil.

Sunday

We brought the tickets to Luxor! And then decided to go and see the pyramids and the Sphinx. It was such strange timing; I was tired at 11.00 in the morning. We came across a little hotel, Mayfair. It was old-fashioned and particularly rundown, but it did have a pleasant terrace looking over whitewash and streets. Anyway, from 11 until 5, we slept, and then we washed, changed and decided what was next on the agenda. It was to go to the World Trade Centre; there were many shops and much fashion for men, nothing particularly good for women. Suddenly, hunger struck, and we chatted over sandwiches and lots of coffee.

Monday

Day in Cairo, we woke up early to horns beeping and dogs barking, the hustle and bustle of the city. Anyway, we got ourselves breakfast and decided to walk to the station where we were able to sort out bus tickets to Israel. We managed to visit the markets, which were bright, colourful and smelly! Awful hagglers. Anyway, at 10.00, we caught the train to Luxor, relieved, dirty and tired.

The Temple of Luxor is far more coherent than Karnak because it was mainly built by two kings.

Caleche!

Karnak

Boat trip

Taxi

Food

Sleep!

Temples!

The magnificent setting of the Temple of Queen Hatshepsut against the Theban hills.

Friday

What an adventure!

Dahab, a relaxed, tranquil town on the east Sinai coast.

Saturday

Dahab is a quite chilled out hippy place. We are staying in a little hut with one bed, no a/c and loads of mosquitoes, getting eaten alive. There is great music and a perfect Tiran wind to chill the air!

Dahab, I have lost all sense of time, the day, date, months, etc. My goodness, my mind has just been flowing here, thinking, watching, and observing living! My Lord.

Monday

Interview with the university in Australia.

Still Monday

Thinking straight and acting properly has never been my forte. Anyway, destiny is in my hands, taking immediate control over the present situation.

Dirty

Smelly

No smiling people

Traffic (Tres hectic)

Ugly buildings, horrible looking

Charged excessive amounts as a tourist

Remember who you are and be afraid of nothing!

Energy is an eternal delight

Suicide is a permanent solution to a temporary problem.

I have now arrived back from Dahab. Australia dawns! Either the novel will continue, or it shall cease right now!

Friday

Leaving Egypt tomorrow; I shall be flying to Rome.

Friday

I received an offer from Australia. Thank goodness, I am sorted; whatever happens now, my intention is to be in control.

15ᵗʰ November 1999

Art exhibition, I went to at the Royal Academy.

13ᵗʰ November 1999

Went to a fab Mexican restaurant: it was great fun!

19ᵗʰ November 1999

Watched Blood Brothers, it was an excellent performance. They got a standing ovation. Amazing, very much recommended.

Sunday

Went to the Cathedral to watch the Songs of Praise, excellent!

Sunday

Shooting weekend! Relaxing, cleaning, dog walking, swimming, artwork, emailing, phoning, TV, eating.

December

Australian embassy to obtain Visa.

Went to the Tate Gallery for a while and then cruising onto the London town, we laughed into the early hours and had a blast! Lots of yummy food, delicious wine consumed. Steve Winwood happened on a Monday night. The band was amazing. Excellent memories. I even managed somehow to get my visa from the embassy under control. What a relief!

Monday, December

Australia seriously is calling. I cannot wait to go out there. Tomorrow is going to be serious packing and getting things totally under control. I am not going to allow anything to overtake this. I desperately am going to get there safe and well. It is just very expensive now.

My little heart, please take time for youself.

I will wait for you.

I will respect your choice.

I just want you to be happy, now.

Think, and make the right decision.

1st January 2000

Edinburgh was the town at the turn of the new Millennium, fireworks, and a marriage proposal. I woke he was by my side. There are many reasons that we could be together and many reasons why now it's slightly difficult.

It was a glorious morning to wake up to, blue skies, slight frost, and a sense of a recovering morning; last night's events were certainly memorable. I couldn't have been happier. We had great chats about our future, what was going to happen between the two of us. 'We shall see' was the conclusion.

2nd January 2000

We packed and then drove into London for lunch, Camden Town in Anzori Bas; all is well. I must look forward, not back, the future looks bright and cheerful, and I cannot wait for me to enter it!

9th January 2000

I have decided to get more organised with events to do with going to Switzerland and Alicante.

18th January 2000

A well Juliet after 18 days of being in the year 2000!
I spent the entire day cooking today. I woke early and went straight to the kitchen. I made everything from scratch, which was incredibly satisfying. I cooked a fish soup, roast sirloin, and apple charlotte. I was pleased. Good chats.

20th January 2000

I woke early this morning and drove straight to Luton airport. I was all in good time, rather tired; I am certainly not good at this early morning business. The Easy Jet flights were sorted, I slept practically the entire journey, arrived in Geneva (Switzerland) early and rented a gorgeous Golf GTI, a very pleasant car. I am a very, very fortunate lucky person being able at 21 to do this kind of easy transportation business. I cruised to my music and met friends in the centre of Bulle, chatting to people from the past, catching up on the latest gossip, really just spending a wonderful few moments with old friends.

Friday, 21st January 2000

I drove up into the mountains; thank God I had rented a car... All went well and I didn't think about it hardly at all. The weather was miserable until we decided to go all the way to the top, panoramic rest. My goodness, it was stunning, a layer of cotton wool bedding the mountains, clear blue, crisp skies. I drove off to Montreux, 'Glion'

Saturday, 22nd January 2000

I would have regretted not going. I woke early. I said my last goodbyes. I had spent two lovely days. I captured one last view and then cruised off to Geneva airport to then catch the flight to Alicante/Spain!

Sunday, 23rd January 2000

I'm in Spain. He and I were out late last night and no time to catch up. We woke around 11.30 and breakfast, which was prepared in the conservatory lovely, lovely!

Saturday, 29th January 2000

My last day in England for quite some time, what is going to happen? I can only go forward with positive hope, ambition, and success (focus, girl). I am very happy now; it is all going very well.

Chapter 7

Another World – Another Exploration...

"Exploration is really the essence of the human spirit." –
Frank Borman

17ᵗʰ February 2000

It is now the 17ᵗʰ of Feb, my god, where has the time gone? I have been here in Auz for 17 days. Life is floating past at wonderful times, we are creating lovely moments. I was in Sydney which was perfect. Bought a car, so I can do some escaping to see all the sites, do work away, research for work/appointments, etc., set myself up. I must get organised people, we all here for different moments, creating their own unique lives. To manage your business well is to manage its future and to manage its future is to manage information.

Has anything you've done made your life better?

By the better ends of our nature!

23ʳᵈ February 2000

Egypt was the transition process. Faithless kiss! I would never leave anyone alone at the end of the day. Never! Sweet pea, enjoy life and everything it has! I must sleep!

Wednesday, 8ᵗʰ March 2000

Well, life has been cruising past before my eyes at an immense pace. I have been having a great time, participating in all aspects of fun and enlarging up my life!

Been in Sydney

Sleeping on the beach

Mardi Gras

Driving

Out partying/drinking, etc.

Looking at Manly

Life is running smoothly which I like, perhaps I am making big mistakes! Perhaps I am not but I do enjoy being here, leading and living my own life, free from relationships and hectic nightmares!

Thursday, 9ᵗʰ March 2000

I went to the Sugar Ray live concert, which was excellent, I love Sugar Ray, and it was brilliant to have attended! Been there on their Circuit Tour, why not here!

Love Ya, Jules!

Cautious romantics who want a better quality of life are more interested in job satisfaction than in sacrificing personal happiness and group for promotion. Their prize – experience, not acquisition.

Monday

Travelling is one of my favourite passions. Admiring, exploring and absorbing, truly outstanding, and breath-taking experiences. I have met some very random people on my travels. I am sure that it is great how I'm approaching the entire environment!

Last week was rather manic. Busy with exams, organising the party 'Spy v Spy'. Being on the committee is brilliant on the CV and leadership, professional mode. The road is sometimes under construction, but I believe that there is a light at the end of it!

Wednesday, 22ⁿᵈ March 2000

See what will happen
Capture each moment
Happiness is worth… Perfection!
The success is the way to survival
Always a positive attitude Juliet!

Monday, 27ᵗʰ March 2000

MET THE QUEEN OF ENGLAND.

28ᵗʰ March 2000

Even those little naughty teasing attitudes you have. Sarcastic/wise in only the cheerful environments.

Message from…

I love you very much but unfortunately must fly to NZ tonight.

Saturday, 1ˢᵗ April 2000

Happy April Fool's.

Well, a lot has been happening as per usual. I have been having a great time, although I am very lacking in motivation and seem to be perfecting the art form of procrastination. I am, however, a very happy hippie chick, really enjoying the moments that are happening. Do not expect anything, just love and capture each moment.

Monday, 9th April 2000

Projects and presentations are going well; just be planned, structured, relaxed but aware!
The tranquil moments nearly moving down capture enhance…
Words just don't want to flow this evening
pour quoi!
I am free.
Free from it, I am.
Free! Free from it all!
All the vampires, walking through the valley!

Easter Monday

The world passes us by within the glimpse of an eye! I have had a great week: working, studying absorbing every moment that has been given. Who knows if I am doing it for good or bad? Success or failure! Who cares!
I am being aware of myself, my position on the planet. The hope for more freedom, love, and laughter!
I have met such a unique set of friends out here! Australia. Is it destined to be my humble home? For yet am I still searching for even more special beauty! Irresistible here and heartache! Delicious food and perfect companionship. We shall see who I share this world with. Perhaps no one? I desire to have children, special and pleasurable individuals. In the meantime, I am absorbing, getting high on life, plus all its offerings. I should thank Jesus for this time of year. Am I a Christian, this is when you died for us all those thousands of years ago?
Dates rollover, nights come with starry skies. Moonlit beauty.
Exchange and trade
Love and laughter
Investment in the great outdoors.
Australia, perhaps it is simply an age of pure enjoyment. No serious commitments, other than to just appreciate life. Realise how fortunate I am as a

wee English 'chick' to travel and experience what I do. Observe, analyse and be naive when necessary.

I truly am uniquely confident to say that I am in control and will remain, until necessary, until the moment I get rocky that I need a lesson in depression again. And when it does, I would approach it as yet another great experience and realise to my heart and mind there is always a way out. Look at the planets in the sky. Listen to tuneful music and always have a deep heart that knows the road to success is always under construction!

There are many fish in the sea, stars in the sky, cars on the roads, grass in the meadows, trees in the forest and people in the world. You are one! A true human with: two eyes, two legs, two arms, and a large heart; ready to spread the word of enjoyment, of life, freedom, and continue of lessons of understanding. Love yourself and be good to yourself... If not to you, to others.

Friday, 28th April 2000

I must undergo more treatments, which upsets my wee heart, but I suppose it shall be for the best. I am living on the philosophy of we will see. I am in no hurry to rush things on and on.

Reflections on the past is always are great ways to observe the character that you are. The people you have met before affect or enlighten your life! I wouldn't be where I am if I hadn't met such great and special people!

I remember listening to a CD a lot when I was in Egypt. I must have been on an unbelievable level. When I went back that time, I was fine! I must have cried very minimally. I had a clear understanding of what was meant to happen for the time being!

Saturday, 29th April 2000

I'm sitting by the lake in Canberra. I have been here quite a lot recently. It is a beautifully tranquil and calm life. Everyone is experiencing different emotions and adventures.

Although I love my freedom, I do miss what it is like to be constricted sometimes. Freedom has brought around a direction of movement! The abundance of understanding and perceiving your own goals through life!

I am not worried about what goes on in the relationship now. It probably would be good for me to some extent, but I want to be free, to explore, I have had enough of people influencing my life. I admit that I am truly grateful to some! But I am not going to get married till I am 25/26. I think that right now, I have moved through a complete transition stage, loving every moment of it! Enjoying, partaking, learning about new and wonderful people. I believe that it is important to find a balance and reliability. I love to earn money, know what is coming in and going out.

Now it is the time for reflection, observation another unique adaption. Let's the planets spiral! Days take their unique moments. I am looking forward to going to Bali!

Sunday 15th May 2000

This book has been to:

England

Switzerland

Spain

Australia

Bangkok/Thailand

Bali/Indonesia

Australia

Trust me! It is paradise.

This is where the hungry come to feed. For mine is a generation that circles the globe in life, in search of something we haven't tried before. Never refuse an invitation, never resist the information, and never fail to be polite. And never outstay your welcome.

Keep your mind open and sucking the experience and, if it hurts, you know what? It is probably worth it. You hope and you dream but you will never believe something until it is going to happen, not like it does in the movies. And when it does, you expect it to feel different, more real. I am waiting for it to hit me!

Go with the flow

Smell

Colours

Thorough

Different lands, cultures

Get in touch with the mystery of life

Smells

Taste

Texture

Colours

On our beautiful planet.

We again will see what Bali (Indonesia) will bring. I am not expecting anything, taking it completely as it will come! Absorbing, adapting, thinking, believing, enjoying, loving, dreaming, drawing, photographing, drinking, eating, sleeping, washing, swimming, talking, chatting, dancing, researching, understanding.

My God! Thank you. I am fortunate!

Monday

Bali. Enjoying the uniqueness of this special place. I am staying in the Hotel Aston; it is gorgeous. The sun has been incredibly warm, and I have got amazingly sun kissed. Went for a long walk and took photos, colour. Will get some black and white ones too! Breakfast, swimming, reading, sunbathing, walking! Even had a massage, glorious!

Tuesday

Took a trip up north, which included: eye-opening Bedugul Mountain and Lake Bratan (seeing the snake man), magical Git Git Waterfall which was truly stunning and very refreshing, feeding the monkeys and the dip in the natural hot water springs, drove briefly through the old capital of Bali, Singarajai and devoured a delicious lunch at the Black Sand Beach at Lovina. Coffee beans, cloves, local fruits, and rice being grown!

Wednesday

Seriously, overcome the devil and allow the angel to always be in touch!

Serenity of the shaded areas, off scuba diving tomorrow, should be excellent fun!

Thursday

Nusa Dua to Sanus Sanur was just a little further north. So, the early morning Bali comes to life! I am very much alone, but feel content in my thoughts. I have reflected much on the past and haven't had streams of thoughts on the future. Just that 'we will see' after the operation. I am pleased that I am doing this; it is giving me time to read and write. Engrossed in the tranquillity of Bali and the nearby island Nasa Pendida, where I did my scuba diving.

I ventured off to dinner, serious long walk, got myself rather lost, managed to let my legs just go, I saw quite a lot. The festivals, beautiful garments, endless people travelling on bikes, deep smells of incense burning spices. Beautiful. I took myself out for a delicious dinner of calamari and got eaten alive by mosquitoes.

The uncertainty drives a certain amount of thrilling risk and excitement. Keeping composed! Enjoying, observing, absorbing, allow time to take its toll, destiny capturing the road!

Saturday

Watching lots of CNN news, catching up on all the political and economic turmoil that is occurring while I am in Bali! I went to Kuta today, which I was looking forward to. Change, changes are important!

Destiny again is taking its toll! Firstly, I haven't been able to obtain any money from any ATM, which is rather frustrating considering I have very minimal amounts. Oh, well, we will see what will happen.

Of all places, I am now at Kuta beach, surfing capturing excitement and waves. The breeze is beautiful. Hopefully, I will capture some of the sun today.

I don't mind people hassling me for drinks, massage, manicure, pedicure, sarongs, etc., it just gets rather too much when they start touching me, it is this I cannot stand and gets me very irritated! I suppose it's a custom and way, but believe me, it is rather off-putting.

I can see why people like it here, tranquil. The days go on and people enjoy as much as they can. I look at the news, I was lucky not to have gone to Fiji, they seem to have a wee crisis over their political leader, the prime minister being taken captive!

Kuta is certainly a more touristic destination, strangely. Not that many people speak English…

Give you good price

You beautiful

You need, you need

Sunday Morning

I am sitting along the main street in Kuta, busy and people still hassling. Christian day of rest? Not here; too many people shouting in their separate directions.

Sunday Evening

It has transformed – my single life into three more people, they picked a Brazilian chap up en route!

Tuesday

I am now in the centre of Bali Island by a lake, we spent last night in Samur, which was great, very relaxing, and peaceful. We had a full day at the surfers' beach (Paradise) and went back to NuraDua (Aston Bali) Hotel.

Today, we visited a temple. Relaxed on the beach first thing this morning, catching up on serious sun rays. Drove through the island: paddy fields, stunning scenery, took loads of photos to add to the collection.

Tuesday

Back to work in Canberra.
I miss Bali!
The power of the woman
Entering sacred space
Touching future
Yet to come
Bringing eternal grace
I am willing to accept whatever the future holds as it is presented, without trying to change it. I will surrender to the flow of the spiral and trust what I am shown. It's the perfect thing sometimes.
Went up to the mountains this weekend, it was perfect, simply amazing!

8th June 2000

Change is an important and beneficial aspect of life. It is a form of choice; people decide and lead the lives that are placed in front of them. Others organise somewhere and form a regime! It is an important understanding to make the most of the lives we are partaking in. Changes happen an immense amount to me! Being in different environments, absorbing unique cultures, travelling, and enhancing one's change of scenery. We all come and go on this planet letting each moment occur, some don't – however it is important to grasp, we must absorb! All nine lives' offerings. Which road to travel, direction to take, door to open? Change, I believe, is positive; it opens minds, brings new light, and new understanding.

I must sleep. I have an early start working at the races tomorrow!

Friday Night

Today, I worked at the GMC car races in the corporate booth.

Taking, absorbing little. Believing the communication flows. Accents prevail… Allow each passing moment to unfold. Perform with accuracy. The adrenaline! Keep moving… Allowing you to stop repeating yourself! And get on with tomorrow.

Saturday, 10th June 2000

Well, another day of work accomplished at the racetrack. It was great. I met a great bunch of people who say thank you and with much appreciation. It was wonderful. The beginning of something, people's observations! But we shall see.
The Lynx
You know the secrets very well
The Dreamtime and the magic
But you'll never tell
May I learned to hold my tongue
Observe like the Sphinx
Powerful yet silent
Become worthy of trust
The secrets will be available

Tuesday, 20th June 2000

I have finished this chapter; it's drawing close! It's all happening in its own good time. I am a very lucky chicky. Taking every moment one step at a time. Absorbing, loving, appreciating. The course on the weekend was very intense and I am rather tired from it. My energy is low, and I need to open my mind. Speak to others about organising to go to Cornell and see if it is possible.

Sunday, June 2000

I am shattered.
End of an era, allow the music to flow!
Trust me! It is paradise.

This is where the hungry come to feed.

For mine is a generation in life that circles the globe in search of something we have not tried before.

Do never refuse ad invitation, never resist the unfamiliar, and never fail to be polite. And never outstay your welcome.

Keep your mind open and suck in the experience and if it hurts, you know what, it's probably worth it.

This is the opening of a new chapter of my life! I have just finished my book from Thailand. I feel very refreshed and new. I will write in this every night, to collect and absorb all creation and share it amongst my many gathered thoughts!

Monday

You have been working hard, just trying to pay the rent!

Say you want to live your life without tears.

Well, today was excellent. It started with a phone call. Two great surprises. Life takes its toll and direction – 'Job at the Hyatt'? Drawing, talking, and getting well into work mode. Accounting department, satisfying.

Thursday, 6ᵗʰ July 2000

Career?

Family?

Friends?

Monday, 10ᵗʰ July 2000

I worked most of the day at hotel operations II and accounting, I feel none the wiser…

Sunday, 16ᵗʰ July 2000

He was here over the weekend, which was lovely. I showed him around the various places, and I hope he had a lovely time.

I went to a rave, passion, last night which was excellent. I had a wild night, lots of manic dancing, perfect. I have been revising accounting all day today.

Saturday, 22nd July 2000

Life is confusion between good and evil, right, and wrong. I jumped in the car and disappeared. I hadn't meant to worry anyone, far from it. I just need time to myself, away from stress, moments, and people. Everyone knowing my specific movements.

Anyway, on the positive side, I have done plenty of work and spent time truly alone, away from the bubble. A break in Canberra. The hotel operations project is due on Monday. I have placed much of my devoted time and energy into it. So, fingers crossed I will do well.

I've been able to jog, long walks in the fresh country air.

31st July 2000

Well, plenty has been happening in my world lately! Three months is nearly up from my last check-up!

The wheel keeps turning, the skies keep changing.

Listen to the whispers.

In the surface of the sphere.

Trees will thud.

Owl, magic, time, space.

Does the truth emerge?

Casting out deception.

Silent flight

Keen, silent observation to entwine

Some life situations.

All conceived that which others cannot

The essence of true his door

Where others are deceived

The owl sees and knows what is there…

Work is regular. Sorted quite a lot in my normal life. Taxes, car, health! Joys, joys, hey! Capture new ambiances.

Tuesday

Had the tourism debate this morning. It is good practice to do this public speaking lark.

Today will be rather full-on! Lots to do, people to catch up with, classes to attend! The joys of being a student!

All too dramatic. Novel material. If anyone will be interested. Fabrication. Take it as it comes. Summertime is coming.

The trees are sweetly blooming

Purple Heather!

Where are you going? Lassie! We will all go together!

Flowers of the mountains.

Prayer and abundance

You bring us the gifts of life

Here at our prayers

Smoke rising like Phoenix

We are reborn

Within the sacred words!

Sacred Manner

To give praise for the richness of life to be shared with all race's, creatures, nations and our life. Energy is a friend. You achieve nothing without the aid of a great spirit. It is time to make peace with another or inner completely. Walk my balance again, the smoke of prayer and praise. Change your robe to white, answer to the praise of the world.

Friday, 4th August 2000

It is just I have a few issues which I would like to resolve, I suppose it is going to take a lifetime to do these.

Men – why do I always get confused and attached? Why do I let my life focus on them; it is ridiculous. I feel too open and ready to be attacked at any moment. I deserve it to some degree. I just wish that I didn't overdo it. Just took one day at a time and just let someone love me for me.

Work – work is always a constant issue in my life. I love to work, and I love to learn new and wonderful things all the time… But I am lacking in curiosity, I want to explore more and for people to appreciate the effort I place into everything a lot more. Anyway, enough of my average approach. I know that one day I shall become an important specimen.

Future – I am unsure about the future now, I suppose to some degree everyone is, how they approach it, what road to take. Who to listen to, the constant question of am I doing the right thing here, am I loving what is happening here, right in front of my eyes? Is this all helping me get to where I am going to be? I always wanted to be a doctor or a nurse when I was younger and look where I am now, in hospitality, anyone and everyone can get into this industry, it is diverse and interesting and there is an unbelievable amount out there to capture. Should I be doing art and photography, or even specialising?

Absorb everything, stay slightly mysterious, don't let others put you down; they are probably doing it at their own expense anyway. Believe.

There is a place for every person on the planet. Experience and emotions happen for a reason; a well-deserved meaning and perfected understanding that we are only placed here for a certain period. Allow adaption to play a key role in your life. Believe in the moments. Allow people to lead their own lives at their rate. This is belief and happening. Occurrence is such a unique space. Strive for the understanding of yourself; allow no one to deter you away from your character! Of perception!

I do love to write though! I hope some of it makes sense to the reader! There actually shouldn't be any readers; this is my unique mind happening on this planet right now!

A comprehensive approach!

Could it be a psychological imbalance in the brain, childhood deprivation and faulty parenting, or the cumulative effect of stress over time that onset the reading into us?

Some right is given to us.

What 'cure' is necessary?

'Habit', 'attitude' and 'lifestyle'

Physical

Emotional

Behavioural

Mental

Interpersonal

Whole self

Existence/spiritual

Recognise, identify, learn, and communicate

Will, go with it!

It is when encountering other people, their morals, their expectations that you allow your mind to freely wander…!

Distracting your mind,

Becoming physically active,

Abdominal breathing.

Foster and increase capacity and actively cope, rather than passively react to the bodily symptoms of panic!

Recognise your thinking patterns and when encountering a distraction, reconstruct and fully support. Confide, and be strong. Absorb the moment. Allow creation to resolve, love all of life, experience, acknowledge, and believe in number one… I cannot believe this is all happening! All I can say is I am very lucky!

Tuesday, 15th August 2000

The joys of living a student life! I would like to know what is happening, the true possibilities. I am trying to do my best with all the understanding perhaps a lot of comprehensions. As always, we will see. Everyone experiences that!

Wednesday

Whale

Of mighty oceans

You have seen it all

Secrets of the ages are

Hard within your cool

Teach me how to hear your words

And understand the roots of history

Of when our world began

People who can turn into the universal mind of the great spirit. Only later, when they receive confirmation, do they begin to understand how or why they received the impression.

Playing the power for your chosen destiny heads to your pathway of knowing

Unique beyond records

Sound of the whale

Sunday, 27th August 2000

Butterfly

Butterfly that flutters

Into the morning light

You have known many forms
Before you took a flight
The art of transformation
Sharing colours and joy of your creation with the world
Is it a thought or idea?
Do I need to decide?
Am I developing and doing something to make my idea a reality?
Am I sharing my complete idea?
The clarity to your mental process
Assist you in finding the next step for your personal life and career
Need for freedom – vacation – new job
Persevere!
Represent courage
Known realities – no longer applicable
The New World demands that you use your newfound wings and fly!
Well, I believe another chapter of this book is to emerge. I, fortunately, finished last semester in the mind of allowing things to happen, float in the wind like a feather, dancing from place to place; encounter new people, different places. Sydney, Working September 2000 Olympic Games, made it happen.
Hosting the Olympics. It is great. I am a very fortunate individual!
I am going to write down some things that I want or would like to do during my week break before heading back to Canberra, to complete yet another semester! Museum visits, music festivals, thriving, Palm Beach, back with a camera, catching up with friends.

Chapter 8

Holding Patterns...

"Life is a balance of holding on and letting go." – Rumi

Sunday, 10th September 2000

I picked him up from the airport yesterday morning very early and ever since we have been taking life very smoothly! This morning, we woke early and cruised off to the rocks, saw the Olympic rings on the bridge, Opera house and absorbed! The morning ambience, chillin, chillin!!

Wednesday, 13th September 2000

Sydney is a lovely city with much spirit and atmosphere with the lead up to the Olympics, which are happening in two days. Plus, also, I am turning 22, hoorah! I seriously enjoyed being 21 though. The Olympics is exciting, I cannot believe that I am here! I truly wanted to be! Work, work!

Tuesday, 14th September 2000

Staying at Bondi Beach, it is beautiful, people are swimming in the sea, surfing, relaxing on the beach.

15th September 2000

It is my birthday! What more can I say! What a dream, I'm here!

16th September 2000

The Olympics have opened! The spirit is immense, sport, sport, and more sport, it is great fun. I am leaving Sydney today, Bondi Beach, sayin'.
Work
September
Byron Bay!
Kokopelli play for me
So, my heart missing
Magic Flute of mystery
Fruitful dreams you bring
(Kokopelli – fertility)
Song of Aztlan
Fertile fire
Canyons of my mind
Sacred union

Heart to heart
Speaks of the divine
It is time to listen to Kolopelli song
Fertility
Asked to use your talents to create fertility
In some area of your life
Whatever you intend to plant currently
Will be productive for you!
Planting seeds for the future takes effort on your part, now it is time to use your skill and resources to make use of the magic.
The timing couldn't be better.
Shift away from the old limiting ideas and move forward.
Time is now!
The power is you!
It is a wonderful, wonderful life
To be here!
I can tell you if I die tomorrow, I can truly express that I have had a splendid life. Very special, perfect, I am an extremely fortunate individual.

Saturday, 23rd September 2000

The Olympics are overtaking the atmosphere! It is great fun! Lots of spirits. Life is proving to be very interesting. I have calmed down a lot more, I am certainly not jumping to conclusions as quickly as I used to.

Patience and guidance, protection of my soul. I cannot get hurt again! I never want to feel low. But I believe that there is much to absorb and see in the life of true perfection that does not need to be gloated over!

I do miss home quite a lot at the moment. I worry about getting back to the UK though. I am slightly unsure why, but hey, we will see what the future has to hold. I miss many of my friends as well! But hey, I am sure when the moment arises to see them again it will be a truly unique occasion!

He is being random, interesting and perhaps mysterious! Anyway, we will see what will happen in that department. Temperamental. Take it as it comes. Why, why? I just want to know what he wants from me! I am not a difficult individual; I am pretty much not difficult to get along with.

Keep smiling with interest and please Jules don't allow yourself to get distressed and hurt again! It is not worth all the pain and anguish!

Future looks bright, happy and cheerful, directions, choices and moments are made! The power is mine! And I have much of life to enjoy and approach!

I know that I am meant to believe in God now; it's giving me an immense lesson. I will see the Rock, go to Alice Springs, over to Perth, up to Cannes, and down to Melbourne, and then back to Canberra and living reality. Get back into the rhythm of work.

Tuesday

Well hello again. I am not really sure whether I have made the correct decision or not but I certainly regret nothing because what I'm doing now, I had dreamt of doing for a long time. Whether it is working or not we will see. I have to think in reality that my studies and career come first and after that destiny will continue, and I shall remain a positive, happy and unique character, that is on this planet for some reason. Some people find that freezing and others don't, whether I do or not will certainly be up for questioning, however right now I will approach each day with pleasure. It is a gift to be alive and remain human and healthy!

Next semester, I can imagine is going to fly past and before I know it, all my family will be here. Taking Australia by storm! Should be great fun to see them. I am not ready to settle down yet – actually far from it. I may be writing this to make myself feel better hey we'll need some motive and protection of our souls and wellbeing.

I am looking forward to the next semester and then graduating. I actually cannot wait. I'll be qualified and will have achieved my education. Ready to take the world with storm! Make my place! My positioning and my reality!

Love ya!

One question that is on my mind... why is he here? Why did he remain in touch! Why is he here with me? Destiny? Take it as it comes! And respect yourself. Never get hurt like before...

Monday, 2nd October 2000

School started again for me at 8.30 this morning. I had a wonderful month away from the hustle and bustle of school life. Now I face myself with the fact, that it is so nearly time to graduate. I must and shall succeed, whatever the weather, pattern circumstance. I am an extremely fortunate individual that has the world at her doorstep.

Everything happens for a reason! I must just make my reason worthwhile. This semester I can imagine is going to pass by at the rate of knots! Flutter! Flutter!

I am a lucky person extremely fortunate.

Sleep.

It would be another day in the glorious life of Juliet Fisher, that is, I am taking it all as it comes. I think that I have been absolutely far too self-involved and the belief at present is that I am stupid, insecure, and lacking in all trust and future for myself... Which I know is a pathetic excuse because I have so much more to live for and believing!

I miss my family an immense amount; it is probably that 10 month mark.

Anyway... I must get on with being happy and living life and making the upmost of all that has been given to me! The future will be bright, it is bright already, I just have to gather the courage of letting go of the past and taking the right now into my present and then just live life.

Work is also proving to be another adventure, I must admit. I must be a more achievable human... I have so much to offer my workplace and the people who I am with... Let go of the thoughts that managed to get intertwined and allow the moments and study to take control.

7th October 2000

Well here I am again, it is Saturday night.

I am unsure of what is happening. I just would like someone to tell me that I am a wonderful person and I have much to offer life. I truly do, I am just sorry that I cannot be the most splendidly special person on the planet.

I don't really care much anymore in the way that people have their judgements and interactions in a negative attitude in my life! I have to carry on and live. I know that I have much to offer people, the world, and the environment – I believe and pray that I will succeed I am sure that I will... Pray, pray to everyone and everything.

I am unsure why I even write like this, in my diary every night, it is not every night though, and it really depends on my motivation! But I do it as an achievement; it is a type of security somehow... I take one day at a time, I write about people who interact in my life... How I believe, where I am going, what I am doing.

Destiny will take control... Achieve honey... You are a darling and have much more to live and believe...

My thoughts are muddled... Actually who's aren't?

It is strange, when I arrived out here the beginning of the year; I was so in control of my life and the direction I was taking... Why this guy, yes a person who has entered into my heart... This was two years ago now? Why has he come into my life? I can tell you I am not a happy person, I am happy in the way, I just let life happen, I have been hurt more than once, twice, three times more and more by this person... It is just madness, I mean madness.

I am just questioning at the moment, whether I am weak or being stubborn, who knows, actually who really cares, no one really gives a flying piece of shit do they? Important characters have departed from my life recently. These people have all had an enormous impact in my being, and truly have created the person I am today.

Directions and enjoyment will take control again, I must admit I am in my depressive stage at present, but by fuck, I deserved to go through this, it is the time. I have had an extremely great year, I truly have.

Anyway... We will see what will happen tomorrow. It is a new day thank God. I have been too badly affected; perhaps it is my own interpretation! Fuck I don't know... We will see. The direction I will continue to take will be a special one. I am sure of that, I know that I have to remain in control and I actually am! Pathetically stupid, I am scared of being alone, but I seriously don't think that I will ever be alone, which is a major treat... One huge treat.

I will grow up and become in demand, no one really wants me at the moment, which I can understand. I am not really a character worth having at the moment... We will see. I just have to take it as it comes; allow the moments to happen... You hear me.

One thing I just wish is that I was able to truly succeed in my studies. I don't really know what has gone wrong in the past... shit happens hey, well that is not true because I do pass. Not amazingly but I do get by. I would be particularly interested to see what will happen. Take it as it comes, it is my usual saying... Or we will see!

No. We will see, I WILL SEE. More to the point!

Anyway, I am just writing and writing this evening, my friend is a bottle of wine and cigarettes...

Who knows, the planet is continuing to turn and the sky will be in my vision tomorrow.

Sunday

Well I have woken and feel rather despondent! It is Sunday morning I suppose. I am going to get my feelings out because I need to get back in control of my life, not saying that I have lost control, I certainly haven't but I really want to get realistic. I should be alone for a wee while, I don't mean seeking solitude but a certain amount of understanding where I am at and what is going to be happening next.

I should do some travelling within Australia, especially where I am. I want to see the Rock, go to Alice Springs, over to Perth, up to Cannes and down to Melbourne. I should let the past go and stop trying to live my dreams, my dreams will happen and moments will continue to occur.

I am hoping that I get back to Canberra and start living reality. Get back into the rhythm of work and the understanding of where I am at and what I am doing!

I really need to talk to my dear friend and express my deep thoughts, she is my soul mate, the one true person that I can confide in, she is such an especially important character, she makes me realise my qualities, I hope that I do the same for her. I admire her passion for life and her love in people. I know that I am similar but I just forget about happiness in myself and the moment of I am still young and should be making the most of what is happening right now!

I know for one thing, I really miss my siblings; they are all going to be coming out at Christmas, which will be a brilliant surprise. I cannot wait to catch up.

Sunday, 22nd October 2000

Early morning peaceful, quiet, birds call their morning, joggers float past, hot air balloon high in the sky.

Here I am, I haven't slept yet, but then again I don't want to until tonight. Today is Sunday, day of rest, day of designing to your own. My day. My daylight stream.

I am no poet, no great intellect, and no beauty. I am myself Juliet Fisher, and I deserve to be happy to allow me to be myself and not to care about others negative judgements.

I have been very confused over the last week, then again who hasn't; it's been an interesting vibrant term. I am not 100% sure it is really working out for the best.

I have decided to give up smoking. We will see what will happen! Take it as it comes. I am sure that I will be able to overcome the tensions, the immediate need for cigarettes. I started it alone. I must be able to complete it alone. It is just all those times that I am not smoking what will I be missing! What more can I benefit that is more to the point? Well, I will have the money to spend...

Sunday

Well, Miss Juliet what has been occurring recently in your life?
Not an immense amount. I did get very sick, which was not good. I got very low and depressed but now I'm beginning to pick myself up and face the music. I am living the student life, so exams, lessons and assignments etc. are what are on the cards! Joy! Joy!
I have spoken home to mum quite a lot recently, I miss her so much, actually I miss all my siblings, family and friends and of course dad.
It has also been a week of birthdays, Melbourne Cup with betting going down. Better sign off, really tired.

Monday, 12th November 2000

I am back in Canberra after having been down at the coast for the weekend, perfect to be away from the hustle of the city...Anyway I thought a bit about everything going down, controlling thoughts, emotions, feelings, and again reflecting and channelling thoughts through for the future.
I have and am still experiencing a wonderful life.

Tuesday, 13th November 2000

School today – Training, Economics and Venues!
Take it easy girl, respect your human self. Treat your heart and spirit; believe in loving you, the person you are and the direction you want to go!

Saturday

Again... I have been away and I am now back in Canberra. I am not a happy chicken. I don't really know what has happened. I feel like being totally alone. The last week has been different; I am controlling and completely whatever. I have given up being competitive and striving. I really know that I shall succeed in whatever I do. But I have had enough of people...
I feel pretty useless at the moment.

I just think that I miss my friends and family too much and I am so totally unsure of what is going to happen next.

Wednesday, 28th November 2000

I so cannot wait to finish this term now and there is not much I can change, and there is actually not much I want to change.

I cannot believe that it is nearly December. Means that Christmas is coming! Makes life exciting, vibrant. I cannot wait to see the family. I am so excited. It is going to be such fun when they all come out. Really it truly is! Special, special stuff. All lovely!

Wednesday, 6th December 2000

I dropped him at the airport today after having spent our last night together, romantic and emotional. We both work flat out.

We departed on good terms. Happy. We made love the last night he was here!

Sunday Morning

I'm happy!

It would be 23rd December and I have not written in my journal for a good amount of time, actually more to the point, where has the time disappeared to! All is well and good and I am living a perfect time. All my family are with me on their different levels! I am so honoured to share this time with them all.

I am living the moment it's been so long since I wrote anything in here!

Sunday, 30th December 2000

Another year is coming to a close. I am a very lucky person, which I know I write all the time!

What has come over me lately, I have been feeling ever so strange? I wonder why and what has happened to me? I don't mean to cause such confusion in my head. I really want to be a perfect unique individual on this planet that has much heart and enthusiasm for life. I believe lately I have been hurt and troubled, but it is me pushing myself through this. I have been very confused on relationship front. Who knows why, but it is the way it is…

Happy New Year

Something came over me last night. I could not stop crying. I was so depressed! Unsure why! Perhaps it is just a stage that came over me.

I have never been like this. It is like my world is not here. Transition I reckon. It is good to be with the family tho!

What would I be doing if my brothers and sisters, friends, parents weren't around. I would be a different person altogether! I am 100 % sure.

Saturday, 6ᵗʰ January 2001

Here I am again mesmerised by this amazing place!

Yes, it is all perfect. I couldn't ask for more really I could not.

I would love to construct or even develop the patience to write a book someday. But we will see what talents arise and what is to become of my life.

I am rather nervous to get back to the UK. I am not sure that people are going to be around, so I will research for my strategic project.

I do somehow wish that I was perfect and people honoured me as being that way but hey, time will tell, I will not lose sleep and one day accept myself for me. The date now is 6th January; we are almost a week into the year 2001. What have I achieved?

Monday, 8ᵗʰ January 2001

It must be time to write in my new passages again – my random chatting hey! Change is the only constant in the universe. Continue to get used to it! Love it, honey…

13ᵗʰ January 2001 – Today

Oh hello. I am in the states again, arrived two days ago. LA: Shopping along Rodeo Drive, seeing the stars (pavements) Universal Studios, dinners and lunches, the gym, the Paul Getty Mag (Museum), all just incredible.

I have had a special break and I am seriously looking forward to getting back.

Remember Juliet, you have again experienced your life. Enjoy England. Of course you are going to receive negative anx! But love it Juliet. It's life and it's yours, so be happy.

Well, what a change. I am a very lucky young lady I cannot believe that I am 22. It has been interesting venturing back to the UK for a wee while. I feel very relaxed and my emotions are rather un-scathed at present. I have been very open and giving of my emotions to friends and family. London, I found rather depressing, unsure why! But it is certainly another eye opener in the way that life is evolving for all of us. It is fascinating and there are some of my friends who I am truly proud of. They are doing stunningly well.

I arrived back the 15th Jan, rather jetlagged to say the least from LA, USA another interesting place. Visited the Paul Getty Museum there I was astounded by the artwork it was absolutely out of this world. Talking about art, while I was in the UK, I went to the V&A, Tate, and Royal Academy. England is truly spoilt for choice and the arts/culture. When I venture into an art gallery, I am absorbed.

Well my last night in the UK and I reckon I am leaving in a few hours. I again am venturing onwards back to Canada. It seems such a short trip. It really is! Now, I used to think it was a far off place, but no I arrive soon. Very soon!

I don't want to talk about relationships in this book either they might be… or they might not… For the time being, I want to walk a line. Find my unique self in the world that is cruising around me.

31st January 2001

Believe it or not it is Wednesday again…

I have started off on my travels. Dad dropped me at Heathrow and I was randomly selected as a dodgy character and had my entire luggage checked. Joy oh joys. Cruised through and jumped on the aeroplane bound for Boston! Good Lord America dawned upon me again. What a great surprise. No change from where I have left really. Rain, rain and more rain. I had much running through my mind on the flight. New destinies, horizons etc. Fun and games. People to get involved with, work to be done etc. around 6.00 I arrived in Montréal and ventured off the plane into minus conditions, snow!! Beautiful though.

1st February 2001

I had a special day yesterday catching up with people from the past. Truly there is not much of a change, I do love Canada. Everything feels right, although it is freezing cold outside. I can see why I had a lovely two years here! It is strange how I make sure that I come back!

2nd February 2001

On the road again. Actually in the air! Ran all the way across Montréal airport to grab a flight to Chicago!

I could probably write forever, but I won't. I have a whole day of travelling; I don't know how I am going to feel when I arrived back in the land of Auz! Extremely jetlagged and ready for a big amount of sleep! Excitement.

My last semester.

As for my men? My blasts from the past! What can I say, other than we will see…?

Suddenly I have the urge to write, not sure why but I suppose everything happens for a reason! I am happy and I am not questioning that, I am not. I just am slightly unsure of what the future has to hold. I must end up repeating myself again and again through these diaries. C'est la vie!

Saturday, 3rd February 2001

6.00 in the morning. I have woken up quite late for me which is excellent. Thank the Lord. I am not surprised I was shattered yesterday!

Salt Lake City is not a bad place; it actually looked really pretty as I was cruising into land. The mountain's, the sun peeping through, really I had a lovely moment of reflection on God's beauty!

Anyway, I have had a lovely break here in Salt Lake City and then on to LA.

I feel rather dodgy at present, unsure why. It's probably the mixture of jet lag, graduation, school, friends, work. We will see what Sydney has to offer again!

It would be about February 8th I cannot wait to get finished here! I have had a perfect semester and everyone is enjoying themselves. But honestly, I am ready to switch off and move on!

It is Sunday already. I have been back in Australia for nearly a week. What has happened to the time!

Might as well make the most of my last semester. Work hard, play hard.

Monday

I am in the rhythm of writing again, this is perfect! Very enjoyable.

I have started dancing classes, my new adventure, and I would like to start the physiotherapy class on Thursdays. Just thinking it would be particularly interesting.

Wednesday

Back in the swing of life, I haven't stopped really. I don't know what has happened to the last week but all is well and good. I went out drinking last night; it was good to be back. I am sure as the workload increases, I will be totally underwater and finding it rather a challenge, but I suppose to some mad degree… It is what I love "a challenge!" but see it as an opportunity! If I could keep this feeling forever, that would be great.

Well! Hello again. It is Saturday night and well all is going well! Happy as actually. I had a pretty perfect day. Set out what I wanted to do.

Australia is a beautiful place, stunning actually. It has much potential. We will see if I stay here. Not sure what I'm going to do next. Hello/goodbye! Sleep now.

Monday

All is well and I am really enjoying being back in the land down under. I am rather shattered so there is plenty that I should be doing. Work is going well, but I do wish I was more knowledgeable!

Tuesday

I had a mad sense that he was going to call me this morning. Very strange and he did. It made me feel very happy. We will see what will happen with it all. I really am very relaxed at the moment. I cannot wait until this semester is over! Fin!!!

Dancing classes are going well. I am in no way as floating and flowing even as beautiful as the other girlies! But some day I will feel a glow!

Saturday

I should again write my diary. I am not too sure where exactly I am coming from, but hey! Take it as it comes we will see!!

Weekend consisted of Thursday night. Dance class… Interior design. The Ranch! Friday. Work. Seeing the play, it was brilliant.

My life is my choice. It is interesting, the whole entire scenario. I am asleep. I am very tired!

Good weekend.

Friday, 2nd March 2001

Where does the time go? Fun and games. I have had a jam packed week. Full of excitements. I feel very free. Like a hawk. Hovering over...

3rd March 2001

I really feel very good at the moment. I realise that I have so much to live for and many places to go and see. I suppose I should make the most of it before I settle down and have kiddies. No way… Certainly not yet, when the time is correct. I am sure they will arrive. And with whom? Who knows Jules?

The greatest essentials to happiness in this life are something to do, something to love, and something to hope for! – Joseph Addison

4th March 2001

Don't exclude yourself from precious moments, warm emotions, beautiful attitudes, majestic discoveries, flowing intimacies, sensory development for those are the jewels placed in the crown of your destiny. Walter Rinder.

5th March 2001

Just watched Sex in the City. What an excellent TV night. I have had rather boring day of work. Same shit, different day.

I am tired I had better sleep!

Be willing to do what your soul directs you to do, if you want to create what you are asking for. Sanyana Roshan

Wednesday, 7th March 2001

Do you what you love, the money will follow! Marsha Sinatra

After tomorrow I will be a lot more relaxed. My exam will be over!

I wish I had drunk more champagne – last words of Maynard Keynes, Economist.

Live as you will have wished to have lived when you are dying – Gellert.

It is 4.00 Friday morning **9th March.** My goodness, what has happened to the days? It has been a month since I arrived here in Canberra. It is all well and good. I think I do require a change of scenery though. See something different other than the life here.

My sister is here at the moment. It is totally what I need. To make me feel who I am right now, thank you for allowing her in my life. The honours.

Never place limits on yourself just be free at all costs. Pelei

9ᵗʰ March 2001

What can I say about this evening other than great times! All righty, fun and games. We are having a smashing, excellent, perfect time hey. I am really luvin it all! We are in Thredbo, which is ski capital of the Australian Alps, although currently there is no snow. There is a great crowd here for the mountain biking. We climbed to the top of Mount Kosciuszko, it was a four hour hike and worth every moment of it. Quite beautiful. I am tired now it is Sunday afternoon!

16ᵗʰ or 15ᵗʰ March 2001

4.00 in the morning. I am back in Canberra. Tired and I have to be awake tomorrow morning. Somehow, I need to get it together. Concoct some articulated speech about mobilisation; we will see how it happens.

What a day in my life. It was great. I am very content. My sister is here. I love her very much!

Cannot wait for the degree to be over! Out of hell. On my way again. Seeing new times, lives, people, places, fascinations, bad moments, they always happen. Sleep well!

Time midnight! 19th March

Well, what a day, I have really been working non-stop since my eyes open today! Shattered is an understatement. Anyway, all is well and I am very much looking forward to May.

22ⁿᵈ March 2001

Sunday morning, clocks have gone back an hour so I can have a wee lie in! An hour!

Anyway we have just had an amazing weekend in Sydney… I love it there! Not to live I don't reckon, but we will see!

Good Weekend

Top stuff. Have a good week Juliet! You'll get it on! Success is a road, there are turnings, straights, bumps and diversions; however, right now, the sky is blue. You are 22! Life is on your toes! Itchy.

Sunday Evening...7.00 am

£50.00 to my name, no more, no less! Hummm...
Life – success, love, family, career.
Car – Jeep 4x4, Wrangler or Range Rover.
Dog – Dalmatian, Labrador, Alsatian.
Colours – blues, yellows, greens.
Kiddies – what I'm given.
House – villa, near water, stunning views.

Saturday, 30th March 2001

We had a gorgeous day in the sun, sea, sand, and surf. No sex, though! It will be interesting to go back to Europe and see what happens there.

"When all the world is sleeping, I stay awake thinking of you!" – Perez 1971–95
The planets will spiral, and my leaf will fall, float and regenerate, and the feather I am floating on will continue to pass on by and absorb the moments that I am meant to!

Sunday, 30th March 2001

Deep sea fishing. It was a great eight hours; we caught 14 fish between us! Impressive. It was such an achievement considering the last time I went fishing was when I was about seven years old. A wee rainbow trout.

Thursday, 5th April 2001

Alice Springs, Central Australia. As if by magic, travel and exploration has taken hold. The land is dry and the air is clear. Blue skies and glorious sunshine. I am in heaven.
Carry on the story. I am still on the same chapter. I cannot believe that my time here in Australia is drawing to a close. I love it here. The sun, sea, sex, surf.
Campsite Ayres Rock and the Olgers. We had a gradual day, the sun rose, and we saw stunning sites... feet are sore! We climbed around the Olgers for about six hours in the baking heat!

Saturday

Walked around the base of Ayres Rock for the sunrise, which again was a tranquil and memorable experience.

The days get hot, 35–40-degree heat! I don't think that I'm made for it. I love the heat if there is shade around. I must collect some firewood for tonight.

I've been thinking about what's going to happen to me next, I am not too concerned. Just allow the planets to take control! I would love to have a European summer though. Take it as it comes!

Sunday

Tour around the Northern Territory. We had quite a stunning walk this morning around Kings Canyon, into a huge rock pool, where of course, I jumped in and viewed the top of the waterfall down the valley! I am currently in the van on my way back to Alice Springs. Complete exams, assignments, travel, the last time to have a smashing exploration stage!

Monday

Run around Alice Springs. Beautiful, there are a lot of aborigines here. It's good to see as there are practically none in South Australia, NSW. I must admit they are scary looking. It is quite right that their bodies are different, with certain deformities by new diets. I am sure it is the same with their approach to us! Anyway, discussing the whole racial scene! I believe we are both very open-minded. And accept who we are and others for who they are. No racial conflict in our lives. Thank the Lord! Religion is another story!

Anyway, after my jog, swim, then work…writing up assignment. I'm mad to open my eyes wide before the birds even start singing. We wandered into Alice Springs town centre. Many tourists scattered the streets. I felt far from being in a unique place. Faxing through my Strat project were the next missions on the agenda!

I have nearly completed this section of my life. The chapter is nearly complete! Excellent. Not that I'm desperate for the next stage to occur, but hey, life is taking its toll and I am on an airplane out of here! Back to Canberra!

J – Just

U – Unique

L – Liberal

I – Intelligent
E – Exciting
T – Talented
What was that? POSITIVE THINKING!

Tuesday, 10th April 2001

Flight to Sydney was quick, watched a film and did some finance summary work, eventful! I am glad that I saw the rock scene! It was stunning and we had a perfect time. Tiring, but excellent moments. It is a very spiritual place. Honoured and fortunate! We left Sydney in a rightful mood and managed to get to my dance class on time.

One month.

Easter Sunday, 16th April 2001

Sister time and the Great Barrier Reef, scuba diving. Stunning stuff. Saw sharks, turtles, beautiful coral. Was amazing, I really had a perfect day yesterday.

Leaving tropical Cairns and heading back to Canberra. Oh, joys! I am quite excited as I have under a month to go now. A lot is going to happen! Graduation, exams, work! Packing. I cannot wait to complete this section. I know that I am never going to have moments like these ever again.

I have lost count of all the journals that I have. This book must be number 13 or 14. Anyway, let's get down to business. I finished all my classes, lectures yesterday, and now, I just have three assignments and one exam to take. Excellent stuff.

We went to see Monet in Japan at the National Gallery. It was a stunning exhibition. Saw the water lilies, haystacks, '360 views of Fiji', man, mesmerised!

20th April 2001

To the left of me right now, I have the Sydney Harbour, stunning views of the Opera house and the Harbour Bridge. The Monet and Japan exhibition was stunning. I will return to capture another sense because we were filtered through very quickly. Three weeks and it's complete. The perfect situation of another stereotypical, 22-year-old: living, breathing, searching, believing, exploring, much here to accomplish and absorb.

Sunday

I was woken to him playing the guitar and singing the Romeo and Juliet song. I am real. The planets move in mysterious ways, he is gorgeous.

Tuesday, 26th April 2001

Oh my Lordie, all my assignments were due today, and I completed them. Congratulations Miss Juliet. Feeling rather relieved, I am shattered at the moment. I feel like I could sleep for 100 years and wake up the prettiest and most refreshed Chica ever!

JC has been sectioned back into a hospital again. It is awful, what a terrible shame but if that is what he wants! That will probably be the safest for him and everyone at home.

Tuesday, 1st May 2001

'My student days "degree days" are so nearly complete. These days seem to be taking forever but this time next week at this exact time, I will be on the aeroplane out of Australia.

I wonder what the future has to hold. I am really so far from the next stage. It will all be alright. Silence, is or isn't the way. Heaven is all the way!

Tuesday, 8th May 2001

I cannot believe that I have been out in Australia for all this time and I am in my last 24 hours, it is rather a huge shame! I am really excited about getting back to the Great Kingdom though. Truly immense last few weeks

Friday – finance, car, dinner, first floor! Trance, have heart, morning walks, airport, Adelaide, Sydney, emailing lark! Lark!

Melbourne, Chapel Street, exhibition house, sanity, departure. Walking away! Involve and absorb.

Trips, many a happiness, abstract diversity.

London – homeward bound for beauty, uncertainty, exploration, and many pictures, photos to be another achievement and success.

A full moon must be a huge sign! Stunning!

9th May 2001

Sydney airport, bound for Kuala Lumpur – London. Arrived safely at the airport after spending a stunning last night in Flounders, South Melbourne by the sea! There was a beautiful mystique sunrise! Truly spoilt. The journey to the airport was successful. Cruise control

Seeing the sunset outside of my cubbyhole window! Exciting, stunning. I wonder what the next stage must offer. Life is a bandwagon. We are all on it. I am fortunate not to have anyone sitting next to me. Space to breathe… Space to write freely and just to be me.

From time to time, I wish I was in the mind of a writer; able to be fluent, expressive, and downright legible and possibly interesting to sum up myself at present, after, yes, the accomplishment somehow of my Bachelor of Business that many nowadays frown upon, to the 'relaxed' approach, to yes, higher education, and of course, my laziness of expression in another language. Man, you will see!

I am only 22. I am being centred entirely on being a girl. The year is 2001. I have graduated.

A new era is bound! Destiny! Quite possibly forever until I die! Will be my world! I wonder from time to time who I will end up with. May it be a collection of many, a handful? We will see. My epic journey of being young has pretty much come to an end. Travelling the world alone and finally, I am on the last leg home!

He was a special man, it is rather weird to just let go and follow my way. I am far from being ready to be in a relationship. There is more I would love to capture, absorb, feel, and approach my way, rather than sharing or even bringing someone else; such as a child of my own into the life I have currently. I know when I will be truly ready though and the person I will be with will be the luckiest man alive, Baroness Juliet.

Chapter 9

Seeking Summer...

"If you seek peace be still, if you seek wisdom be silent, if you seek love be yourself." — Becca Lee

Tuesday, 15th May 2001

I got myself pretty organised today for the next stage. I spent this morning getting in touch with work areas! Employment and career orientation

Two minutes for the bus, immediate movement of authentication. I have been travelling all day, arrived here at Le Manga in Spain. I can tell you no one particularly gives a damn, but then again, are they supposed to? Not really.

Travel writing is that my section forward?

I know that I am very low. I repeat <u>very</u> low on cash again...

I cannot say indisputably that it is a modern oasis in a commercial and modern man time! Right rich bitch, if I need to be one! Left home again and ventured into the unknown. What is known, however, is that I am regularly always fine, until emotions and uncertainty hit me.

All will come out in the wash, bleach, bones, man! Where do you step off! When can you quit?

The dream and the desire to take hold and allow that dream to move forward. Look at me. I must be mad. Good day though, interesting, absorbing, sensitive, possibility, adaption, movement.

Thursday, 17th May 2001

Even got me a job around the corner in a jazz bar if I want to take it! We will see what will happen in the future.

Saturday, 19th May 2001

I met his friends and family today. It was a good day that just flew. Lots of good food and drink, which was excellent, I will give the Spanish that. As in relation to emotions...we will see. Speak soon.

Sunday Morning

It is difficult here in Spain, only because I don't speak Spanish. I suppose I must rely on my patience and just take it as it comes. See how quickly I can do it.

Monday

Emotional stage possibly...

I have organised a flight back to the Great kingdom to see the family up in Scotland, there is something truly related to my "movement". I feel so stationary when I am not doing anything.

So, Thursday I venture away again. Things have definitely changed with him and I am glad that I came to Espana to capture another sense. But time has moved on. And I don't want to feel like chewing gum, stuck to someone's feet. I have my life, career etc. to move on with.

Tuesday

Time, the key to all doors!

I am sitting alone on the beach. The sun is shining; I am alone with me and my thoughts. Just taking the moments in.

I am not really sure whether I will be back here in a hurry. Time has moved on and I cannot stay stationary with my heart open for more aching and unflattering. It is good to be here though and get a sense of peace in my mind.

My next stage is to sort out my life. My room, photos, art, do some drawing of how I feel and most probably what I have seen. See if I can go to some exhibitions. Colour, black and white. Drawing from my heart.

I am sure that I will find myself an important person again.

Things will never be the same. The song is quite right.

I do miss Australia a staggering amount. The past has happened, and I shouldn't really run from the broken hearted.

Travel writing is not really my forte at all but I suppose I'm just doing it. Writing whenever, whatever and however. Making my own impression. I am in no way far beyond my years, actually probably in the past younger. But I love being alone.

There is definitely a streak of wildness inside me, good wildness. I fly places to study art, creativity, photography, languages. I love the solitude for a while, a time for thinking, the simple act of recording the beauty in my life, with my pen, pencil, mind every day! Dad is quite right I am like a yoyo with my emotions.

I am not sure when I am ever going to read back to what I have written but I'm glad I did right now. I remember feeling the pain from love whatever it is.

Time to move on!

Wednesday

He got the position as night manager.

I am the type of girl that makes a one-night stand last for three years! I don't want to say goodbye tomorrow. Happiness is like the clouds, sometimes there are many and sometimes there are none and you get the day with scattering.

We made love. Is a holding, a kiss, a hug mutual? None is nothing all more or less than complicated. I am young and have the energy!

Don't you cry tonight. I love that song by Guns n Roses.

Sunset over the Mediterranean, quite beautiful. Over the summer, get a job, draw, and paint, make love…and allow progression and more understanding and knowledge to capture. Engross me.

Engrossed in time, a wave of movement, the desire to be perfect, admired, liked, and the necessary progression of my life. From being ill, confused, the escape scenarios of moving out of normal circumstances, and the influence substance – to swimming, travelling, good moods, bad moods, sensitive and manic, angry, and obsessed. Researching my soul.

I would like to get a dog, call it Tan or Seal.

I am on an airplane out of here. Not that anyone cares; I almost don't really care for it myself.

JC needs help, requires an immense amount of focus and direction, but only if he is going to ask for it, or admits that he needs it! It is difficult to comprehend such a lost soul, or perhaps he is not, he is regarding us as all, the exterior is manic and wired.

Wednesday Afternoon

I am on my journey home now, waiting patiently at the airport. Ready to just get home and get on with my life. I feel kind of strange, not much emotion at all.

Saturday Night

Scotland, Langside. Excellent times, with all the family.

I must sleep now. Writing – it is good for your own wellbeing.

Without salt, no sugar
Ashes come from burning
The cassock is to hide a fool
He is deep down because you are high up

If the priest goes to the right, then
A teacher must without fail turn to the left
If a man is a coward, it proves he has will
A man is satisfied not by the quality of food
But the absence of greed
Truth is that from which conscience can be at peace
No elephant and no horse, even the donkey is mighty
In the dark, a louse is worse than the tiger.
If there is 'I' in one's presence, then God and Devil are of no account
Once you can shoulder it, it is the lightest thing in the world
A representation of Hell – a stylish shoe
Unhappiness on earth is from the wiseacring of women
He is stupid, who is 'clever'
Happy is he who sees not his unhappiness.
Gurdjieff – Meetings with Remarkable People

Sunday

Dreams and breathing in fresh Scottish air. A truly stunning place. Was out for about an hour, I went for a cruise in the car, viewing more scenery. Distance and discipline are key criteria. I am moving onwards and outwards and must play parts in my society.

Perfect indulgence and great to be having a feast with my current nearest and dearest. Deep in contemplation. I would like to get my love out of my head. Part of the rich tapestry of life and progression occurs like this. Exploring down at the loch…Oh, flower of Scotland.

Monday

Cawdor Castle, Macbeth, Shakespeare's based story! Dinner in Elgin. It was sweet, all of us chappies together, sharing the special moments. Be positive and smile with your eyes. Believe it, girlie!

Tuesday

Inverness to Edinburgh. Not much of a journey currently on the bus down to London from Edinburgh! Departure and tomorrow a new day. Interview. See what you will work!

I arrived in my capital city at 7.00 this morning after rather a manic journey from Edinburgh; it was kind of crazy but a journey that required experiencing. I walked to the Egerton Garden! I wandered down to Brompton Road, looking at fashion and expense, and up Park Lane to see the cars. I arrived at my interview early. Absorbed got rather non-attitude. Caught up with friends, for lunch at Oriels, which was perfect. Bus from Victoria to home.

I need a good cry! This is all that is mine now. See ya.

Factoring in uncertainty is an essential ingredient of my experience. In my willingness to accept uncertainty, solutions will spontaneously emerge out of the problem, out of the confusion, disorder, and chaos. The more uncertain things seem to be, the more secure I will feel because uncertainty is my path to freedom. Through the wisdom of uncertainty, I will find my security!

Today, I shall judge nothing that occurs. Non-judgement creates silence in my mind.

Thursday, May 2001

I cannot believe, diary number 15, here we go.

Energy caught hold and I went for a run along the park. I spent most of the afternoon planting flowers and shrubs…Contemplated deeply about the next stage, although didn't feel entirely close to the conclusion.

My dream catcher 'catcher' is making a few times; I believe it might be close to switching off time! The future holds many uncertainties.

We outgrow people, places, and things as they unfold.

We may be saddened when old friends say their piece and leave our lives…

But… let them go…

Caption!

Even a happy life

Cannot be without a measure of darkness

And the word happiness

Would lose its meaning

If it were not balanced

By sadness

Carl Jung

Friday, 1ˢᵗ June 2001

True colours shining through!

Silver lining! Shining when the night is burning red. Shining in the twilight. Was I born with my eyes wide open? Time after time, I get dragged down. Frozen in the madness all around. I must scatter myself like a diamond and place in the morning all day through. Innocence! Close.

Friday, 1ˢᵗ June 2001, Night

Greenwich Mean Time for the time being is the place to be! The next stop. My step forward. This time last week, I was on the journey up to Scotland. Passive thoughts and song. When do we step up? Certainly not yet.

I like to sleep under the stars with no mattress underfoot. I am just living in a dream world for others to intervene because they love me and that is what they 'need' and possibly what I need. It will all fire back in my face one day… I am waiting patiently for it to happen, this decade or next. We won't know for now! Race day at Newmarket!

Monday, 4ᵗʰ June 2001

The number you have dialled has not been recognised, please check, and try again…

Man, whatever! My story seems to say that my life may go on, with or without this character.

Tomorrow, I have an interview in the army.

You have no idea of the tremendous release and deep peace that comes from meeting yourself and your brothers totally without judgement.

Here is the way it is! The way you see the world depends entirely on your vibration. When your vibration changes, the whole world will look different.

It's like those days when everyone seems smiling at you because you feel happy.

Tuesday, 5ᵗʰ June 2001

Hardly the beginning of a new week. I went off and had an interview with the army! The British Army!

Wednesday, 6ᵗʰ June 2001

"The meeting of two personalities is like the contact of two chemical substances. If there is any reaction both have transformed." – Carl Jung.

7th June 2001 – Election Day

The country is incomplete diversity. Where to go? What do you think about the next few years ahead? The votes will be counted by tomorrow. This is the first time I have been home to vote after I was able to. Had another interview with the army – it is going to be a lot of hard, hard work. I am unsure, but I'll take it as it comes.

Friday, 8th June 2001

London bound today the 8th June. I enjoyed being there for a wee while. Inspiration as it comes. Decisions will be made.

"You are in physical existence to learn and understand that your energy, translated into feelings, thoughts, and emotions cause all experience. There are no exceptions!" –

Saturday, 9th June 2001

It is only an illusion
That you do not
Have what
You want
Sunday moments

Don't exclude yourself from precious moments, warming encounters, beautiful attitudes, majestic discoveries, flowing intimacies, sensory developments. These are the jewels placed in the crown of your destiny.

Sunday, 10th June 2001

I am very committed to writing in my diary lately. It's not that I even have much time on my hands. It is probably because my mind is in a strange state and my thought patterns are rather hectic.

You have a kind and generous heart. Allow the music to play and the wind to blow. You cannot prevent these; however, you have one of the greatest gifts in life and that is your health.

Smile, you have a charming grin – open, play the notes, take the photographs, create your life. You are in no rush! Beauty is in the eye of the beholder! Quit your illusions.

Every man takes the limits of his field of noises for the limits of the world!

Monday

A serious amount of production is necessary now!
The only aspect of time that eternal is now!
As for Monday, I rose at 7.00, got the twins their breakfast, and went on my regular jog; it is always good to exert energy.

Tuesday, 12th June 2001

Cannot describe how I'm feeling now. Music, words, and the many will provide pretty much what is getting me to where I'm going. Much has evolved forward. Never waste time and energy thinking that you were somewhere else doing something else, accept your situation and realise where you are, doing what you are doing, forever a specific reason. Realise that nothing is by chance.
Learn lessons. You can move upward and onward.

Wednesday, 13th June 2001

Mind is floating off to Hawaii, Canada, Europe, Australia, New Zealand, but I reckon for the moment, my place is here in the UK, I have been travelling for six years,
You never live fully, as when you gamble with your own life.
Don't tell any other players the rules – you are a winner,
Plans for the moment, aged 22
Helicopter pilot's course
Work –full-time
Hawaii – university

Thursday, 19th June 2001

Hawaii is my next stop. Fingers crossed. I can feel the motion, smell the sea breeze, and feel the sand! See the sunrises and sunsets! Make my own life. Calculate costs and what is necessary and what is not. This is when I would love to be left-handed.
Feelings are the holiest force in the universe (they are the only reason for life), and a feeling of love is the holiest of the holy.
I never came upon any of my discoveries through the process of rational thinking.

Friday, 15th June 2001

Hyatt Regency
Surfing accommodation
Flying helicopters
Cocktails!
Sun and sea!
We will see, hey!
I could leave tomorrow if I had half a chance but nay!

Sunday, 16th June 2001

Drove to London in torrential rain, we ate lunch down Ken High Street.
Then Royal Albert Hall and saw the Ballet Romeo and Juliet.
Suddenly, I wonder why I write these books, number 15 now, register! It is a good release of expression and my interpretation of life! I keep having flashbacks, destiny moves in mysterious ways!

21st June 2001

London proved to be good fun, had a great time catching up, partying, interviews, seeing friends. I had a good time.
The interviews went well. It is good to get them over and done with, wonder what inspiration will cause! Take it as it comes, destiny in the work world.
JC hit rather a rocky patch again, which is a shame. But I suppose it is all part of the learning curve, and movements of the globe will allow him to explore and lead his own life.
In time you will do it all differently anyway, why not do it differently now?
"The past existed in multitudinous ways, you only experienced one probable past. By changing this past in your mind now in your present, you write you can change not only its nature but all its effect and not only upon yourself but upon others." Seth
I must construct a dissertation of 10,000 words then we will see…

Friday

Strawberry picking,
A driver is not just a driver
A husband is not just a father

A job is not just a living

A person is not just a statistic

Why! Perhaps it was all overcoming my fears last night

1 Public speaking

2 Accepting of people's togetherness

3 Evolution

4 The matter of not understanding

5 Sudden movement, for example, moving to Australia, Hawaii without any planning.

Mistrustful suspect people who set out to punish!

Sunday

Bristol

It is only an illusion

That you do not have

What you want!

Tuesday

What is this turning into? I got very upset last night, surrounding the JC scenario. I am all rather anxious about this weekend! Learn to accept and move on. Celebrate it all! Make the most, who agrees? Decision administrator! Life-saving scenarios! Have it and love it!

Imagine you only have one year to live, what important things would you be doing? How would you be allotting your time to accomplish the most you could? This exercise was motivated for going after your priorities.

The only way you can live forever is to love somebody. Then you leave a gift behind when you live that way, as I've seen with people with physical illness, you have a choice of when you die.

Rich in choice, rich in decisions, and of course devoted to the great creation 'sense' my origin where I am from, where I am going, etc.

I wish I could speak my words.

I wish I could know the lessons of love.

We are each of us Angels

With only one wing

And we can fly only

By embracing
Each other

      -   *Luciano De Crescenzo*

Journey home just slept. I keep switching off from reality, which I really like. Although success will eventually come; at present, right now, past or future, I am still me and I will remain always. Cheers for the day. What a gift!

"Most decisions, possibly all
have already been made on
some deep level and me
going through a reasoning
the process to drive at them seems
at least redundant. The questions
'What do I want to do?' Maybe a
real reaction to the subconscious
the decision I have already made."

–   *Hugo Prather*

The most beautiful thing we can experience is the story!

Monday, 2nd July 2001

Walk down the street, be you when angel sayings, there are greater things.

I never thought I'd miss you half as much as I do!

Don't think about it. Allow it to happen, excellent. The worst thing you could do is worry about what you could have done.

The question is what do I want to do? Maybe a fearful decision 'reaction' to the subconscious decisions I have already made! Cheers for it!

3rd July 2001, Wimbledon Day

Cruised off to Wimbledon today, over the Dartford Bridge. We had such a lovely day, Great chat, good music and great company, champagne, strawberries, and beautiful sunshine!

I am tired!

I drift off with questions, wait for answers.

Good things come to those who wait.

Cluttered closets

The universe loves symbolic gestures.

Juliet, use your ability to visualise!

4th July 2001

Had a helicopter flying lesson. I was the pilot now and then, which was unreal!
I'll always remember size and sensitivity; it was a stunningly sunny day and an
excellent chance to do it!
Patience on silence, always great degrees.
Divine luck! The only aspect of time that is eternal is now.
Let the comings and goings of life continue, but you stay here and now.
This exercise is to bring you to the eternal present where it all is!
Don't panic, destiny is on your side!
Music forever.
Congratulate forces, right and fermenting with sexuality! You are a late 70s kid,
your lucky star!
Crucified!
Dare to be different.
Be proud.
Attractive.
Open heart and particular quality open mind a celebration.

5th July 2001

Dublin, Ireland. Wimbledon week. Pleasure. Pleasure. Don't make a big deal all
the time Juliet. Moments occur naturally. You know that time provides
experience; you are very young now with much to give life.

Friday, Dublin Airport

Life is an opportunity and not an obligation.
You get around girl! Somehow, I wish I could travel like this forever!
Enhances amazing experience of delving into new places, although Dublin is
only a hop skip and a jump over the Irish Sea!
I sense a relaxed atmosphere, friendly smiling faces. More than you get walking
along the High Street in London. Horses for courses though. Remember the
opportunity...
I caught a flight back to England quite early on Sunday morning, drove to
London, and had a swim in Chelsea pool. Followed by lunch with Grandpa, his

80th birthday, which truly amounted to seeing everyone; the entire family together.

Monday

The union of feminine and masculine energies within the individual is the basis of creation. Female intuition plus male action is creativity.

Put the female in the guiding position, this is her natural function. She is your intuition, the door to your higher intelligence.

The true function of the male energy is absolute clarity, directness, and a passionate strength based on what the universe, coming through your female, tells you.

Tuesday, 10th July 2001

I had a flying lesson for pretty much the entire afternoon. It is going to cost a small fortune to get my PPL.

Exhilaration or what! I must get my mind straight though, back to the drawing board, getting complete and steadfast for the future technical details now.

Nothing
Is more dangerous
Than an idea
When it is the
Only one you have

      -   *Emile Chartier Alain*

If you are seeking creative ideas
Go out walking
Angels whisper to a man
When he goes for a walk

      -   *Raymond Immon*

What's next? Humility is the acceptance of the possibility that someone else can teach you something you do not know about yourself.

Conversely, pride and arrogance close the door of the mind.

Confession with an identity crisis!

'Do what you love, the money will flow...'

Had a flying lesson, turns and ascends and descents– interesting, then basically drove him to Luton, managed to get lost cruising around in the discovery.

Monday

Passport applications, driving licence.
I went flying all afternoon, making myself inspired. I listened to the Spanish tapes all afternoon in the car, no distraction.
No doubt, the universe is unfolding as it should!

Sunday

Clover fields, praise to the Lord Jesus and God in the slight attempt to be going about life and leading it the correct way.

Wednesday Morning

THOUGHT OF THE DAY – 80% OF SUCCESS IS SHOWING UP!

Thursday, 28th July 2001

Flew over London in the R44; it was incredible. I really enjoyed myself a lot. Most of the day was waiting around. I didn't mind too much as I had a lot of reading today. My HM71 and MET. Good stuff. I always seem to be carrying something, too much.

Whoever I am or whatever I am doing,
some kind of excellence
Is within my reach!
> *- John W. Gardner*

Tuesday, 7th August 2001

I've been turning over a new leaf recently. I had a wild and good weekend! ...A Royal party with the sister.
The future is exciting and vibrant! I am looking forward to falling in love! But now, I am not in search of it! Man! Life, a life, priorities, what are my priorities now?
Hawaii
Accommodation

Flight

Miami, San Francisco

Car

Surfing

Helicoptering, choppers!

Find your unique expression of the God force, don't mimic for it is already too late, and create new!

It is a new beginning – live it and love it, you only have one go at this life, don't regret any of it.

Wednesday, 8th August 2001

Cambridge and did some readings! Two hours of it! Quite an accomplishment.

Thursday, 9th August 2001

Today was good; I am flowing with yoga, trying to build some strength within. It naturally progressed, unravelled, it is all good, truly enjoying, great really. Absorbing the English summer air, taking the doggies for walks, eating lots of delicious food. Chilling as well as just contemplating, relaxing, reading, stretching. Man, it is all good. Devotion is the next aim of the game. I suppose.

'I wish I had drunk more champagne

Life kisses us on both cheeks

Day and morn

But laughs at our deeds

Eve and dawn

Saturday

Such a great night in London,

I would like to be more content with my body, now I replenish myself. I am trying to be healthy!

Never place limits on yourself, be free at all costs.

Monday

That lost sense of love! Forgive, forget, and live as you said.

Here comes success.

Success beckons, what a day, what a special day in life!

All living.

I ended up going to do my kickboxing session; it was intense. Certainly, great though. Choices, decisions, what is to become of me next will be interesting, certainly special, it is my life.

Reassurance, I remind myself all the time... 80% of success is just showing up!

Can you feel that my heart is broken?

Find your unique expression of the force.

Don't mimic for it is already too late. Create anew.

Thursday

Define yourself! I am just in a process of reassurance said she who has been doing advanced autorotation and emergency landings!

Those who know do not say, those who say do not know!

Friday

Flying away to Hawaii, I suppose it is slowly coming into organisation. It will be interesting to see what will happen next, I cannot wait to get out of here though.

Monday, 20th August 2001

V Festival 2001 all weekend and had a wicked time. Just excellent: super music, perfect company. It was just totally chilled, a step out of reality and a major turn into... Festival Rock hip chick. It is good times and many more to come hopefully. We saw Top Loader, Faithless, Chilli Peppers, Red Snapper, Nina, David Gray, Muse, Placebo, etc. it was just a perfect break from reality! I must sleep now before I am shattered for tomorrow.

23rd August 2001

Flying

Driving

Aldeburgh

Dolphin pub

Aldeburgh Ball

It was just a good time!

You are a child of the universe
No less than the trees and the stars;
You have a right to be here.
And whether or not it is clear to you
No doubt the universe is unfolding as it should.
          -   Desiderata

Tuesday, 28th August 2001

I am excited and I feel free! Time is a great healer! A good one! Excellent perfect. Interesting, spontaneous, write, what will be will be.

Believing is one thing
Doing another
Many talk like the sea but
Their lives are stagnant marshes
Others raise their heads
Above the mountain tops
While their souls cling to
The dark walls of caves
Any aspect of time that is eternal is now!

Thursday, 30th August 2001

I'm not really into writing in my diary now. Just enjoy the professional. How come I dreamt of getting together with the lead Top Loader!

Wednesday, 5th September 2001

Bags of potential loving, hehehe...

We are all regular humans – that's the reassurance for me, plenty more good times, I hope! I've got plenty to come back to, it is a special place.

Never place limits on yourself, just be free at all costs!

Each specimen on this planet with the ability force and tried! Believe, specialise, and perfect.

It's not a dress rehearsal!

Saturday Morning

My lover! I'm having a perfect time here in Cornwall, meeting people. It's not often that I break loose; it is a sensual environment here though. I'll be interested to see what will happen with my next stage...

Great vibe last night at the surfer's party.

Chapter 10

Merging Clout and Consciousness...

"Out of the suffering have emerged the strongest souls; the most massive characters are seared with scars."
"Forget not that the earth delights to feel your bare feet and the winds long to play with your hair." – Khalil Gibran

15th September 2001

Hello girl

What a week, peace of mind!

How soon will you realise that the only thing you

Don't have is the overall experience that there's

Nothing you need that you don't have!

Excellent

Juliet,

Happy 23rd birthday

A new journal for a New Year – to write down all the dreams and the great times that you will have this year.

Though we travel the
World over,
To find the beautiful,
We must carry it with us
Or we find it not.

> *- Ralph Waldo Emerson*

I asked for riches that I might be happy.
I was given poverty that I might be wise,
I asked for all things that I might enjoy life,
I was given life that I might enjoy all things.
I was given nothing that I asked for,
But everything that I had hoped for.

> *- Confederate Soldier*

Have a great day and success in the future!

Saturday, 15th September 2001

Happy 23rd birthday – More excess baggage; Space, sun, exploration, madness, work Pacific Economic Basin, rest, and play. It's been an interesting year through 2001. And it still isn't over! I am still cruising through my stages.

Sunday, 16th September 2001

It has been an incredibly strange week, after the occurrence in New York, Washington, the possibility of us all going into war. Brainwashed we all are! What is going to happen next, are they going to find any of the bodies, 5000 that are currently missing? It was shocking. I don't suppose I am going to believe it until I see it. I do however find it incredible, and strange; the choreography of the terrorist attack. I was totally engrossed in the newspapers pretty much for the entire morning. Running (which I haven't done in ages), swimming, emailing, ventured off to church. It was deeply moving, praying for the Americans' peace and of course empathy for all the lost!

Friday, 21st September 2001

Today is the first day of my travels.

I am rather blind now, not many feelings.

I am currently in NYC. There is a very sombre vibe in the air. This terrorist attack on the World Trade Centre has had an immense impact. Just so awful. Human remains, it is a very difficult situation! Identify! Military sleeping giant mission. There is no way I would have cancelled my trip to NYC; and perhaps an operative attitude! Consumer spending, the stock market industrial average is dreadful. It's such an emotional scene. I will never forget this day...

I caught up with friends last night; it was very special and excellent to capture their feelings first-hand. They have an attitude, and are naturally shocked, scared, and doubting their normality. Much has happened in all our lives; it was great to share small sections of our lives again.

I am now sitting in JFK airport, waiting for the flight to Miami; I have to go via Washington though. Terrifying. Fingers crossed I am not shot down.

Sunday

Tomorrow is again a new step.

The last time I wrote I was in New York City. Since then, I have been through Washington where I had to take my boots off to go through security. I got on my flight to Washington; I was the only person on it. Extraordinary.

Miami – my only challenge was to find the 'ex-Swiss lot' from Hawaii. I know if I run out of money that will be the greatest decider. Then again, the next work stage will be exciting.

Miami was random, humid, passionate, exciting, and heavy! Hey hey hey, loved it though! Rented a 4x4, lapped up the Atlantic breeze! Directions, paper bag, work, independence, I say! Swimming pool, walk, I cannot miss any moment! Alrighty, but it just didn't do it for me, look at the stars, look how they shine for me, they were all yellows.

San Francisco via Denver, Colorado, excellent! Glad though, what a day, I slept, hung over, patient, charming, chilling!

Work, work, work another very important concept I shall grasp! I am not sure whether it will be Australia, Hawaii, NZ wherever! If I'm happy there, then there is nothing else more important! I have a quick and easy flight, and I settle the other end 'for a week' until I move on again!

Hawaii

Wednesday

"When one door closes another open,
expect that new door to reveal even greater,
wonders and glories and surprises,
feel yourself grow with every experience.
And look for the reasons for it."
- Eileen Caddy

Friday, 28th September 2001

What a last few days. Isolation. Not really, but I am having an interesting time. The events over the last few days were quite amusing. Surfing Sunset, at the North Shore of Oahu!

I must graduate myself to being a more extrovert, positive and focussed character! I am thinking and worrying a touch too much about the 'what if'...My work has been cancelled before it has even started. Everyone is in turmoil now, especially with business and travel!

The flexibility of heading to Australia is always a possibility! Fingers crossed it all works out. No rushing or immense planning more of the week; just be.

Saturday

In a couple of days, I must decide what I am going to do next; as my work job has been laid off currently due to the terrorist attacks. Whatever I choose I am sure will be due to the next stage of happiness and longevity!

Monday

I've been here a week now. Shock, seven days and much has happened

Beautiful views

Surfing

Found a place to live and a horse in the back garden

Fivesome

Law party

Strip club

Sunbathing

Swimming and running

It's been great and I have met some great people.

Tuesday, 2nd October 2001

Full moon last night and first night in my new place des residence! Living with three other guys now, is great fun. We had a BBQ, delicious and all excellently and precisely timed, with no organisation. It is a beautiful spot, and I can see Sunset Beach from my bedroom window, special, very special! I went for a wee run today. Just down the beachfront, swimming hasn't yet progressed. Sure, it shall though. I am going to go to the Hilton Hotel, Turtle Cove up the road. See what will happen!

No job yet. Fingers crossed it will happen though; investigation into the locality, research, adaption, experience, application. We can only pray that it will all work out, man, these are interesting times.

I need a total thought-provoking stage, it is now my very first full day here, I must start getting myself prepared. I am going to just remain in research mode! It shall all float, progression! What an unreal day! Let's have more of them, please! How destiny moves you!

Wednesday

Radical places, it is beautiful here.

I should learn to chill out a little, once I have my routine, change. It is all well and good, perception, adaption, belief but also Man, what an occurrence! I need a job now though!

Today, I'll get myself organised. The state of the earth as an entire global economy is pretty much on the downturn, it is for our generation to create a new, innovative, and powerful place to survive on!

Did Costco shop, just the necessities for one month.

We have the internet now connected, which is brilliant, perfect communication. Not too near, not too far!

I love this place, it's kinda crazy. Certainly worth arriving at or even passing through, destiny takes its toll though. I am in a progression; I suppose everyone is though.

When you are pushed, pull

When you are pulled, push

Find the natural course and bend with it

Then you join with Nature's power.

My life at long last – I am very content; just allowing tomorrow to unravel before my very own eyes.

Monday, 15th October 2001

I love it here and I am certainly not forgetting anything. It is a specialty. I am over the illusion! My heart and mind being confused. Ambition, hope, suspense. I am experiencing more and more each passing day… I am here for a reason I know it! Belief, faith, two of my angels! My special angels, they are answering me now, congratulations! Three weeks and more good times.

Remember they don't last forever!

Next plan – mugs!

You have no idea

Of the tremendous release

And deep peace that comes

From meeting yourself

And your brothers totally

Without judgement!

Love is the way it is

The way you see the world

Depends entirely

On your vibration

Much accomplishment today.

Saturday

I got a job, which is fantastic news, makes me a very content Chica. At least I am earning some cash!

Sunset Beach

North Shore

Haleiwa

Sharks Cave

Swimming

Surfing

Lava flows

Pot

Drawing

Painting

Photography

Boogie Boarding

Sleep

Snorkelling

Job

Dancing

Hilton, Turtle Bay

Aerobics

Yoga

Riding

Parties

House

Scuba

Sunday

I'm babysitting these kids and they have puppies. I am thinking I am going to buy one, a golden retriever, called Thor! We will see what will happen though! I am getting a dog next Monday. Then home to carry me through my next few months, years, lifetimes; it is going to be unreal. Brilliant, remind me of my responsibilities, which of course I have under control at present, a dog is a life, not just an occasion, so! Never doubt your devotion!

Wednesday, 31st October 2001, Happy Halloween

I've got a new addition to my family now that Thor renamed as Ben has arrived! Much goes on!

Today is the first time, I have felt sad, but no tears yet! But I have been upset, more toyed with, used.

Fully blue moon. How fitting.

4ᵗʰ November 2001

My sister is getting married. Simply yippee! A magical and special day to be had. Happy wedding and happy anniversary. God bless our family.

Friday, 9ᵗʰ November 2001

Devil progressed into action, and it was for me to overcome this and sense my anger, attitude. I am now living back along Sunset Beach, after, I might add, an interesting week at Turtle Bay. How strange, it was special and total independence.

Friday, payday today. It was rather crazy moving everything around again, backward, and forwards along the North Shore. The waves are beginning to get huge; the winter season is certainly settling in.

We achieve a sense of self-flow in what we do for ourselves and how we develop our capacities. If your efforts have gone into developing others, you are bound to feel empty.

Soul – soul description, of the happiness of the life I lead, possibly a perfect one. Who knows what destiny must capture? Life must hold. I hope and have faith that it is all right. Look at what is around you. You look just fine. What complications and confusion? Now breathe! Lady, breathe! All naturally takes its toll! Circulation flow! This is certainly far from being my home though. I have a passport for Ben Dog; I will be out of here. Far, far, away...

Monday, 12ᵗʰ November 2001

The last few days have been mad. One of the room mates went mental at me, dreadful; he pulled me off some exercise equipment outside. Being mad and depressed isn't going to help much, weird times.

Work, rest, and play! I am no surfing genius far from it! I am a real beach lover though, viewing the sunrises and sunsets. Today has been packed, Rocky Point, Kavala Bay, work, home, Halawi, Sugar Bar, home!

Tuesday, 13th November 2001

Flying again – helicopters; it was another excellent experience. I should have perhaps worked a touch longer, but I did have many things to get sorted.

17th November 2001

Surfing well is an interesting one, a profession of understanding water movement.

Sunday, 18th November 2001

Hawaii is certainly an eye-opening place. I must see more of the islands though, capture more! And more! Visit all islands. Maui next. Ben dog should be coming, he will! He will! Not to Australia sadly! But I shall make sure he will be cared for!
Painting – I am glad that I'm getting motivated to paint again.
While swimming I saw a hammerhead shark! At Kervela Bay where I go swimming every morning!

Tuesday, 20th November 2001

Well, hello!!!
An immense change has come over me recently. I broke my heart and am now pushing the limits! I worked this morning, Sharks Cove. There are some yummy-looking chappies around. My strange scenarios with getting heavily involved, is it truly necessary? I think not! I am sure the mirror will accept itself one day. Don't think twice, just follow the trance. The question of the deed. The eyes and experience. The gravity of life. Power pilot.
Beautiful area, wonderful life, it is a holiday tomorrow, great excitement. I might go flying, I will see. For the moment, yesterday was such a fantastic flight. I cannot believe I pilot these creatures, these machines! Good times, I am not sure what's going to happen.

Friday

I arrived back in Australia last Tuesday, which has been incredible. Rather a bang in my face, but I am glad about my spontaneous decision to catch up with friends down here. I'm looking forward to graduation, degree paper then another start to a new chapter. Cool!

Wednesday, 4th December 2001

Another day in paradise, contemplation, panning planning, visualising, and focussing.

20th December 2001

Journeying on again. New Zealand.

Leaving the great land down under. I am seriously going to miss it! NZ 106 here we go again, not worrying what's going to happen next. Flights. New relationships. What happened to me in Australia? I slept around...! Thank you for giving me the best days of my life!

I cannot wait to see my Ben Dog, my treasure. His arrival in my life is just the most comforting feeling that I've possessed. It is truly special!

Front page of the Canberra business! Hehehe! For gesturing and winning the student service award, excellent! I don't go away empty-handed!

Christmas Day, Tuesday, 25th December 2001

What a year. I miss my family environment currently. However, it is a decision to be here. I am just gathering problems from others. Not my own doing. We will see confusion somewhat over this period. Back to work New Year's Eve

31st December, Last 2001

Maui – another unique destination. The life, the paddles, and the kicks. It is all good, allowing the planet to spiral, the ways to crash, the sets to occur and I as a human, breeze through, enjoy and allow the next year to enter in with a positive vibe, spirit!

Anyway, allow me to get back to writing and involvement.

Nothing too serious, just pure appreciation of love and understanding. Spirit, acceptance of the dead, ocean views, feeding the circle of life! I am not out of it! I am just natural. Hardly in charge of me! I am in a society of being who I'm not! I wonder where in the next year we will be! The reminder of the fact that we are here for one reason! To live life! Accept and be passing, who knows more experiences, new cultures, another in my life.

Young Ben dog! He is a pure creature! He is my responsibility. He is a good boy.

Year 2002

Be a butterfly!

3rd January 2002

Passing through it again, another stage on the journey back to Oahu! It was a lovely stay in Maui, but I feel somehow, it was away from the necessities of life! Hana was a quaint place. Lahaina was more of a Haleiwa travelling around and absorbing the ambience, then disappearing and then showing up again proves to me how bizarre the life is here, the encounters and of my wallet getting stolen.

Monday, 14th January 2002

New diary cannot believe I have just spent the weekend on the North Shore, a wee retreat from the city.

No homelessness will occur. I do pray I am fully enjoying moments though, and particularly having Ben Dog addition in my life. This will create a challenge, a responsible one by Juliet, what a name, the sun! Shakespeare described. I must understand myself more this year and not allow people to bring me down. Now and forever – strength is my goal and my guidance.

The North Shore is a beautiful place though, with beautiful people.

Thursday, 17th January 2002

Ben dog is four months today, good stuff! Excellent!

I am well, with plenty of stuff going on, work, tennis, surfing, flying.

I have just found out that my parents are coming out.

Exciting. I cannot wait! March time.

31st January 2002

Oahu was not far away, and I arrived back here on the gathering island! I decided I would move into a quiet, tranquil, safe neighbourhood, touchwood! Also, it's a perfect place for Ben Dog.

Flying, working, tennis, surfing, and photography. These have been my main priorities for 2002 far! Flying is fantastic though, I cannot believe how fortunate I am to be flying over such a staggeringly beautiful island.

2nd February 2002

Involvement in the entire Romeo and Juliet scenario? I am tentatively confused. I am missing intimacy, contact and interaction, with someone I care about and vice versa!

3rd February 2002

North Shore sensing the winter air.

4th February 2002

I am at Sunset Point again. Beautiful day. Truly gorgeous.
Writing in the glorious Hawaiian sun, what special uniqueness is that?
Another perfect day of fluid occurrence on the North Shore of Hawaii. Watching the sun disappear!

Thursday

A fantastic episode flying, how incredible I flew to Koko Head solo. And saw amazing whales, a mother and her baby swimming between Hawaii Kai and Koko Head. It was staggering, quite a spectacular view. What kind of perfection was I living in! There was no way I could share this moment, other than treasure it for my memories.

Yesterday

Acceptance – allowing a progression of understanding. I cannot change the unforeseen and what has already occurred. Progression of the movement, understanding.
Anyway, what more can a person ask for in the acceptance of what we are? The days unravel, the ocean is deep with mystery, being here absorbing it, creates me, very simple! All we do is live!
Connections, that's how we are all exceptions of our equilibriums, progression.
Qualities, from emotions from the oceans fatties what I believe I'm nourishing myself on!

Monday, 11th April 2002

New business idea – Town and Country, developing photos.

Wednesday, 13th February 2002

I have organised photos and I'm meeting the guy from Town and Country tomorrow.

I'm locked on holding on for my brother. I pray for him. I do hope that he is alive and believing in the strength of tomorrow, survival.

14th February 2002

Excellent. How come I spent the entire day just speeding through it all! Substantial rest and respect for the female kind! It was an interesting time! Surprise and don't be embarrassed, embrace your beyond.

Analysis of the market and development. Foreign interest and development. Injection of the capital economy. Put together a proposal for the elective courses.

16th February 2002

Excellent aura. I had a fantastic surf day today out at sunset. It was quite unreal, one of the best days that I have experienced.

Favours, favours, work, work, I seem endlessly to be doing favours and working for people. I suppose to some degree, it is a good thing. No, I must however learn to say no! How often here I said that to myself! Always and always, with no discussion.

I have had time to think though. I must somehow conjure up $3000 US to complete flying.

19th February 2002

Dear...

It is good to hear you are still working hard! You seem to be excelling in the hospitality, hotel world. Much admiration, as it is a continual battle to achieve satisfaction with guests, but with your capabilities I have faith that you will progress and get fully what you deserve!

Workwise, I am working for a local backpacker's 'Sharks Cave', check-ins, checkouts, reservations, etc. usual repetition. Business wise I am in touch with a company called Town and Country, I am becoming one of their exporters, clothes, surfboards, skateboards, shoes, logos, etc. It is starting well, and hopefully will give me the option to trade between the UK, Europe, Australia, New Zealand, and mainland America. Retail is an interesting area. The phrase that you continually used with me! Finally, my photographs are being recognised, and I'm in the process of designing postcards, greeting cards, posters, etc. in that 'sepia' tone, it is ancient-looking. It is enjoyable and I'm always being guided by creative professionals.

Flying these choppers is my main challenge currently, it is staggering viewing the world 2000+ feet high – a feeling that I would love to share with you!

Trusting a girl behind, or in control of, machinery like this takes a great deal of understanding from a masculine point of view! It is thoroughly amusing but is always great conversation.

Relationship-wise, you know me!

I have no one special currently. I am rather apprehensive about getting into a relationship again! It is good fun being free and single.

I do however miss the intimacy and sharing thoughts and my life with someone! I experienced some of my best and worst emotions. I'll allow the planet to spiral and continue to believe that I'm in no rush now!

Life is fully open to surprises! Priority is for the creation of own satisfaction.

Love, Juliet x

20ᵗʰ February 2002

The journey is the destination. Who is running well? I have been deep in thought about what the next step is. Look at what else is happening in the world. Acceptance of life itself and help those who are not fortunate.

Anyway, I've spent today sorting myself out really; getting all my photos organised and all my books. Later I'm off to babysit the kids. Got into the surf for an hour and a half this afternoon!

February 24ᵗʰ Sunday, 2002

Second Sunday of Lent

Jesus Christ destroyed death and brought life and immortality to light through the gospel. All that is seen and unseen, gracious of appreciation!

Beauty in all my imperfections...

Everyone falls!

Why do you give?

What about friendship?

Nothing must end!

What if the world was a little more perfect?

Tuesday, 25th Feb 2002

I have decided this weekend to cruise off to Maui firstly to capture the scene and secondly to escape how I feel here on Oahu and thirdly to catch up with this other pilot friend. Wink.

Saturday, 2nd March 2002

Maui! I woke up this morning in another unique frame of mind. Maui. Spent the night on the North Shore – totally special and somewhat different from anyone else I have experienced! Growth and understanding are what it all amounts to – a certain form of perfection. The day flew past, the sun shone brightly. Conversation flowed – views flashed before my eyes.

5th March 2002

Top totty!

Back in the rhythm of the spirit here on the island of Oahu.

Finished education at university – not learning forever!

Troubled relationships, abandonment and spending time half in reflection and half in what would be good for the future!

Work. Visualisation is a key ingredient though – I am in a new stage though. What of intelligence, I'm not sure how clever I am, making time, allocation, we will see!

Dreams come true!

The Grand Waiakea Resort Hotel and Spa – Maui – Hawaii

We made passionate love. I haven't been with someone good and someone who made me feel good in such a long time.

Still trying to make things operate with Town & Country.

I'm off surfing!

March

Mum and Dad have arrived, hoorah!

I am at peace now – not too concerned about anything other than spending time with my parents. I rarely have time alone with them both, and it's very rare currently that my parents are together. So, I am blissfully content that I have this opportunity to spend time with them both – much-discussing life.

BBQ yesterday with a whale dance, sunset.

This week has been jam-packed with events. I have been doing loads and loads with Mum and Dad!

Pearl Harbour

Kaena Point

BBQ's

Aloha Tower

Dukes

Turtle Bay

Dog walking

Swimming

Hair cut

Still Aloha Friday, next week, I must pay my bills $400–$500! Where is the Romeo – to fit the Juliet? Certainly undiscovered right now although somehow, I wish I could shut the book – open a new chapter. Perhaps…

Watching the moon and even seeing Venus – that was special. Ah, shooting stars and spending time with my parents. Setting off from HNL to the North Shore. Where again in transition, all special moments occurred. Humpback whales were performing their midday dance. The sun shone brightly, and we continued to cover conversations such as the political-social situation in the UK.

The addiction is malicious, undeserving, disrespectful, and damaging.

The island is very seductive! I'm living in a dream world to some degree at present, which is totally perfect. I am however feeling rather edgy and in need of a certain degree of routine!

My mum and dad left today. I was very sad about the entire occasion. Somewhat hurting in my heart, my creation, they are a special couple, and I am totally fortunate to have them all in my life.

Obedience to God.

The perfection, who knows what specification is for the next phase, of course we will see! Have I had enough of that, certain controlling, never, unique, understanding, perception, and natural acceptance?

Tiredness.

Finally, I am writing again, perfection really, floating on a cloud of paradise. I'm happy but somewhat confused about the entirety of it all! I had a big night last night, today I was recovering well until now and I feel great, rather mellow, at peace, it's all good though!

I'm thinking of going over to Maui next week. We will see how it all pans out.

23rd March 2002

Ah, refreshing, an adequate night's sleep, along with a stunning wake-up call at Lizard's Point. A few photographs. Stretches and thought processes! It will be interesting to see what feelings occur in the next two months. Contentment, satisfaction and the natural progression of life unravelling each day.

31st March 2002

I opened my eyes on the way up to Tahoe from San Francisco… To just see the pine trees, sun decreasing, what a magical moment. *How perfect life can get*, I thought. You pay, you accept, excellent! Perfection to the greatest!

1st April 2002

Excellent day, fantastic, spring skiing and snow, what a treat.

North Lake Tahoe to San Fran – Delicious.

Returned from skiing, currently on the island of Maui. The magic island! Stunning. Well, the trip is just beginning, let's see how it unravels.

Sitting at 10,000 feet on the summit of the Haleakala volcano. Quite incredible, very beautiful, a good 4,000 feet above the cloud cover. Lonely – well, alone with my thoughts.

Having been in the water today is total refreshment. I feel one hundred percent more alive. There is friction within the ocean that generates power and energy from within. What a fantastic treat after my mega depressive thoughts earlier on. We will see; however, what I do know is that the ocean is waiting for me to jump in it again – at one with the elements.

The thought process today is one of reflection and of course, the ongoing question of what the future must hold.

The volcano crater was remarkable, what a treat to walk. Like up there – rather a dream. Surf was good. I miss Ben dog though.

I bet it's that place where you can't remember, and you can't forgive. Tenderness!

Daze... you left.

Stages – life cycle!

Delights as high as these

Bless my destiny

Why do some human beings desire with such urgency to do such things; regardless of consequences, voluntarily, conscripted by only themselves
Conquer nature
Physical capacity is the only limit?
I will start putting my power into a stream of thought.
My life has turned upside down since the last time I wrote – Maui, last Friday
It is now Monday – I've moved to the North Shore – unpacked endless quantities of my stuff and finally have a room with views of trees and the ocean, a kitchen space and living quarters – fantastic.

8th April 2002

April, so far, has not been my month; apart from skiing for a couple of days and naturally, the excitement, adventure, and pleasure of travel.

- Had my stuff stolen
- Bad fever blisters
- Period
- Moved house
- Credit card cancelled
- No choppering

Ah, well.
Relates to communication and perception of the world right now! One thing I am incredibly fortunate to have, is a roof over my head.

9th April 2002

Ah – I reckon I should approach my diary differently. I don't think I write directly from my emotional level, probably partly because I find it difficult and I can never find the correct words to use and again because I'm afraid that someone is going to read it.
The wind has picked up anyway, and I have a stunning view from my dining table. Just had strawberries and yoghurt to boost my immune system, as I feel that it is low at the moment. C'est la vie!
Drawing!
Exercise classes

Sorting insurance out
Helicopter piloting

Thursday, April 11^{th,} 2002

I feel rather strange at the moment. I think it is more to do with not feeling settled; although I must pull myself together. Just cycles of feeling good and bad. Ah well! I'm just going to let it all happen, progress.

I also am rather lonely, not that I require people in my life. More to the point of the acceptance that my friends are everywhere and are all doing different things now, finding the time for participation! Who knows? I also would quite like a boyfriend.

State of mind

Is it me or you!

The flame burns on!

Confuses – can't believe it!

Shall I be a nonachiever – load of time.

Wednesday, 17th April 2002

I surfed pipeline today – wise, scared, achievement, waves. Interesting swell! No major dramas apart from the feeling of being caught – somehow. I am in a trance of time.

Let the moments happen, girl. You are fortunate to have arrived here, leading the ambience. It is a free environment, an opening passage, and a sign of the natural.

ALOHA

The beauty of this place is a true attitude, passion and flowers. Stunning. What a treat to see rainbows every day, prisms of the reflection.

It feels like everything now is an episode – my mind is floating through imagination currently. I am stunned by the silence, the waves and, of course, the blue skies. We are extremely fortunate individuals.

Sunday, 5th – Sunday after Easter, 28th April 2002

What a week – another one in paradise. Ben dog was rather sick (he is allergic to rice), the surf was fantastic in town, good parties, harmonisation. It was special, incredible.

Thursday, 2nd May 2002

I've moved back to Sunset place again, it is perfect, but I do however feel rather set back. I have many ideas rushing through my head but very little motivation, not sure why really, but I suppose all the moving around – upside down, packing, and unpacking bags, being in all different places, adds to the confusion.

Silly or not silly – I'm not prepared to go home quite yet. And I wish something was more stable, but everything is a choice, decision, direction.

Honolulu – Waikiki
North Shore sunset, Turtle Bay
New Zealand, Auckland
Australia, Canberra, Sydney
Honolulu, Kahala
North Shore, Sunset Point, sunset

Friday, 3rd May 2002

I went for a run to Pipeline first thing this morning. The air was crisp and fresh, it felt good to take Ben dog along the bike path where there was very little distraction; followed by a swim on sunset, then coffee. Worked at Kaneohe on base, it was an interesting day. I read a lot of the pilot book and did many emails. Aloha, Friday.

Monday, 20th May 2002

Country surfboards
Airport
Hotel
TGI Friday's
Surfing Three Waikiki
Hot tub
Pina Coladas
Cha chacha – Mexican restaurant
Saturday night
Walk to Diamond Head
Beach
Church

Cheeseburger keys
Hotel
Surfing Diamond Head
Food
Extreme IMAX Theatre
Sandy's Surfing
North Shore
BBQ

Tuesday, 22nd May 2002

Working the Sunset on the Beach event, working at Country Surfboards, return ticket to the UK. I think perhaps I require a touch of guidance: good, evil, right, wrong, happy, and unhappy. Distinguishing moments, certain and uncertain.
I am training to fly helicopters, through the entire truth and understanding of it all, the enriched life of university, travel, excitement, passion, involvement, and yet I am here analysing my life!

Diamond Head Crater – fantastic view of the surf

The last time I wrote in here I had climbed Diamond Head crater. It was all impressive and stunning views of the surf. I went sailing in the afternoon, had been surfing in the morning at sunset, rather an aggressive sunset crowd, good swell from the Northwest had come in! A famous long board surfer had his memorial service out in the ocean about a mile from Haleiwa Beach Park. I went with friends; it was fun and chilled out! All the flowers dropped. We all went to Rosie's Canteen afterward and downed a few margaritas, got a good Saturday afternoon/evening flow going. Then all followed by having a BBQ, which again was fun, open, drinking, listening to music, playing music, surf videos, etc.
Sunday brought on new excitement: the church at Waimea first, then in another church on the NS, surfing at Chums Reef, chilling. Sunday of course.
Another diverse crowd but an awesome full moon… We went for a surf session early, which was perfect, clear, nice breaks, worth the early rising. Caught up with friends at Sunset this was total madness for a Monday morning before 9 o'clock, ah, well! Drove to Pearl City to spend the day researching and gathering first-hand footage for the Sunset on the Beach event! The day was a fantastic success and very much enjoyed, the film was Pearl Harbour, treasurable sunset 30" screen, Pearl Harbour, in Pearl Harbour on Memorial Day.

Thursday, 30th May 2002

Girlfriends left back to the mainland, end of the girl chick era. Very different now. Ah, well, I must move on and enjoy the Hawaiian Islands.

Over next month:

Working

Flying

Reading

Surfing

Flight organisation

Ben dog organised

Drawing, painting, and photography

Enrich your life continually

The brilliancy with it.

Saturday, 1st June 2002

It's a true shame all my surfer chichas have left – I'm down about the entire scenario – however, life continues to progress.

The face of you!

Today has been unpredictable, flowing with my position here. I'm realising I have friends which is important, but I'm unsure they are a substitute for love.

Routine for the coming month –

Run to Pipeline

Swim – depending on the surf

Call surf report and helicopter squawking

Priorities

Collection of progression

The realisation of your priorities

Conjunction with perception

Sunday, 2nd June 2002

Yeah, I woke up early this morning and went for a run – which opened my Sunday, followed by a dip in the ocean! Then to church, the church on Waimea it was good. Perfect to thank the Lord for everything and of course, the continuous pleasures in life that He enables me to have.

I seem to be endlessly in my journal in the search for something though. What would I change right?

Monday Morning, 4th June 2002

I started work yesterday; it was all right, however, it needs a huge amount of attention, which is positive, new innovative minds, conjuring up ideas, etc. Rather placid, enjoyable, the co-workers were friendly, no complaints at all! The surf world was an interesting one! Selective! My approach must be right, correct, pleasurable, full of passion and unexpected joy and respect, trust for each other! Understanding is important.

Commitment, attitude, no challenge too great for me! It is with heart, the justification, Jesus – to show his love – this is what we can believe in our lives.

Is your heart, right?

Having the mind of Christ.

Monday, 10th June 2002

Somehow, I am in a trance, goodness. I pray to my angels though, please may they guide me through this time; for respect, honesty, trust and belief in understanding and comprehensive logic. Relationships are an interesting, comprehensive logic – relationships are an interesting sage – involvement, participation, and sharing.

I woke this morning with beauty by my side! Naked comfort, talking, and sexual intercourse, followed by running and swimming with Ben dog, lovely! Work dropped posters and brochures off! When I was out surfing, a stunning rainbow captured my attention – lovely!

Tuesday

We both went out surfing this morning, which was lovely, a real treat.

I like this guy, I really do, scared to some degree by how much, but I suppose it's all right, who said they don't believe in love in first sight.

I'm still on the planet! Alive and well and respecting, living, loving, and enjoying. Allow it to happen, change nothing!

Wednesday

- I have a place to live
- A family to see
- A dog to take care of
- A computer to set up

- A run to take every morning
- A swim in the ocean
- Flowers to smell
- Sunshine to capture
- A mind of intelligence
- Capturing level of understanding, comprehension

16th June 2002

I am the breath of life.
Volunteering at Vacation Bible School

17th – 21st June 2002

Questions and answers.
Who is the greatest in the Kingdom of Heaven?
Whoever humbles themselves
Those who welcome
Listen and hear the answer.
Gentlemen have a new definition.
Forgiveness of sins – how many times?
We all struggle with the applications of teaching.
General life

Tuesday

I skipped writing yesterday – I don't know why! Probably because I got a fantastic massage and was pretty much working on the Sunset on the Beach organisation stuff, which has been fantastic, I'm enjoying it coming towards completion – everything, I'm sure, will come together!

Saturday

Perfection to a fantastic deal, new week, peripatetic, I love me! I love my life – and hopefully, I am going to capture the guy that I really like! Unsure about love but I think about him as if I should love him. We will see! True prayers shall be answered tomorrow, church! A domain! Please allow perfection to take hold!

Monday

We went out surfing at Backyards and got it on romantic in the water. Stop being impatient, unnecessary really! All this time...

We will see.

Surf swell is fantastic, watched Big Wednesday yesterday.

Talking to the moon, keep the protection

She will promise you her light

Bring the light and shine till morning

The wind pulls the clouds across the

Quietly while you were asleep

The moon and I were talking

I asked that she always keep you protected

She promised you her light

That you gracefully carry and bring the

Light and shine like morning

Then the wind pulled the clouds across the moon

Your light fills the darkest room

And bring the miracle that keeps us from falling

She promised all the sweetest gifts

That only the heavens could bestow

You bring the light and shine like the morning

Her light if you live

I will always remember this moment

Keep the groove

And of course, the life on tracks

Quietly while I was asleep

The moon and I were talking

I asked if she would keep you protected

She promised her your light!

So, you shine till morning

Keeps me from falling

Promising me the sweetest things

Light for a living!

Description – who knows?

Tall – Taller than me!

I haven't written in here since the sisters arrived; it is now 07/07/2002, a Sunday.

What a fantastic time has been happening – truly special to be sharing the Aloha spirit with them! Perfection to a great degree. Let it flow!

Go driving. Monday, the beginning of another beautiful week in the Hawaiian Isles. Perfection, with my sisters being here, great!

What have we been up to over the last week…been in town, Dukes, surfing, cinema, Turtle Bay, fireworks, Kavala Bay, movies, party here BBQ, drinking, drawing, Haleiwa Joes, glider ride, flowers, Kaena Point! Dali.

I am in the process to get a new job at Turtle Bay Hotel and Resort, fingers crossed, and we will see!

Sunday, 14th July 2002

Interesting energies in the house. Almost television! Story of life – characters!

Belief

Perfection

Yeah

Breaking through – was doing all the breaks between Backyards and

Rockies the complete journey of occurrences. It's all good, great!

Priorities: work, and of course a change of breath.

Energy, power, strength

Exuberance and determination

Enough is enough! Take the risk!

Vitality and empowerment!

Dawn through transformation

Surfing first thing – yeah – it seems to me that departure is inevitable.

Thank the Lord for the swell.

Writing from San Fran. Have a wee layover, which is rather frustrating, but I'll be flying home soon, just a lot of travel!

I slept the entire flight from HNL-SF, thank goodness for no sleep last night. Yeah!

Thank you for a fantastic year – Hawaii, Oahu

Cannot wait to return, yeah

Surf, art, work, fun in the sun!

Chapter 11

Back to the Bosom of Blighty...

"KEEP CALM AND WELCOME BACK" – Anon

Saturday, 20th July 2002

I have arrived home. It is rather a strange feeling. All good though, very happy back in the bosom of my family. I feel strength, warmth, and plenty of security.

Monday, 22nd July 2002

Many interludes and adventures
But always because they bring you joy.

Happy Sunday, 28th July 2002

Yeah – well, all is going well, very content to be home right now.
Strength playing
Record
We will be free!
Flow and believe
Who knows?
Who feels?
Who cares?
Live a spirit, sense of motion.
Create a floor…Juliet

Sunday, 4th August 2002

Immense weekend in London. Drove against both peak hours.

Tuesday

It is great to be home; however, I miss Hawaii loads. Much too much in fact. It is good to be back here though, living the feeling, having the summer holidays, home – hope that I make it back to Hawaii with a positive, ambitious, and open frame of mind. Surf!
Naturally I miss Ben dog; he is a fantastic dog to have around. I'm dying to take him for a walk and swim in the ocean. We will see what happens until I return. Return to the stunning islands.
All of September I'm planning on flying at Cambridge, get in the air as much as possible, take photos, etc. I'm able to return, ready to kick arse. Yeah!
Not crazy, chilled

Play my game
Graphic
Fine line
Trademark.

Tuesday, 13th August 2002

I haven't been in touch in a wee while. Been busy –
Catching up with the Suffolk crowd
Jubilee Party Friday
M and D wedding anniversary Sunday
Who could ask for more? Cannot wait to return to the islands, Ben dog is doing fine.
Blessed am I!
Thank you, dear Lord, maker of heaven and earth. I truly am grateful for your appreciation and love in my heart and mind!

2nd September 2002

Arrived home. Good vibes Portugal and Cornwall perfect.

September 2002

Portugal and Cornwall, I am now back in the rhythm of enjoying my time at home.
Since I returned from Cornwall...
Flying mainly, back in the pilot seat and heading to Cambridge every day to gather more hours and ground skills. It is going well – lots of work but excellent to be back there again! Flying is amazing and I'm incredibly fortunate to be able to devote time, energy and another passage in my life towards it. Just finish it, girl. Remain committed – it won't take long. Shouldn't be too much longer now!
Was up in London last weekend, which was fun.
I went for a BBQ, drinks, lots of good mates around, which was fun and games; that is new! It ran sweetly, had a late-night though and was completely washed out the following day.
Sunday – woke early and made it to a church service at eight in the morning followed by a swim in the Chelsea pool, old haunts, cannot believe I'm still doing it!

Made it to the airport around 11.00 and did my Met exam, which was all right. Very interesting, read up on a load of navigation, and finally completed the day by taking part in some fun solos. After circuits, excellent fun!

I am rather apprehensive about heading back to Hawaii, I suppose it is due to not knowing where I'm going to be living quite yet, also, getting back into the lifestyle, which I know won't be too much of a problem. It is just sorting out motivation again.

I'll continue getting hours in the air and I would like to take up kite surfing, these are just things that have been rolling around in my head. Artwork, surfing, BBQs, Ben dog, driving my car, photographs, settling into a new place, skateboarding, running, gym, Turtle Bay – Helicopters, who knows what will be in store! We will see, I suppose that I'm kinda nervous – live it, let it, love it, learn it, have fun with it!

"Thinking about life:
The great essentials to
Happiness in this life is
Something to do
Something to have
And something to hope for"
> - *Joseph Addison*

Wednesday, 11th September 2002

It is exactly one year after 9/11. It is incredible to sense how fast time has flown past.

A day of remembrance for all those victims in the awful attack.

God our father in the heaven above, please keep watch over your flock. As we all partake in the ritual and gift of life.

May I become a servant and a guide to those in weak positions – a shelter for those without a roof – a refuge of tranquillity – enjoyment and acceptance of the passions that occur!

I'm tired – thank you for a wonderful day.

"The worst thing
You can do
Is worry about
What you could
Have done"
> - *Lichtenberg*

Thursday, 12ᵗʰ September 2002

This is me right here now, surrounded by my material possessions – books, paintings, photos, artwork, computers, flying, material, clothes, flowers, etc. Ah, yeah, graduation certificate, the works, but who am I and where am I going? I know that I'm flying every day between now and the end of the month. Then off back to Hawaii.

Wanting what we can't have – I know the story!

22ⁿᵈ September 2002

My time here in England is nearly over and I'm heading back to the mid-Pacific to take on more pursuits and to develop more creation, hope, understanding, passion, love and adaption to the environment over there. I don't want to be fighting for what is rightfully mine, correct. But I pray that my prayers are answered. And I'm able to settle into the striving passion of surfing, sea, sun, and sand.

No complicated relationships, that's farfetched. To move to the same rhythm and develop a trusting friendship and compassion, watch this space…

I'm not here to make life difficult or complicated; I'm here just to move through the pace. The breath of life, from the awakening moment of every day, I'm out there absorbing.

Survival of the fittest

Flying

Instrument work

23ʳᵈ September 2002

Today, I was instrument flying, which was all right, the wind was strong. Hopefully, tomorrow, I'll do my navigation x country. We will see. It'll all depend on weather conditions. I'm not too stressed, just hope that it goes well!

25ᵗʰ September 2002

Well, aloha, ha!

Another application in my beloved journal right now! It is plenty of hours, years, moments, and minutes that I have applied myself in writing. And not once have I believed in becoming that unique, successful person. I'm completely non-coherent. Why? Decisions shall probably be decided later, when I can believe and understand and quite accept that that I am a unique specimen on this planet. Until then and that realisation, I suppose I'll continue to fly helicopters over here and defy what is represented to me elsewhere.

Monday, 30th September 2002

Passed my pilot exam! Yeah!
Fantastic – no looking back
Forward, far forward, understanding
Live it all to the most full
Believe – astound! And live for the moment
Be you girl!
Fly high

1st October 2002

Yet another day in the great tapestry of life, however this time…it is my last night at home for some time… I'm not sure when I'll return, but we will see! Pas de analysing what other persons decide to accomplish, believe, because I'm far from ever judging them!
I'm rather chilled, relaxed, and ready to open new eyes to another perception. Hawaii, all right is it a hard life, who knows it is for my discovery anyway!

Glion, Switzerland, 1998

Laurentian Mountains, Canada, 1998

Monument Valley, America, 1998

Sphinx, Cairo, 1999

Sydney, 2000

Prince Phillip, St James' Palace Duke of
Edinburgh Gold Award, 1999

Queen Elizabeth II, Australian
Commonwealth Event, Canberra, 2000

Graduation Ceremony, Parliament House,
Canberra Australia 2001

Uluru, 2001

North Shore, Hawaii, 2001

American Flag, New York,

Ground Zero 2001

Honolulu, Hawaii, 2002

Norfolk, 2009

Chamonix, France, 2010

Suffolk, 2013

Land's End, Cornwall, 2015

Isle of Wight, 2016

Chapter 12

Again, Aloha Hawaii!

"There is no such thing as work-life balance — it is all life. The balance has to be within you." — Sadhguru

4ᵗʰ October 2002

Aloha Hawaii

First day back in the islands! All I can say is thank you! I'm not meaning full-on daydreams but progressions, counteractions, balance.

I can get Ben home and move on.

Turtle Bay

Alligator Rock

I've just moved into this place at Alligator Rock. It is quiet and local. No distractions or madness just chilled.

I'm fortunate to be here, living the life of a princess, an angel. Who knows what is going to happen over the next few months, other than really being a soul with a heart and mind?

What am I searching for right now?

Peace of mind

Set straight – Alligator Rock – beautiful place – very calm – far from tourists being around – pure tranquillity – perfection really

Ben dog is with me now – I can hear the ocean and smell the refreshing breeze – what more can I ask for right now – other than someone to share my life with. The Lord will show. I know he will; he is right now, fortunate timing, true, true, true, pas de problems! I have hope and trust, that I'll be blessed.

12ᵗʰ October 2002

Surfing since first daylight, which was a beautiful, totally perfect beginning to the day. As for progressions, who knows? Certainly, I don't. I wish I did. However, many aspirations for happiness, accomplishments and devotion at present moment! I must admit I enjoy my own company, spending time alone, living life.

I'm surfing as much as possible.

It is very special that these people have entered my life and what gatherings I can have and will continue to do! Anyway, it is interesting how we all focus on our aspects. What takes us, holds us, breathes us! This time last week compared to what happened today, fantastic treat! Good swell finally came through – another journal addition, fine company, the touch of cleaning here and there.

Wednesday

Nearly Big Wednesday. The swell is too big right now for me, very windblown as well! So, I have decided to focus my attention on this new pad, which is truly fantastic. Alligator Rock owned by some English family, incredibly fortunate I am. God is answering my prayers.

Tuesday Morning 12:20!

Whoever made the full moon!
Certainly, thank goodness, today and tonight are over; I reckon the consternation with what I have been going through right now is not the best anyway! I'm ready for another blarblar.
Will I now have this pleasure?

Tuesday

The waves sound meditational; I'm ready to thank God for the day. Breathe and add a new spirit to the dreamland…sleep and dream well. God bless.
Anyway, I woke this morning kinda hung over, went for a swim around Alligator Rock. Rainbow right outside the window again, stunning. I am living by on a pot of gold. Lucky girl.

- Shopping breakfast
- Surfing
- Photographs
- Sleeping
- Surfing
- Dinner
- Newspapers
- Enjoying the simple things in life.

Aloha Friday!!

Sunday, 27ᵗʰ October 2002

Life in the Hawaiian Islands is beginning to settle down, praise the Lord. I woke this morning and paddled out at sunrise, followed by a touch of backyard action, which was great. I caught some good waves, got pounded but certainly was fun to have a change from Alligators. Yesterday, I had a three-session day, which finished me off; it was fantastic fun.

I am scared to get myself too emotionally attached. I simply end up getting hurt again. Such is the rich tapestry of life. We all have our ups and downs, fingers crossed I'm on an up at the moment.

What an end to a beautiful day, truly splendid! What a lucky person I am! Anyway, after I wrote last, I ate some salmon for lunch and pretty much passed out all afternoon, followed by about a three-hour surf session, which was perfect. Sunset, waves, company, was really very lucky, turning into quite the local freak; frog on the sponge had a lovely time though honestly!

Tuesday

I went to bible study tonight, which was good, a really neat setup with fine people. Good sense of direction and respect to the Lord. Yeah, anyway, the food and company was good, chatted and allowed the evening to unravel in song, prayer, and guidance within the bible.

Tomorrow is going to be busy, fun. Fully of joys. Working, kiddies, flying, making papier-mâché fins for the shark outfit will be fun!

Got my email set up even!

Wednesday

Another end to yet another beautiful day of the islands. Quite right, the tranquillity – love – acceptation and complete acknowledgement of being here right now is completely special other than appreciation – thanks – gratitude love and hope and total generosity of abundance in my presence is simply special.

Listening is certainly the art of becoming; I arrive right now. I had a great day. The belief of life flowed and the unique sense of who I am is positively shining through.

What I do know is that on this fine day 25 years ago mes parents got married, I'll call home tomorrow – knowing that the world is sweet and happiness is sweeter!

The waves were beautiful today, sunset, Backyards, Alligators, Halloween.

5th November 2002

Remember remember the 5th of November, gun powder, treason and plot. I see reason why your powder treason should ever be forgot.

Today was Mum and Dad's 25th wedding anniversary.

Tuesday, 12ᵗʰ November 2002

Nada – tres important today; just another candidate for the Game of Life. Did not do much today, other than absorb the North Shore winter rain, watched the waves and popped in for a wee surf.

1st December 2002

I haven't written since I got evicted from the house at Alligator Rock, a serious shame, really, sad! But the party was good fun – and totally worth it!
Starting from,
Backpackers
East-West Side
Surf spots
V-land – Velzyland!
Crazy Lane

5th December 2002

I have exactly 15 days to organise my life here in Hawaii, enjoy the days, capture every special moment that the islands must offer.
For the last few days I've been:
- Surfing, Waimea Shore break, Backyards, V-Land and Goat Island
- Working
- Gymnastics
- Opening of the Eddies
- Finals Van Triple Crown at Sunset

Adios to Hawaii is going to be a touch heart-breaking, but I'm ready to fly away, leave again on a jet plane, don't know when I'll be back again.
Cycles of relaxation
Here we go again…
Last night was fun. Headed off to the Turtle Bay, which was a good time, really enjoyed living the spirit of the surfing crazy North Shore.
Turtle Bay
Organising Ben Dog
Big party
Sex Pistols
Stayed up in Pupukea with the guys; amazing fun, big time, plenty of good spirits.
As for my embarrassment, we never do that – breathe, live it.

25th December 2002

Thank you Alligator Rock – for the memorable party in mid-November. I moved in with three lovely lassies – all hard-working surf chichas – this was fantastic. Finally, I had a chance to be free, sofa surf, and live the life of a pure derelict North Shore bum – surfing everyday – meeting new people. Let my guard down and have intermittent relationships with plenty of surfers – I was consistent with one chap, he brought me to the opening of the Pipeline Contest – the Surf n Sea Christmas party –morning charging at Waimea Shore Break – he lived in a little love shack at Backyards and joined my list of the backyard boyz – which reminds me – I must start on a wee writing caption – the Boyz from Backyards.

Went flying a few times, took photographers up, and caught some awesome island aviation footage – fantastic aerial views. I gave plenty of the photos away – should be making some money off them really – but I enjoy sharing.

The surfing over the last month has been too awesome, plenty of competitions have been happening – Haleiwa, Sunset, and Pipeline.

I had a great house party and went with a lovely skateboarder and– the evening passed in fantastic form – at Gas Chambers' break, I had never seen so much cocaine and so many surfboards in one place.

As for my surfing, it certainly progressed up a level. Surf breaks that I never thought possible and met some great people from all over the world – with free spirits, open minds, and no stresses with partaking in the rat race of life. The North Shore of Oahu truly is the Mecca of the surfing world, and I am honoured to have spent a year and half of my life so far there.

The islands treated me well this year – the yin and yang were in a balance; it started with plenty of yangs – then the yin kicked in. I had an awesome time – a chilled passing opened my spirits to the Hawaiian gods and let them cast their special spells. I tried pushing nothing, enjoyed the time with my dog, the people I met – the moments shared were blasting.

I'm back in the bosom of my family now and rather unsure of the next ventures. Ben dog is back with me – which is lovely – he is a perfect addition to my life here.

The twins are in lovely Christmas form. Opened my eyes at 4.00 to be greeted by Father Christmas and reindeer droppings over the house!

The plan is to go to London town for a while – pay my respects and thanks to my angels for the life that I lead and to remind him about perfecting the world that we all live in. Of course, get surfing and continue flying. Catch up with family and friends.

Most importantly – get a job, keep my health, enjoy every day, write, and draw as much as possible...

Share the love

Peace

Chapter 13

Big Girl Pants

"You were born to be real, not to be perfect." – Ralph Marston

New Year 2003

1ˢᵗ January 2003

Happy New Year, happy new girl! What a fantastic spirit of events – over the last year of pure ultimate living life.

Energy is an eternal delight...

An event unimaginable – here we are – entered another year, time, date – the guiding planet and the glorious occurrences of interactions, depth, understanding – relating to an enormity of 'comprehension'!

The circling globes

Moving planets

Radiant sunshine

Relations

God bless his creation

Amen

No, I haven't vanished. I'm still here – living in the ultimate Great London town – the United Kingdom!

I am content, at peace, alive, focussed.

Hopeful, ever hopeful, full of uncertainty but loving the excitement.

Alone time, reflection, and focus.

Totally without judgement

January

Circumstances allow themselves to manifest.

Now sitting in a London townhouse, near Chelsea Harbour, it is pleasant – away from the madness of too much traffic, the underground and masses that flock the London streets.

Grand Boats in the Marina – it is almost a quiet and cold Miami – just waiting patiently for the summer sun to show its face again.

Back in the Great UK, on a more permanent note than that of the last eight years, it is time to take the passenger route for a while, I am happy to be at home, back within the bosom of English folk. Although in London, how many English people are there?

The days seem to fly by right now, packed with catching up, skateboarding, swimming, walking, running, shopping, emailing, telephoning, setting myself up for the new life I'm about to endeavour here.

Channelled London fashion. I'll be interested to partake in all the moments that are occurring – viewing what you view, taking advantage and capturing the day. I had an interview yesterday. We will see. Patience is my game now. Also, a huge sense of peace.

The January blues – looking forward to the year ahead.

Sunday, 3rd February 2003

What is up in the world? I believe that we will be going into war, not far away now.

Living the life – back to modernisation!

Discipline!

The Great United Kingdom.

We will see what will happen – who can cease to have their surprises!

Happy Chinese New Year – the year of the Goat/Ram, 70 thousand Chinese people live here. China, a prosperous new year.

I'm not the happiest I have ever been in my life. Stimulus – operating – I cannot explain.

Songs of Praise – self-sacrifice, praise your name.

Relationships developed.

How does it happen? Good times. Perfection to the utmost – believe and breathe on.

He is certainly an individual that has entered my life again. It is pleasing to be on a calmer level with him right now. No dramas, no confusion! No manic outbreaks, all relative.

Shooting Days have been a relief; tromping over the ancient trodden ground in my life span. Letting lead fire. The smell, the air, the decent company! The praise for how we will farm the land and raise our traditional values, life cycle, and management – preserving God's creation. Am I looking for space right now alone in the city?

9th February 2003

We spoke – Years of growth elsewhere, who knows? Who really or truly cares! Remain constant, girlie. Who knows what the future must hold? Capture you in a storm; hold you in a whirlwind of opportunities, scripts, and words. Who knows?

Perfection. What is perfection? I do know that I'm happy with myself and my life; the enjoyment of really participating in everyday purities. Who cares for the untold – today's gossip is yesterday's news? Who knows?

I must admit, I'm rather lost back in my hometown. Not that it is an unnecessary stage to be in right now. But allow progression to take hold – combine and captivate my self-appreciation.

I miss Hawaii.

Cambridge

Airport

Knightsbridge

Chelsea Harbour

Chelsea pool

I have my second interview with the Dorchester tomorrow, which I am truly looking forward to – I pray that the job is right, as I am sure that the experience that I can gather from such a prestigious establishment would be awesome, fantastic.

Then we will see what will capture me next…South Africa, Australia perhaps? I love the Pacific region; it is different, far away from the madding crowd…and an ocean clearance of more than ever could be understood.

Sunday, 16th February 2003

For many, Sunday is the day of rest.

Probably for myself too, but loaded with exciting ventures, skateboarding, swimming, dog walking, painting, watching a movie, emailing.

Went to the movies last night and watched 'Hours'; it was impressive, rather feminist – but hey, always interesting to capture.

Also, went to the anti-war demonstration in Hyde Park – which again was fascinating – all very interesting. Many people, the most diverse caption of society ever. Even through all my travels, this was an incredible section of history in the making and not just here in London's Hyde Park, simply all over the globe.

I'm rather lonely back in my home town, I have friends passing through. I'm missing love in my life – but I am certainly not missing the chase, the journey, the denial, trust aspects. It's good being free, but again, I boil it all down to the right timing and the right outlook. I'm lucky, very lucky, fortunate, and treasured. I am praying probably for mutual feelings. Feelings that I cannot describe quite yet – understanding, compassion, love, depth, fun, enjoyment, pleasure, adventurous, naturally good-looking. The effort certainly, eyes for me and my heart, and of course, my mind and my physical being. God bless the Sabbath.

Saturday, 23rd February 2003

I got my job at The Dorchester this week! I pray that I'm going to succeed to my potential.

After missing a certain someone – I'm now at home detoxing my body – and spending time with my very close, loving and important family. Also, absorbing the fresh air before I have to head off for this job, I feel like I'm going back to school, but hey it all be good – interesting and eye opening.

3rd March 2003

I started work at the Dorchester; it was quite an intense mission, but it all happened. I made it into work, asked questions, relayed answers and made an impression. Naturally, right now, I'm thinking about what I should and should not be doing, adding to my stress levels…

We are back together for the weekend, what a unique bond.

Sunday, 16th March 2003

Happy Sabbath – beautiful sunshine. Work – tomorrow day off
Sweet. Work hard, my lovely.

April 6th Sunday

Grand National
Boat race, Oxford vs. Cambridge
Work, work, work
Hyde Park
All is progressing well, haven't written for a while. Parents went skiing – same for the next week.

Easter

Spring time
Stars and Sky
Serenity Simplicity Splendour

Flying
Spin class
Church
Rabbits
Lamb
Walk dogs
Trees, punters on boat, horses
JUST LOVELY

Sunday, 4th May 2003

I seem only to connect to my Sundays and writing – right now – organised level – it's been great though – no complaints to anyone or anything. Life is progressing in a manner of steps – matters far from my confusion right now. Who knows what the next undertaking shall be? The continuation of trust, honesty, understanding, belief, compromise! Was in the Sun today – catching the left, believing in the right.

20th June 2003

It has been a while…
Belief, comprehension, here, comparison, who knows? Return dear friend return. I thought it might be about time that I got interacted with my writing thoughts again! Plenty has occurred over here!
Love, acceptance, adaption, love, enjoyment always.
Aloha spirit I cannot describe the ultimate partaking!
Summertime and I'm loving easy. We will see. Work, work.

1st August 2003

Aloha always
Work – The Dorchester
The pen nearly decided to stop!
The urge for captive
New you
Eternity on the bridge is eternal energy.

15th August 2003

I am now 8 months, not 8 years, 8 weeks, 8 days, or 8 minutes into participation here. It seems to be running smooth, enjoyment and guidance. It's all proving to take its toll!

I cannot express the somewhat enjoyment I have here. I have to somehow partake, no dis-satisfaction but yes an acceptance of capability of what occurs next, I'm positive all will be noted!

I cannot describe, but yet I still have plenty to prove and plenty more to acknowledge. Who knows yet the choices I decide for the next adventure? Right now, I'm here in London – living the moment.

1st Jan 2004

Another year complete...Who would have believed so much has changed!
WE ARE TOGETHER
I am pregnant with a baby boy!
Many discussions about names. This time next year, we will be sure! We had a chilled one with friends over. We had a delicious dinner, and I kept my eyes awake to see the NY in!

I felt very pregnant today and spent the morning swimming and the afternoon walking and watching telly. Perfect, lots of food and movies, the perfect end to a perfect festive period.

Plenty to do over the next month:
- Organise midwife
- Dr in the country
- Ticket to Mallorca
- Timings for moving into mews/or another home?
- All my paperwork
- Enjoy the year ahead!

3rd January 2004

Pregnancy is an exciting period. It is lovely to have all the friends and family being supportive.

7th January 2004

All back from St Lucia.

JC has gone slightly crazy and went missing over the last night, 48 hrs. Turned out; he had been to London.

14th January 2004

Time really does fly; I'm now in Mallorca. It is certainly a beautiful change from England. Here the sky is blue, the sun is shining and I'm quite content, sadly not perfectly in my routines yet. However, time again will tell, plenty has been happening this year already.

I've been really sick and unable to move. I pass out, a lot. Under Doctors orders I need rest – now in the Mediterranean for a month on another adventure and exploration. I do enjoy travel. It is different having a partner to share it with and a baby to protect and love!

Sunday, 18th January 2004

The Mallorca life is ticking past at a steady rate – my days are filled with walking around the local village, swimming, listening to the church bells, absorbing the Med temperatures, reading, sewing, and then a touch of telly viewing.

Wednesday, 21st January 2004

Market day in the hotspots of Santanyi, my days have been filled with swims, long walks, fresh air, good food, video watching, and plenty of sewing, my tapestry is coming along. I find it very therapeutic!

Job prospects, he can claim some money back. He is a lovely guy and I'm lucky to be with someone devoted and sensitive!

Although naturally, we hit our rocky patches...

Sunday, 25th January 2004

As for him inside – he is cooking nicely – although I reckon my life will never be simple and quiet again. I do enjoy child stimulation I'm sure it will not be too much of a trial! More a tribulation.

Wednesday, 28th January 2004

Filled out my tax return – about as last minute as I could!

Man, I need to get a clearer picture in my head of understandable forms!! Anyway, had a gorgeous swim this morning. Hopefully, I'll be feeling better soon.

Spain is still treating me well; I'm happy getting fatter and of course, managing to get through the tapestry.

Saturday, 31st January 2004

All is still treating me well here in the islands. Very peaceful. I'm doing plenty of yoga, stretching, reading, tapestry, movies, walking, and swimming. Quite perfect really.

10th February 2004

Last night in Santanyi, it has been a blissful few weeks. I've chilled out a little more, which is probably a good thing. We are heading to Parma tomorrow, visiting friends; it will be lovely to see them. Seeing friends and staying in the glorious Sun Vida Arabella Hotel. What a VIP treatment.

We have been discussing potential business ideas. We will see what will happen. Although we have both agreed that this year, we're gonna make it happen.

I do have hope and I pray that we two work through and discuss our troubles. It is important in relationships. Money is the cause of most of our tense discussions. It is only because we don't have any.

However, I pray in time…there is more to life…though we do need to rely on each other.

I'll miss the peace in this village. It is very quiet. The bustle of activity with the morning markets on Wednesday and Saturday, the strolls around the tight ancient streets that are so small you could barely throw a cat. The temperature has increased slightly, or I've got more adapted. It is not boiling like the expectations of Mallorca. When the sunshine's here everything sparkles. Great blossom on the trees and green grass. Things are coming alive, off to Palma.

29th March 2004

I cannot believe two months of my pregnancy have just flown past quickly. Plenty has happened since we returned from Mallorca. The joys of moving house! We are now settled in the converted stables in the Mews. It is cosy, lovely, and beginning to feel like home.

I was in London for a while, I went to visit a girlfriend from Canada, who had her art show in Mayfair, which was lovely, and I caught up with a few friends, which was perfect.

He is working locally in Thetford on the industrial estate, earning money. Good that he is leaving me to my own devices during the day. He worked for a friend, selling her vodka, which worked out brilliantly as he now has a job to earn more money over the summer.

Pregnancy is now feeling much better.

Hopefully, I will write in here again before I burst. I have not been the best at keeping up with my journal lately!

27th April 2004

I cannot believe where the time has flown this last month. I'm settled in the Mews, which is perfect for the time being. My routine is very calm – or has been at least for the last month. I'm doing plenty of sewing, swimming, walking, internet-based activities and writing to friends. Finally, I organised to get a new camera, so I'll be back to taking lots of photos.

The baby shower happened a few weekends ago on 17th April. Was wonderful fun and God treated us to a glorious sunshiny day. We received many presents – lucky, the baby room is certainly not lacking, and we are overloaded.

I'm not doing much with my professional life right now. I've been having a lot of thoughts and perhaps plans for the future. However, nothing concrete yet. I'll just take what I'm going to do next when the time arises. I've been thinking about getting a wee clothing business online rather like Brother Swiss with Aloha Products. I have also been thinking about doing Teacher Training, there is a course starting in September. Eventually, I might even become a teacher. Must do more research regarding those ideas though…

10th May 2004

Still waiting for the little man to pop out, I cannot believe how overdue we are becoming.

Trying to keep myself as busy as possible to take my mind off what is gonna happen next!

Chapter 14

Welcome to Mummydom!

"The moment a child is born, the mother is born. She never existed before. The woman existed, but the mother, never. A mother is something absolutely new." – Rajneesh

14ᵗʰ May 2004

I have become a Mummy! The labour was intense. My beautiful boy was born first thing in the morning, a water birth blessing. True gracious thanks for the safe arrival of such a treasure.

30ᵗʰ August 2004

It has been a long time since I last wrote.

Much has happened and changed my existence as a human. Being a mum is rewarding especially when a little man smiles his sweet smile.

I am in Menorca now, with the family on the annual summer holiday. The sun is shining, and we are staying in a gloriously spacious villa, lying in the rolling rocky hills overlooking the sea. Tanning is my main mission along with bonding with the siblings and Mum and Dad. We reflected on the time we spent in Australia and Bali! A beautiful time back then. Still a beautiful time now.

We trained it up in Scotland to spend some time with them, which was fun. We went clay pigeon shooting and off to the coast and Edinburgh, a beautiful city, vibrant, cultured, and fun.

Went to the coast of Great Yarmouth with Mum, which was a lovely break away from the normal routine. Walked along the beach and threw stones into the sea for Ben dog.

August 1ˢᵗ, we had the christening, plenty of friends and family came to stay. It was extremely tiring but awesome fun to catch up with everyone and we were blessed with a gloriously, warm, sun-shining day.

28ᵗʰ September 2004

I am proud of my little boy and, his growth, and his interaction, with the adventurous wide world he is developing within.

It has all been nonstop since returning from Menorca.

New dog called Kota, she is a little overweight and a huge personality – hope that she will be all right.

Life is ticking on though. Four months and I'm busy organising my business from the internet, doing little shows here and there. It is fun and will keep me out of trouble.

Keep trusting the Lord to make me strong and keep me level-headed. I don't mean to lose my cool. It is just what happens, especially as everything is close to home.

Drove to Edinburgh.

18th October 2004

The weeks, months seem to have just disappeared. Five months, and he is a fantastic character, I am incredibly blessed to have him in my life.

As mentioned before having the babes – we have hit some high and low patches, however – right now, we are steady as an even keel – business is beginning to pick up – Aloha Products is coming together which is good. However, I am very interested in hooking myself on the property ladder.

Whether it is around here or anywhere – we will juggle the balls now. All seems to be swimmingly passing us by!

January 2005

We have been to Ireland and Mallorca since October, and more exciting news is I'm becoming a mother again! I've been in the morning sick mode; it's nasty and sometimes feels so permanent. But I am being strong and loving looking after baby, my home and the dogs.

Chapter 15

Every Day Is a School Day...

"Learn as much as you can while you are young, since life becomes too busy later." – Dana Scott

17th January 2005

I moved things around in the house, which feels a touch better. The babes will have their room, not having to share with our clothes, etc., their toys, their clothes, and their space.

I am slowly finding my feet in the New Year. It has been a touch hectic time with lots of friends and family staying. Now I'm loving the calm. Naturally, I have company. However, right now, I'm in my routine, structure! Walking the dogs, enjoying wee one's company, getting on with emails, letters, etc. yeah, it's good. The teacher training course is going well.

1st February 2005

I am trying hard to make it all work now, yet I feel like I'm banging my head against a brick wall. I've become incredibly frustrated with one thing and another.

This year has got off to a rocky start. Firstly, Kota breaking her leg and then the power cut over the NY night.

Then, when the NY gets underway, I have lots of people to come and stay.

He got a painting job in Shropshire, and a week after he started it I ended up bleeding badly for another week, becoming sicker and weaker; and eventually through a lot of emotional ups and downs, I stopped bleeding and slowly got on the mend. The doctor says I could have miscarried based on the amount of blood loss, clots, and pain.

I'm trying to work hard, be a good mother, supportive partner. I don't know what to think and believe anymore.

I'm tired, upset, sick, low, frustrated, pissed off.

20th April 2005

I haven't written for ages; however, things are going well, which is excellent. He is now working at the Garden Centre. It is creating a much smoother and pleasant relationship between us both – both contributing to our livelihoods.

I've been busy getting ready for the next babes, whilst looking after our little one and teaching Year Two at the local school as well as painting, looking after the dogs and swimming. Managed a trip to London and caught up with some good girlfriends.

- Ann Summer's party

- Body Shop party
- Granny's Easter party
- Car accident
- Coming and going of the siblings

God is certainly watching over us now. Keep up God good faith!

Balance

Seek balance.

Balance emotions with reason.

Combine detachment with doing our part.

Balance giving with receiving.

Alternate work with play, business with personal activities.

Balance tending to our spiritual needs with tending our other needs.

Juggle responsibilities to others with caring about ourselves.

Whenever possible, let's be good to others, but be good to ourselves too.

Some of us must make up for the lost time.

Today, I will strive for balance.

What a journey!

This process of growth and change takes us along an ever-changing road.

Sometimes the way is hard and craggy.

Sometimes we climb mountains.

Sometimes we slide down the other side on a toboggan.

Sometimes we rest.

Sometimes we grope through the darkness.

Sometimes we're blinded by sunlight.

At times, many may walk with us on the road; sometimes we feel nearly alone.

Ever-changing, always interesting, always leading someplace better, someplace good.

What a journey!

16th May 2005

Darling son's first birthday weekend. It was a load of fun. Lots of hard work, lovely BBQ, and beautiful sunshine.

All has been well. He is working; I am working…Meeting new people, friends for our little boy.

Getting much larger for baby #2. Names are running around our heads. I'm positive an original and suitable name will arrive!

Kota, our other Goldie, has had to be rehomed. So very sad. She needed to be somewhere where she was the only dog and somewhere with extra high fencing! She kept swimming across the river and stealing picnics from people. She could sniff out a sandwich within seconds and would be off! No stopping her. And getting her back even more difficult! I just was so worried that she would have a mishap on one of her many escapades!

17th June 2005

Aloha Friday – I am certainly no way near as good with my diary entries as to how I used to be. I suppose right now, everything takes up my time and I don't get plenty of space for reflection, or even self-meditation.

I'm happy – and very happy to be expecting baby number two soon. I'm blessed with my family around me. We are a wee family and of course Ben dog, Rosie the rabbit and the fish.

I haven't seen many friends. We did pop to London briefly for a fleeting visit for a BBQ, I wasn't particularly well. He got very merry.

Hope to do some travelling; however, I don't reckon it's on the cards for a wee while.

22nd July 2005

Darling son #2 has arrived. Long, long labour. He is Born! Born at home in the front living room, bouncing around in the paddling pool. So good to tuck up in my own bed and snuggle with the boys.

16th December 2005

The boys are both delights – they keep me very entertained and stimulated, never a dull moment – never a moment. I have just gone through a bout of poorliness with them both; last week. I am particularly drained. I don't know how to express this. I am dreadfully confused. I endlessly seem to be making people – other people – happy. Is this the welcome to motherhood!

I suppose it cannot go on like this though.

Our eldest– he is a cheeky monkey – everything is new and wonderful for him – especially tractors!

Our second beautiful boy– all is fresh.

Christmas NY 2005/2006

We had a fab time in Sri Lanka, it was great to get away from the norm and make the most of sunshine and a completely different aspect of life! Elephants and beaches.

Back to the grindstone here in England. It is fine: teaching, working, mothering…walking, swimming, researching, sometimes getting depressed and frustrated. It's no mean feat! I am slightly saddened.

HE COULD DO WITH A REALITY CHECK.

It is crazy. I thought my life would be simple and I could control most of my emotions. However, time moves on and it can all be very fragile. We must be very aware – focussed and remain in a sort of harmony to be placid and content… I've got to stop blaming myself for other people's actions and behaviours.

16th February 2006

He is taking coke in the bathroom by himself.

I am slightly sad, confused, disappointed, angry…

However, I must remain focussed on the children.

I have said he must go to the doctor and get himself sorted… I simply cannot have him like this any longer… I did not set myself up for something or someone selfish!

22nd February 2006

Plenty is still happening here; the kiddies are keeping me very active. Starting a new job tomorrow with the school, this will be eye-opening. Hope it all goes well.

He is getting back on track again. He had been acting rather strange recently, which has proved rather a challenge. However, the future moves on and we must gather strength and remain forward focussed on living life. Who would have thought relationships could add such drama to people's existence. Good and bad. Anyway, we have decided to move from this chapter and start a new life in Spain. Mallorca. It will be a fantastic challenge. I am very much looking forward to a fresh pace of life. Sunny skies and warm temperatures. No more commutes.

14th April, Good Friday, 2006

The end of that – another religious year.

My writing is dreadful now.

Scotland the great.

Oh, land of Scotland.

I am hoping that one day I will be taken care of… I am busting a gut right now!

How is it to be without someone?

It is me… To be without?

Smile, open our eyes, love goes on…!

Chapter 16

Muchos Emotions in the Med...

"We must accept finite disappointment, but never lose infinite hope." – Martin Luther King Jr

4th June 2006

A huge move and change of scene in the beautiful island of Mallorca – Con Concos the village is peaceful, and a wee haven. It is suiting the family and all our needs. Ben Dog has made it also. So, I do feel a sense of relief and homeliness.

All of us and luggage at the airport LHR. It was an immensely emotional day. Firstly, we broke down 12 ½ miles from Heathrow on the M25. Fortunately, a helpful, overworked truck driver pulled us to safety and deposited us on the sidewalk. Porter expenses, the excess baggage and animal welfare. All added to huge stress. All very challenging, but I didn't crawl into a puddling corner. I faced the music and tackled each physical interaction.

Con Concos, tranquil and acceptable for the time being.

Shattered and hungry, we still plodded on with the adventure!

Mountains of unpacking, organisation, focus, planning, jobs and contacts

Easing steadily into the island life

Fish oils and yoghurt, swims, and walks

I'm needed! Talk again soon.

5th June 2006

PS: Visited the kids' nursery. I am sure that both babes will settle in sweetly! Eldest son integrated perfectly. Tractors, kids, walks, swims, BBQs settling.

9th June 2006

We arrived a week ago and much has been happening.

Furniture shopping today, which was a relief to a degree because we managed to get ourselves sorted for our time of settling in here on Con Concos.

The boys both have a cold now, they are both adapted to such an immense change that they are doing great.

We are beginning to get in touch with people. Exterior! And have got the latest in mod communication hi-tech – yippee!

Managed to get an interview, which is another relief, however, it's in Deia! (so much for no commute!) Hopefully, it's not too far from here.

Ben dog is grand, settling quite sweetly into the pattern and the frame of things! The washing machine arrived – have plenty of washing on the go – you would not believe it! About a month's worth!

Anyway, I am happy I have my period, which is a hurdle, however, if my boys are happy, then so am I!

13th June 2006

Well, we are settling into the rhythm.

I went for a job interview at the Residencia Hotel, which was great. I am thinking it will help me with my Spanish and it is only six weeks over the summer months. We will see – however, I am positive it will be for an awesome experience. I am concerned about the long drive and the children though.

Had my period over the last few days, which has added to my cycle of hormones and hormonal behaviour. Inspired, I've been busy planting seeds, writing to friends, cooking, cleaning, walking Ben dog.

17th June 2006

We have been here 2 weeks today and what an adventure mission – it is plugging along quite sweetly really. I have a job at the Residencia Hotel on the other side of the island.

Made some new friends.

Watched plenty of football.

Might be getting a black cat.

Experienced an immense thunderstorm, the weather is miserable – although interesting to watch, like a sandstorm, mud rain.

21st June 2006

We have a Dalmatian, unnamed for now however. We got him from the market at Felantix. Adorable wee pup – with a lot of love to receive!

22nd June 2006

Our eldest has turned one and the new Dalmatian pup has been named Toby.

So, we went to Palma today and collected the social security numbers that we need for work. I faxed them off to the Residencia – fingers crossed that they arrived. Otherwise, I will get them in the post tomorrow.

The children are well and integrating, as they should. Yesterday was busy, making sure that the job for the next six weeks was taken care of.

26th June 2006

I get angry and bossy. I guess it is when I am lacking control. There is nothing more annoying sometimes than busting a gut to make our time here operate effectively – as well as running a family, household, job, etc.

I am feeling a little more relaxed now – still the Telephone guy hasn't turned up though. What a pain. However, this I guess is Spain and it is bad enough in England waiting for servicemen.

Friends came over yesterday for a BBQ, which was fun. England played Ecuador in the World Cup football and the UK won, which is great – through to the next stages.

I start work in Daia for the 6 weeks, things might improve. Space probably is what I need. I love being a mum and within the family – however, I am sensing a touch of independence again.

Still, we wait.

4th July 2006

The job is full on and a long drive.

I miss my boys. I love them too much to disappear off. No matter – they are important.

8th July 2006

What a mad couple of days!

I feel rather ashamed of myself that I have let La Residencia down, and myself. It was just too much of a commute, not enough money and most importantly, I missed the boys. What a tribe they all are. I guess life is important and I've got to start making more professional and grown-up decisions.

Anyway, back to the housewife routine. Hopefully, my brother JC will come out soon along with other family members and friends in the next week. Exciting times, hey?

Well, I must get dinner in the oven, children to bed, the dogs walked, and receipts on the spreadsheet and get the washing on the line.

He is watching the football. Oh, grand – adventures!

17th July 2006

He has done a runner in the family car! I am just completely devastated that he has got to such an extent of pure and utter selfishness!

I go through ups and downs with my feelings. I cannot sleep, eat, think; my heart is completely crushed. I just wish he would return and explain.

The thing is... I've moved our family and entirety down to Mallorca for him! Could it be the whisky and pot combination that gets him so angry with me? This is not love!

The boys are going well. I just cannot tell anyone back in the UK what has happened. They would get angry with him. Does he care? He just must take greater responsibility!

I pray I am a good mum today. I'll ask God again for more guidance and strength! It is bad right now. It can only get better!

We can only believe it! Hope and have faith – remain positive!

I promised the family two years here. So, I must follow my word.

Monday, 31st July 2006

I am kid-free for a couple of days, which is peaceful and pleasant, and I've just had a touch of good uninterrupted sleep.

I have now finished breastfeeding. So, I've cut my maternal pleasures in that area. As a treat, we are off on an adventure. Visited a town called Arta and a castle and are now on a beach Cala Rijula. It is a tourist town, however peaceful and I am watching the waves and windsurfers and managing to catch up on some much displaced sleep.

I am asking God plenty for strength and guidance now, especially as my patience right now with the kids and him is at breaking point.

I am now on the beach. Again, waiting for someone else! I wonder who or what!

1st August 2006

Nearly two months on the island and the first morning we woke up with the sunrise on the beach. It is glorious and *mucho tranquilio*, although the dogs are being walked and swam. The tractor is smoothing the beach and we are slowly dusting the sand and sleepy dust from our eyes.

7th August 2006

I am working in the local Alchemy restaurant helping an English girl, set up. I am feeling a little more positive this week. I think it had all got a little much; however, it is helping me have my workspace.

21st August 2006

I have returned from the UK after a few days. Eldest son and I went over for the laser treatment. It was quite heart-wrenching; however, it was accomplished. Another session was completed for his birth mark.
I am now back in Mallorca. We had a couple of days at home and then in London. It was a good change of scene and pace. I am tired of constantly cleaning, washing, changing, walking, etc. However, we will see what happens with this job at the restaurant, Alchemy. And good times, I am sure are in store and I know the kids in September will be at nursery making friends and that will be a much better schedule for them.

24th August 2006

I am on an airplane to Edinburgh, and we have been delayed for over seven hours on our way for a wedding. Thank goodness, 36,000 not left–right Leed Ed, Vis +14 West running 9.50 local time Apologise for late aircraft. Meant to arrive at 3.00 pm local time. Anyway, we are here. Have had imagination and images of the talking story about the skies! Forty minutes to go, I guess!
I do miss flying myself chartering choppers – Hawaii and England. Perhaps in good times, we will do the same again. However, it's complicated working out funds. Finances! We will see!
I hope that they will be all right still looking after the kids. I am sure they will. It just takes different energies and time accumulation. The kids were good and positive lovelies! I must appreciate them more. However, more not be me anymore!
I am shattered though, tired. Let's wish for some hours' sleep!

Saturday, 9th, September 2006

I AM PREGNANT.
I am back here in Mallorca – things were running fine until I went back to work.

I've been working long hours. No break in the home life and no break in the work. I reckon a lot of my emotions are to do with being pregnant. It is no excuse though.

22nd September 2006

Things I feel have gone from bad to worse. I really just want to make him happy. Obviously, I am really not succeeding and he is constantly mad at me. If it is not one thing it's another. Things are beginning to really wear me down. Especially emotionally. I have absolutely no friends to discuss this with. I feel so alone. It could just be my emotions – pregnancy and all. However, I feel so devastated that I am endlessly battling. I have told mum now that I am with child. I will write and let the rest of the family know.
I know that I moved here for him! Does he not realise this?

25th September 2006

I guess the rain cloud is steadily blowing over. I got myself into a right pickle. Things definitely still need sorting out though. Lots of tranquillity, peace. I have written to the family now about baby #3. Wonder what the outcome will be?
I think JC is alright. We are definitely keeping him moving and operational.

3rd October 2006

I am feeling a little more settled now. I was all over the place last week and really didn't feel all that great. Had spots and cold sores.
Anyway – things are getting on the mend again. I think I need an extra pair of hands around the house. I think I got myself into a pickle though and a touch het up.
JC is back off to the UK tomorrow just to sort some things out. We also – somehow have been blessed with about a 20 day old cat. Boy, another wee lad. God does work in mysterious ways.
I am good!

4th October 2006

Things are getting better. Poor love, I have been ordering him on missions all over the place; however he enjoys doing things like that so all is good.

22nd October 2006

I've been working so hard and trying to be a good mum and partner! We have had people to stay. I've started bleeding in this pregnancy. I am just praying I don't miscarry. The same happened with my last pregnancy.

He is angry at me. I am just asking him to earn some money, to stop smoking drugs and drinking each and all day. I am tired and fed up! And so sad and confused now that I'm the one that may be miscarrying.

I am also trying so God damn hard to make things work.

OBVIOUSLY I AM A FAILURE RIGHT NOW.

2nd January 2007

We have made it to 2007. I had rather an emotional rollercoaster of a new year. I haven't quite deserted the family yet though. I wouldn't do that! Even when I get emotionally tested I could never leave my absolute responsibility. The kids are way too precious.

We had a fun Christmas, lots of goody's cooking, etc.

We did meals on wheels service for about 18 guests.

Anyway, I must get over my little blip. Lack of sleep, etc. pregnancy and start enjoying life, other than cleaning, washing, cooking…

7th January 2007

I still haven't clicked out of this mood. I am really very emotional and also frustrated. I wish there was something I could do. I am getting so angry and so tired. Don't want to go anywhere or do anything. I guess a lot of it has to do with the pregnancy; however a lot has been because he is mad at me. He tells me I'm paranoid, controlling and bossy. Anyway I am not totally happy here, then again when are we totally content…

This year will be a deciding and interesting year on our next step and direction. It is good to be working at the Alchemy and it is giving me a little time out of nappies and domestic duties. The kids are back at school tomorrow, which will be a huge relief. I can organise the house a little more. Do some yoga, swim, work, get in touch with correspondence.

I am having trouble with sorting out the birthing plan and arrangements here on the island.

Need some positive channelling right now. Certainly could do without the assistance of shouting, blasting and arguments.

8th January 2007

Goodness. I really am sad at the moment. I spoke to mum earlier – really I don't mean to burden her with my troubles – dilemmas etc. It is all just really getting me depressed at the moment.
Anyway I should just get on and grit my teeth, be dutiful etc.

26th January 2007

I guess when you love someone – you do become very blinded by people's actions. I have decided to just get on with the situation at hand. Love the boys, the dogs and look forward to the future.
I have been thinking a lot about Australia. I don't like it here fully in Mallorca. I find it a very male-dominated society. It is not quite my cup of tea. I must admit I do enjoy my work at the restaurant and the boys bring me an immense amount of joy. I just never seem to get a moment.
I think it is high time for a break from the routine! I am not sure how long I'm even going to go for; however, what will be, will be.
Number three arrives in May and to be perfectly honest, I didn't get off to a great start. Everything felt a little bit for the show.
I guess I will get on with my life when the time is right. Just being pregnant, I have found, discovered, that it is a lot of demand on the body, and I've just got to know my limits.
I am glad that I am reading more now. I always seem to have my head in a book, which is great for my brain and eye function. I drew a couple of pencil pictures of the boys! Just to spend some time and sense if I could get back into some artistic flair! Oh, we will see!

27th January 2007

My tummy is ever-expanding, which is great and of course, I am happy and excited about the new sprog. So, all in all, a good positive start to 2007 now. It has only taken me a month to settle down and feel right.
Did some drawing yesterday.

Wednesday

I spent the last couple of days in the hospital, which was a total shocker! Rather an eye opener. I bled a lot and spent the days in hospital completely bedridden. Not at all what I am used to! Anyway, I've decided the sensible option is to return to the UK – the doctors have told me bed rest seriously. They gave me an injection today, which apparently will help develop the baby's lungs in case it arrives early, it would be a very premature baby – fingers crossed though it will all go well!

Returning to the UK on Friday and will sort out arrangements for the rest of the tribe!

3rd February 2007

Homeward bound which I am happy about, relieved really; although I miss my boys terribly. I just don't want to be letting anyone down least of all my parents whom I feel like I'm letting down all the time.

I also think he needs the space from me right now. Glad he is with the boys. Sorting out the rest of Mallorca, getting Ben dog a flight. All is well! No news is good news.

I do get a little paranoid sometimes, which I guess is natural. Although I get myself a little worked up. I think I need to trust more. Allow myself to relax and have faith. I am going to church tomorrow. Need to have a word with the pastor! Open myself to the arms of the Lord!

8th February 2007

It is my last day of freedom before the boys get back. I picked Ben dog up from Heathrow today. Indian head massage this morning.

I really have been getting some good sleep, relaxing which helps. Plus think and feel positive for the wee one inside.

Certainly, I am feeling different. Fresher and a little more directed.

Chapter 17

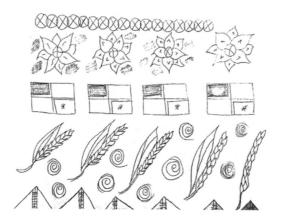

Green Pastures...

"If you look the right way, you can see the whole world is a garden." — Frances Hodgson Burnett

4ᵗʰ February 2007

It is the beginning of a new era! The kids are coming back to England. Ben dog arrived yesterday.
HE NEEDS TO WORK OUT WHAT HE WANTS TO DO – WITH ME AND HIMSELF.

11ᵗʰ February 2007

So, the boys are back. They are a lot of hard work and their needs are of great necessity right now!

14ᵗʰ February 2007

Off to the specialist hospital to get some clarification.

15ᵗʰ February 2007

I was a little emotional today. Went to the hospital to get reassured. Things are a little pear-shaped right now. Confused to a huge degree! Please Lord, aid me with decisions.

16ᵗʰ February 2007

Who knows what is going to happen, although I think it is time that a plan was put into action. I feel terrible that I am invading people's space. However I guess at the end of the day, all is trucking along.
I've told mum I am not keen on going back to Mallorca I have also broken the news to him. Although he is fine with that he also doesn't want anyone to know about it yet. We have options though; although I am pretty confined at present. Not much I can actually do.

22ⁿᵈ February 2007

Sometimes I really feel like giving up on it all. That can't happen though, I try so to make him happy and obviously what I do just isn't enough or isn't right.
I cannot give him his every wish! I don't want to even mention the 'I'm tired card'!
Anyway, today is an important day. Going off to discover what is up with the pregnancy. Work out the placenta issues, etc. then make the birthing plan as it

comes. Saw the midwife yesterday, which was great and she has given me some greater confidence! About time.

23rd February 2007

I was upset yesterday during the WSH visit. I couldn't stop weeping.
He was in London with his friends, drinking, and smoking.

2nd March 2007

30 weeks pregnant thereabouts.
He has returned from his episode in London.

3rd March 2007

Went off to Fun 2 Play with the kids today, which was great. My eldest angel is a little fragile after his operation yesterday. He is brave.
I am a little shattered, although I am good. Breathing and managing the best I can.
He is heading off next Friday for about six weeks; it will be strange without him. Focusing on what is happening right now. The kids, the pregnancy. Tick tock! All will be fine!

15th March 2007

It has been a week since him and JC left back to Mallorca and surprisingly I am feeling much calmer. The house is calmer, more steady and relaxed. Still of course I miss him, although I think it is important to have this separation time. The boys are happy. I am cruising along well in the pregnancy now and for the first time I feel very at peace with myself; relaxed and as if I can do my own projects for a wee while. Of course I share my ideas.
Had a look at a house although I don't think that is going to happen – sadly. I will, must, focus on my direction.
Planning this house move – again!

21st March 2007

Did a lot of paperwork this morning and the Alchemy want me to carry on working with orders, marketing, menu planning; which is excellent.

1ˢᵗ April 2007

I have just spent a lovely weekend in London. We had a lovely time. I drove up with the boys both very excited. 'London'. Saturday was crazy busy with shopping. Went to the Rower's sponsorship wrap party, which was excellent. A very good presentation was put on; I was particularly tired by 10-ish, so got some food and then headed back to Pooles Lane to relieve the babysitter. Sunday morning the boys were up with atom. Very adventurous! Another beautiful spring day. We have been lucky. Saw friends and went to the church service! Two donkeys even came. Palm Sunday!

Had lunch at the Chelsea Ram, followed by a great walk around Battersea Park. Everyone was out! It was a perfect, busy London Park afternoon.

6ᵗʰ April 2007

It is Good Friday nearly Easter time. How exciting the boys are both good and I am ready to face the holiday weekend with them. I do hope that the one inside just stays warm and cosy.

Calor gas man and builders at the new place we are moving into. However, the carpets all must be laid and troubles at Giles Lane with the woodworm and the removal company haven't got back to me yet, which is rather annoying.

Anyway I finally have my health back on track. The dogs and all animals as well; the boys are both energetic and we will do something fun with them today!

Hopefully I remain positive. I don't want to get disheartened by anything! Especially as I have come this far.

8ᵗʰ April 2007

It is Easter, family engagement and I am excited for them both. The ring is stunning. Blue sapphire. They are very lucky and beaming. So, through the Atlantic Row, Desert Marathons, 9/11 they are together and strong. I was honoured to be around. It was such a privilege and to be sharing a wee drop of delicious bubbly with them also. Just fab news. I want to tell everyone.

10ᵗʰ May 2007

Actual estimated due date today, my third beautiful boy arrived on 8ᵗʰ May 2007 at 8.43am weighing 9 ½ pounds; exciting natural delivery in the water pool at WSH. I am happy, and he is a delightful and verbal and greedy little thing.

Many happy days ahead of us, our little family; bringing me joy and hope. I am praying he lights my path! Our paths!

July 23^{rd,} 2007

I do get moody, angry, judgemental, and critical. I just would like situations to be calm and not part of my involvement a lot of the time!

We have probably had quite a rollercoaster ride, with a car situation; we have probably gone through at least three or four cars in the last month. It just hasn't been our lucky year on transport.

I am very much happy being at home though, and the boys and I manage to get out once or twice a day; even if it is just taking Ben dog for a walk or popping to the store! Even better catching up with the Tuesday Crew! Lots of parties for the kiddies over the summer!

Our eldest is such a vibrant little man, and his speech has come on amazingly well. We have varied conversations now and fortunately, he is managing to explain, describe and act on what his needs and wants are.

Our second son turned two yesterday. I think we had about 60 people (adults and kids included) come over. I was proud to be a mum and so pleased that he has made it to two! We had a lovely day within the midst of summer floods. So blessed here, although I feel rather guilty that we are witnessing these deluges and people have incredible droughts. 1/16 England is under water really and the worrying situation is that it doesn't look like it's going to stop! Drought, I mean there is an abundance of water; however it cannot be drunk as specialist water filtrations have been over worked and flooded themselves. It is a concerning situation!

He is a great little chap. We have some fairly fascinating moments. He talks, walks, eats, runs, plays, swims! He is an abundance of bubbling cuddles and fun! I am completely fascinated as to what kinds of people they are going to be. Charming, clever, happy, and healthy? We will see!

I am extremely happy to be back at Heath Barn though. It is a lovely dwelling and I enjoy the feeling of a touch of remoteness! It is great to see so much sky and not feel pressured.

It has been a while since I last wrote some thoughts on paper. Months have flown by since #3 arrived, well only a couple. He is now 10 weeks and I feel totally blessed to have him in my life. I love being a mum more than anything. He is growing and developing each day. Such a pure angel.

I reckon I have been being a little harsh on myself lately and taking negative situations a little too much to heart. Blaming myself for when things go pear shaped or when people are pissed off and angry! I feel very much grounded and the children are my priority!

We have settled into the cottage and the typical Virgo that I am sees me working hard each day to be a home maker and for everything to be comfortable and clean! From the moment I wake up each morning to the moment I go to bed, I am pretty much shattered!

As for him… well he drives me a little insane at the moment. I think it is because he needs reassurance for everything and anything. It's almost like he needs his hand held.

Maybe it is because I am focussed on our lads?

I just simply cannot be there for every occurrence and I must admit I do get frustrated at times. He does make me laugh and smile though and I do feel protected by him.

I just love the fact that family members are close! My family, siblings are more important to me than pretty much the air I breathe. They are an incredible emotional support and I truly am grateful for all the assistance with me! And the little lads!

It is also great to be here with some good wholesome friends! I am very blessed, God is certainly watching over me at the moment. I do hope that I succeed in being a good person, calm and collected. A good partner and a supportive and interactive mum to the adorable lads I have!

21st August 2007

We have just returned from a week away in our caravan. It was a lovely summer break. We drove up to Scotland to see friends. It was rather emotional. We took the boys fishing, where the Golden Eagles live. We saw them on a ridge, but they were far off. Went to Alton Towers, the boys loved it! Went to a Monkey Park and Bird breeding place. Excellent.

23rd August 2007

We spent all afternoon in the sunshine and garden, which was fab. I accidentally put the wire through the hedge cutter! Joys and short-circuited the caravan!

4th September 2007

We went to Wells for the weekend with the boys and the twins, which was fun in the caravan.

Wells, N-N was fun; I went to a friend's book signing of her wonderful travels in the TukTuk across Asia back to the UK. What an amazing mission and fantastic determination and the right inspiration.

So, I am spending my days now cleaning and looking after the kids. It is continuous, great fun, and good times. I must create a routine and schedule. Eldest starts pre-school tomorrow. Very exciting. It will be a refreshing change for him, new insight.

Oh, yes, I started netball last night. Excellent. I need to pick up fitness! But I am sure given a few more sessions, I will be back again. It was a good energy blower.

8th September 2007

Started the day getting the fence complete and secure, so the dogs cannot get out. They have already found the pig food and indulged as much as they can!

Eldest's first few days at school were a great success.

4th October 2007

In Mallorca, I flew over yesterday from the UK from rain to more rain.

5th October 07

Soller is beautiful. I do like that side of the island. It is peaceful... Stunning mountains, plus a different vibe. Even found my candle things to put in the air. House viewing. A townhouse and a beautiful end terrace mountain house. I liked the airy feel of it.

Had to stop at the hospital on the way back to sort out the mucus on youngest son's chest.

13th November 2007

A whole month has passed since I last wrote; I cannot believe where the time has gone. We have been busy been working, playing, socialising, meeting new friends, and getting in touch with old church visits. Working now, new colleagues and a lease of life, which is great. It is a lovely change of pace. I am glad to be away; I love the boys. But it makes me appreciate them more and working to provide.

All is well, loving netball, breastfeeding, dog walking, and swimming with the Tuesday Crew. The kids are all growing up fast and well. It is all good right now. I am in a peaceful place!

Goodness hadn't written since our trip to Mallorca.

20th November 2007

Poo, paint, puzzles, puke, and piles of clothes; once I get some time and motivation, I am going to write a comic story about the five Ps and the importance of having a sense of humour!

All well, spent the weekend in London socialising and moving the boys in the direction of the Natural World at The Natural History Museum and The Science Museum. Good times had by all. Took the boys out. He and I had a lovely time together out on the razzle-dazzle. We went out to the Mandarin Oriental, The Berkeley, followed by singing at the Lanesborough.

November 2007

We have secured the rental of a B&B property in Suffolk. Hopefully we can make it happen. With all new adventures, there is an element of risk, fingers crossed we manage it correctly.

Anyway, life ticks on. The boys are healthy; we are healthy and happy.

I have got my menstruation back after giving birth 6 ½ months ago. It is strange because there is a full moon. Very exciting and spiritual. Guess tomorrow the guys will come and pack it all up. Then we will be in the B&B. Pray for belief!

14th December 2007

Just as I thought we were moving forward…

I am being constantly pounded down by someone.

Trying to make everyone happy, I am making no one.

Shattered.

I am completely heartbroken now.

Why can't we be left to just get on with living instead of being judged/analysed! My goodness, it is endless!

Anyway, the boys are bringing me much joy and I am blessed to have them in my life. Just to stir things out. Talk about pushing the boundaries! I am destroyed now. Why live in such a beautiful place and be crushed by many judgemental and negative words? Soapbox. Anyway, I am moving on. We have plenty to be just getting on with. Work, business, the houses!

The list is endless!

15ᵗʰ December 2007

Saturday – day out at Center Parcs with the Tuesday Crew. It was a lot of fun – the kids enjoyed themselves and it was a good change of pace and a good weekend break.

9ᵗʰ January 2008

Happy New Year! We have had a very busy Christmas and NY plenty of fun! A lot of stimulation. The boys all had a great time. I was motherly, busy, and very busy with my boys!

2008 – An awesome year ahead, I know it!

10ᵗʰ February 2008

We spent a night in London, our first 24 hours together away from all the boys since our youngest arrived. It was a pleasantly perfect time. The sun shone for us amazingly; we set off to Greenwich and stood on the meridian line and saw the most amazing view of London. We ate a delicious lunch in the Trafalgar Tavern and caught up with friends who are heading off to India for six months. Staggering. We went shopping, to movies and dinner.

We are going to spend the next 40 days, working through The Purpose Driven Life – what on earth am I here for!

In 40 days, we will see if the purpose changes.

21ˢᵗ February 2008

It is only a few days to go – heading to Hawaii. I am very excited if a little apprehensive. All is going well though. We are busy setting up the business and getting known. It will be a big promotion focus when we return!

28th February 2008

Back in Hawaii: unbelievable, special and wonderful. Jetlagged. Perfect to be sharing Hawaiian times.

Caught up with some of the guys at the airport, a great Aloha welcome.

The Dukes in town, a night in Honolulu, followed by an early morning Denny's as they had to leave to fly back to Switzerland. Returned rental car followed by another rental car, trip to Kmart cheap goods, and flip flops and up to the North Shore, Haleiwa, and then Sunset House, Hawaii Joes, Haleiwa for a Hawaiian lunch, and of course, trips to the surf beaches and dips in the ocean and photos and relaxation. Pure quality! Very different and perfectly special.

Next day early wake up as we are severely jetlagged. Time for breakfast at Rake's canteen followed by a Waimea shore Break, Waimea Falls, OH, and then wedding welcome party on the beach followed by Big Sleep. Today – Kaena Point and lots of Albatross. Shopping, lunch, Poly Centra, artwork. I am tired and very much must sleep! God bless and greetings. Rick Warren's book is very insightful, and I am very much enjoying it!

2nd March 2008

Mothering Sunday, now back in the UK.

All is going well, and we are having a special time. The wedding was simply beautiful and organised, 100 weddings in one, magical and totally unreal to be able to come! And share! Ticking along and relishing each moment. Capturing the sunshine and the gleaming ocean and the steady flow of the waves. Could not be more appreciative now.

28th March 2008

Aloha Friday again. It seems like our holiday in Hawaii and lent was far away. Totally I feel like I've been back here for ages, never a dull moment.

Focussed and appreciative in writing words again. Sometimes I feel it is a form of relief and positive enlightenment for channelling correct patterns.

God has certainly put me in place right now, I feel lucky, lucky to be living here. It is such a unique slice of absolute heaven, which leads me into the creation. He has been opening me recently to the birds, creatures, plants, seeding. Amazing creations. I am loving viewing the scenery. The sky, the changing weather! It is snowing, raining, sunny. Everything is keeping me very much alive!

We had a staggeringly amazing time in Hawaii; it was a dream come true-although it just went jolly quickly!

We were totally tired with the jetlag. However, we made the most of each day and did as much as we possibly could. We had about three or four missions every day: visiting friends, the ocean, seeing nature, wildlife, flora, fauna and the sunsets – stunning endings and appreciations to each special and miraculous day. It was great to appreciate it all without the kids; they just would not appreciate it all at their ages. It would have been amazing to share it with them though. We went to the movies together, walks together, ate patiently, and went swimming, surfing. All amazing, special, and memorable moments.

The wedding was staggering, very organised. It all seemed very much in control, unique and ticking along with their lives together, excellent – fantastic, honourable to be sharing the beginning of their unique journey! The greatest excuse to get our acts together to enchant such a slice of life.

HE RAN OVER TOBY DOG! Truly devastating moment, we had to make the terrible decision… we had to put Toby down. Simply heartbroken.

He opened me up to a new meaning on dog patience.

Ben dog is still very much within our family body!

Lent

The Divine Purpose. It was a very interesting and enlightening book. It very much brought the Bible and beginnings of understanding God's mission and purpose in my life!

I am honoured he decided to open some special biblical captions, stories, and instructions. I am open to more understanding of the Christian faith. So, for 40 days, each day, we read the Purpose, the map! And points to ponder, verses to remember, questions to consider.

I am tired now. But honestly, I do hope that I write properly on these pages. Include the angels in my next chapters. They will help and guide.

29th March 2008

The sun has got his hat on this morning; it looks glorious outside. Let's hope this weekend is a bright and sparkly one!

I know that I am an extremely blessed and privileged individual and I do hope that I will continue to nurture my boys and grow them into strong, independent, and reliable, focussed, and dedicated characters. I pray for their understanding and sensitivity to the world.

3rd April 2008

So, I woke up and got on with being a mum to my lovely lads. God's creatures that require stimulation and life! Never a moment goes by without energy, questions, and understanding. We went to the Farm Park and saw lots of lovely animals and a farmyard structure. Tractor rides, picnics, chicks, rabbits, horses. He has not turned up and I am going to work tomorrow. I have a feeling he has done this on purpose! To see how I will cope! NOT WELL!

5th April 2008

Took the boys to the Farm, and we got six hen birds. Some good layers! So, we will be inundated with eggs.
Anyway, I think I am going to do some cooking, get some brownies, cakes and cookies on the go! Sweet tooth for the church congregation!

April 21st 2008

I must snap out of my mood, it is unhealthy. I am a little upset, not crying or anything, I'm not sure if he is happy at all.
I wrote him a letter and he hasn't read it yet.
Anyway, I have thought about being a single mum, but it really would be twice as difficult.
My life other than that is going well, apart from the car failing its MOT, and then getting around to sorting that out! We have customers in the B&B, which is just excellent, just need to make sure they pay us lots of money.
Monday morning off to work today, Wednesday and Friday. It will be a great week.

27th April 2008

The business is making money, which is great. We just need to make that double over the weekend and then over a four-week period. Anyway, better than nothing!
Happy with all the animals, they make me feel very peaceful. The boys are all well too, vibrant, and alive.

3rd May 2008

So, I have just spent a very special few days back in San Francisco; it has been awesome. I arrived on Tuesday – flew in from LHR on a very comfortable British Airways flight. Rented a car and then found their great home in Mill Valley. Have been surfing and skateboarding, eating, and drinking, helping and then being very lazy.

The wedding happened yesterday and went for pre-wedding morning surf; it has been totally special and honouring to be part of their network. Really loved being here. I even got mentioned at the speeches! Honoured. Truly!

It has been wonderful to have some me time again and notice how I manage situations, get on with life and be happy. It is just awesome to be surfing (in the cold). Just great and I love the fact that I was able to do it! Skate, surf!

I am very much looking forward to being back with my family!

13th May 2008

This time four years ago, I pretty much was a single white female. Now I am a mum to four great kids – well, one dog, and three kids.

My eldest turns four tomorrow and I am totally happy and excited with him.

20th May 2008

Was busy this morning getting paperwork, bills, etc. organised, to be honest, I am a little stressed with one thing and another, then again, I am sure it will all be all right and I am hoping tomorrow we will focus our strengths and direction and allow Father P to bless our new venture.

Went to Fun2Play, which was great with kids, and they all had a fab time; running around, burning energy and playing with their friends!

31st May 2008

Well, plenty has happened since the last time I wrote, I have had a miscarriage – although just how I know my body – I have not felt right and it has been a shame – as of today, I am not pregnant – hormones do have a funny way of playing havoc with the body. Deep sadness.

It was great to have Father P come around for an afternoon of tea and cookies and blessing the home, which was great, and the kids really enjoyed him and his kind and guiding wise words.

Today was an interesting day. The business is picking up.

God certainly has a path, direction for us all – we are just cruising along with it all.

I am happy, unusually frustrated sometimes. Placid and happy with: plants animals, friends, the business, properties, and work at Center Parcs.

Please continue to guide.

1ˢᵗ June 2008

Again, I stupidly lost my temper. I must go and see a doctor to control my hormones. He is off partying and having fun – not off working and providing.

10ᵗʰ / 11ᵗʰ June

The B&B is beginning to take off, which is excellent news! I am a little nervous and apprehensive; however, I am sure that is just normal natural.

We had a lovely special weekend last weekend flying to Florence for a friend's wedding– followed by a family wedding in Devon – magical really and full of emotions.

We managed to catch up with a few familiar faces. The Canada lot and family and friends; fun times.

Back to business now though, back at work, which seems all right; managed to achieve everything, followed by umpiring netball exam.

Animals and plants all doing well!

Kids are grand!

Chapter 18

Fields of Gold...

"I never made promises lightly and there have been some that I have broken, but I swear in the days still left we will walk in fields of gold." – Sting

22nd July 2008

Second son's birthday – he is turning three. He is a delight.
A lot has been happening: working, B&B, plenty going on, boys growing.
He proposed to me in the fields of gold. God does move in mysterious ways.
We are blessed – very blessed.

2nd August 2008

Already eight months have flown by and the boys are changing and adapting
each day. We are sharing a great life together and I hope and pray that we will
continue to strive and support.

18th August 2008

Trip to Disney and work then weekend, Olympics are on.

9th September 2008

It has again been a busy few weeks with plenty going on: parties, work, kids,
celebrated a wonderful 30th birthday party together.

9/11

Tragically, this time seven years ago, lots of lives were lost in NY; I flew over
there – it added a new dimension to my life. Incredible, such a completely
different and uniquely captured adaption in my life!
Our lovely boys bring incredible warmth, love, and happiness in my heart! I love
and appreciate them more than anything in my life.
Lord – guide me over the next few days – turning 30 and the new direction and
paths.
Dedication
Spiritual
Heart
Direction
Success
Drive
Compassion
Devotion

Dedication

That is what it is? Life is too short – look what happens sometimes?

15th September 2008

I feel a little hung over or pregnant, cannot be though! Ticking along and breathing in the day!

28th October 2008

This year has been a rollercoaster ride. We married on 15th October romantically up in Scotland – very special and perfect that family came and shared our venturing time.

Father P married us in Eilean Donan Castle. Special and very momentous! I feel a little overwhelmed with it all – however – now back to the ever-going domestic life.

I am pregnant with number four! I cannot believe – blessed. God must be shining a unique ray on us now.

We pray that we have a good and smooth sailing pregnancy, and the boys grow and adapt to the new additions.

30th October 2008

Back to the grindstone. Photos from the wedding have arrived.

Terrible cluster flies in the house.

Guests in. I know they are unhappy – cold! Well – extra jumpers are needed. Always something – such is life.

A new puppy called Honey! A Golden Retriever to add to the family mix.

Happy days – remain focussed, positive, and blessed. God is certainly watching over us! Let's hope it continues

3rd November 2008

It was the eldest's first introductory session at school today. Such a milestone. I do feel a little pressured by that and the remarkable success that he wanted too…
He was excited. It was time for dinosaurs and all. Friends. New water bottle.

4th November 2008

I try very hard to be a good woman and mother and yet he continues to belittle me all the time!
I work hard in work, with the business and with the family.

5th November 2008

Obama in the White House
New times
Change
Beginning
Improvements
Let's hope that the world economy has taken shape.

8th November 2008

Today is the first day of true morning sickness in this pregnancy and I was rather poorly! I felt and still feel a little dodgy. The first time I am going to decline a party invitation. I was meant to be going off to the Hunt Ball. But I do not feel at all well. I need to curl in a ball and totally snap into another world.
Sometimes I wish I could delve deep into my imagination and write from the heart. You know, like people would be interested if I would be interested. I seem to feel and write insular now. In fact, it is what is going on in my head and usually has to do with himself upsetting me or making me angry.
I need a switch-off button sometimes. Just so I can just live, my way.

9th November 2008

Autumn is such a glorious time of year. Garden, amber, red, orange, burnt umber!
Animals' calling their last calls before winter descends.
The wind blows straight through the skeletons – leaving leaves dancing freely.
Fertile the soil for next year's growth.
The new beginning.
It is time to cuddle up, close the hatches, and enjoy the breeze. Moving us on…
Blowing in on the next season!
Birds gliding
Trees blowing
Leaves dancing

I'm hibernating, with child and of course, happy. I have absolute terrible morning sickness. Yesterday, I was unwell. Sick and had the most terrible headache.

I wish I could just share some of this carnage.

13ᵗʰ November 2008

Feeling terrible morning sickness! Ginger tea and a couple of biscuits.

I have a 'show day' in finance today. Will be interesting to have a change of perspective, even if only for a couple of hours as I would like to do another job selection proves to see what job would suit me best.

The boys are my angels, and I must make sure that my parental duties allow them to become individual, hard-working, helpful, and supportive people. Of course, I would like them to be happy and healthy. I need to work out a way to generate more money, especially so we can relax and not stress too much.

November

My head feels like twigs! All caught up and mangled, confused and not directed. It has never been this tricky before.

I guess I must listen to what my husband wants and needs, and I have got into marriage for better or worse, richer, or poorer, sickness and health, honest and obey and cherish – honour till death do us part!

Anticipation, excitement, confusion and no direction. Who knows…? I know and trust in the Lord, that he will look after us! And take care!

Tuesday

Another new day and waking up with complete morning sickness, which is a good sign, I guess I'm making the placenta!

Number one with the changes financially and physically.

New beginnings, new understandings, new directions, new investments, new fluidness, new support, new family members, new routines, new openings, new focus.

The year 2008 had been amazing.

20ᵗʰ November 2008

It has been an emotional few days.

Delusion and confusion

Today I did my bloods, which felt better moving on.

Went out for lunch and a walk around the Abbey Gardens; loved the ducks, the swings, and running freely, dancing with the leaves.

30th November 2008

I had a break in London last weekend, which was simply perfect and just what I needed; I did take my youngest with me – wonderful bonding time with him!

Advent service at St Andrews Church the boys were very well behaved.

Lots of customers in the B&B, very positive.

14th January 2009

Process of a real love story: blessed with three glorious boys, a business, a job, animals, and a busy, loving and judgemental family. I must remain focussed on the priorities in my situation. Pregnant for 16+ weeks now. Growing a new being, feeling much better now.

I love the sky, the freedom, the changing seasons, the air, the garden. The pure blessing being here – we just need to focus on the business and make sure we get more customers in and paying to help with the rent, the relaxed life. So, we can work hard and step back – focus on my family. My boys, my man, my animals. Work. I am a touch unsure what to do about my job now? Work through all the politics and woman emotions. Battle the broken. I guess it is just the nature of the job, keep a low profile, focus on work, holidays, and the mat leave, develop a shield, and be resilient.

Friday, 6th February 2009

Second scan and the baby is healthy, active, and another boy. True mother of sons! Pleased and relieved he is healthy. I feel a little abandoned by my girlfriends, probably a touch-sensitive. The doctor had to come out and annoyingly I had to miss work due to illness! I think I really must decide what the right direction is for me with work and business, and take an amount of time for some reflection. Maybe I have a little too much to deal with now and am ultra-sensitive right now.

Promoting the business

Exciting times with the discovery of a new life, new names, discoveries!

26th February 2009

Every pen won't transmit thoughts.

2nd March 2009

March already! This year is racing past. Have had a peaceful weekend with my three little lads. It is Lent. I said that I would be more helpful and giving and that I shall!

The business has been a little up and down, which is highly frustrating – with bills coming and going. It is tricky to keep on top.

7th March 2009

The business, which I am trying to be positive about, is making me low and a little hard work.

We have had three cancellations in the last few weeks, which I am confused about. What am I doing? I know pregnancy makes things a little personal. I need to feel better, more positive – more spiritual! More focussed. I thought we were doing well. I guess 8/10 and 7/10 are all right. I just take negative comments to heart and I must just improve!

Carpet in front room

Curtains in Rose bathroom

Labels for the guest doors

10th March 2009

Watercolour room names and sitting room. Maybe I do this on Saturday?

Individual bathrooms with deodorant, cotton buds, homemade goodies

Breakfast menu

Bird book

So, I went to the doctor with my youngest this morning and he knew that I wasn't convinced. I will see him again in two weeks. Maybe it was me and my attitude he wasn't convinced with then?

Let's remain strong, with faith and gathering quality thoughts and interpretation for the coming months.

Relax, work hard, focus.

3rd May 2009

Switzerland – stunning I am a godmother. We drove down yesterday and arrived safely with the boys. Arrival in Switzerland, lovely old-fashioned chalet, cosy and warm and enough space for us all. Hot water and TV, lucky. The church service was in German and was enlightening, special, and unique. And stunning, a boat ride, a funicular, a castle in the sky. A walk, sunshine. All a pleasure. I am tired, the boys are happy, and I am blessed, truly blessed.

Hope that we can provide a smooth and happy well-run business over the summer period. Rock on #4

10th May 2009

We have quite a lot of bookings, which is brilliant. The pregnancy is finally running well, and the baby is moving.

It is good to breathe and our break in Switzerland was lovely. Christening was glorious. The sun is shining, the birds are chirping, we have customers in and doing the right thing. Confidence, subtle.

12th May 2009

Had a terrifying couple of days with our youngest in A&E. Then the Rainbow Ward, blue lights, resuscitation…Simply terrible

Another day and another collection of dramas. It is non-stop now. It just seems to be a non-stop moments of gathering crazy and annoying events that seem to stress me out.

He is the next episode, police interception, and possible charges; what an absolute crazy nightmare! All beyond my control though. Probably a good thing – justice will prevail.

11th June 2009

Run down until the baby is born.

Nervous a little... about the labour, Ahhh! However, it will be worth it. Look forward to meeting the new addition!

All going well, am on my last holiday days this week, then maternity leave starting next week. Oh, the great joys. I am keeping myself calm though. I really must, I can feel when I get stressed, my baby reacts, and my body turns! So, I should stay relaxed and make sure I have no other intervention!

Starting our youngest on a new diet. Gluten, wheat, and dairy-free – let's see how we go feeding a 1-year-old that… Hum.

15th June 2009

Had a great day yesterday on the Lady Florence River cruise boat around Orford and Aldeburgh. I am on maternity leave now; had the ladies around from work. Now getting ready for the baby – the nursery is sorted and I am generally spending time at home and with the business. Kids are still at school. The eldest has recovered from his tonsil op; our second son is a communicative gem, although a little trying sometimes, and thankfully our youngest has much improved since the change of diet and detox.

16th June 2009

There were huge thunderstorms last night, very exciting lots of flashes, pours, and rain. I am very pregnant now and feel very ready to have the baby. I am hoping it comes next Wednesday 24/06/09. We will see though. They come on their agenda. I do hope it is not this weekend though, as we have guests in.

19th June 2009

Another wonderful day – beautiful outside.
I am feeling a little morning sickness, this is the hormones starting. We have a full house of guests this weekend. I am hoping that the baby holds on until Wednesday. That would be perfect…

26th June 2009

It is the due date today – for the arrival of the new wee one. I certainly have been having movement/contractions; however, it is playing the waiting game now. Never dull, as you can imagine. Still, he will come when he is ready. Just wish it was already. Just relax and let the vibes do their calling. No judgements or anything. Pray, pray, pray.
I have had a great few days with my youngest, whose skin has massively improved with the new diet and some Chinese herbs.
The contractions will build when ready – spoke to the midwife yesterday, who told me what I already knew. Shame, I don't think the little one is going to show his face today. Well, maybe today. Just not this morning…

27th June 2009

Saturday 1.21am

He has arrived at home

Natural water birth

Two midwives!

Excellent. I am shattered and very happy!

He is a day old now. What a special babe.

Murray won tennis yesterday.

Michael Jackson has died! Terrible news.

Glastonbury is on! Just been in touch.

1st July 2009

Feel very blessed with my boys now. What absolute delights – not sure whether it is the Nurofen I have taken! Anyway, the sun is shining, guests in the B&B. Sun is beautiful

21st July 2009

Three weeks since last I wrote. It has been non-stop since our new arrival and we now have another new addition, Jack, or Mr. Tan, the puppy dog who arrived on 10th July, never a dull moment in this household!

Summer holidays, which is a relief not to do the school run; however, it is non-stop entertaining the children. We are getting on and we have plenty of fun times to be had! Just organised chaos! Streams of weddings, gatherings, etc.! Joys, serious joys.

Stream of motherhood. The eldest is five and second turning four tomorrow! Ahhhh – that hits the spot with adorable, turning four! And don't we know it? Complete excellence!

Spaceship – 40 years ago the lunar landing happened!

Went to Pleasurewood Hills yesterday. Had the kids' party at the Lodge.

The B&B is steady.

30th/29th July 2009

Had a glorious massage today – perfect. We spent the morning around Bury. Got me, well the family, a new iPhone. This will hopefully revolutionise my life. Spoke to work

Have got guests in the B&B
Need to get some help
Did lots of filing yesterday

    Proper phone
    Proper business
    Proper job
    Proper pets
    Proper children
    Proper husband
    Proper home
    Proper future

I am blessed. I must remain focussed and willing to help and serve, remain strong and supportive towards friends and family.

4th August 2009

Already – tick-tock, tick-tock.
The boys are bundles of pure energy, pure light, laughter, and loud moments.
Plumbing nightmare – Damp spots! Just waiting for the lights and the signs!
Need signs up and more customers in!

13th August 2009

Motherhood – oh the pleasantries...
It has been a wonderful few weeks with the growth of our precious little one, puppies, and floating happy hormones...
Now back to reality... demanding sex – morning, noon and night.
Ahhh, get off now! Let me breathe, rest, understand.

7th October 2009

Summer holidays over back to school runs, which strangely enough I don't mind now, a little relentless. However, I seem to be managing.
I managed to get a massage in today. Total bliss. Truly what my mind/body required. I just need to relax and let free! Of course, remain on top of controlling the boys, dogs, etc.! Plenty has happened though after the month of writing absence! Our youngest is growing, smiling, gurgling and being a general delight in my life.

21ˢᵗ November 2009

Last week was a complete disaster, firstly, the Halloween party, which was a great success and was completely spoilt by the fact he didn't get out of bed for days.

Now Chairperson for the school PTA, which is great, although another responsibility. It is fine for me.

I am exhausted, remaining strong for us all. I seem to be the only one taking it seriously.

<u>He must gain a focus – a direction, a purpose.</u>

Second son managed to end up in hospital with pneumonia. I think he is very much on the mend now though poor chap; had to cancel New York trip.

13ᵗʰ November 2009

I feel like my heart is in a tennis ball match now. I feel in limbo-land – maybe broken to a degree?

I don't know where to find my strength from. I am trying to be strong. Trying to be involved, trying to get on with courage.

What exactly are we meant to do at the moment? I am angered, saddened, and alone by his actions. I don't really know who to turn to – where to turn to. It is such a strange feeling.

19ᵗʰ November 2009

We are overrun with builders at present, along with the boys and non-stop enlightenment.

24ᵗʰ November 2009

Had a couple's counselling session – much improved he is certainly helping more.

15ᵗʰ August 2010

I haven't written in a long, long while – a lot has happened over the last few months. Going from strength with one thing and another. Barely get a breathing moment. Full into an unreliable English summer – an abundance of rain. It's fine though. The sun peeps through occasionally.

I am pregnant with #5. Exciting times. Just gone on maternity leave, which is a weight off my mind as now I can focus on the jobs at hand here at the business.

The boys

The business B&B

The Gallery

Never dull – always, plenty a moment to relish, enjoy, indulge.

He is now for getting into action each day – with breakfasts to cook and a happy face for customers. We are caught in the real swing of the summer months, holidays, joys, travel plans. Non-stop and an excellent non-stop.

This pregnancy is ticking along – my leg (the right one) is not in a good way and will need some attention. The baby, fingers crossed, is fine and I am coping the best I can. Driven, if not a little demented! Generally, the boys fighting and squabbling before 6 am!

Love is almost a form of confusion – peace, tranquillity, and progression are what we would like to achieve.

Had the boys, playing football

Fun birthday parties

Animals

Sheets drying

Cleaning

Gallery progression

Exciting times

20th August 2010

Summer holidays, planning, cleaning, organising, baths, kiddies, customers, and gallery – all seem to have taken its toll. I am quite pooped.

However, looking after me and the growing baby – I do like being pregnant.

Priorities, homeward bound. Simple, calm, relaxed, at peace. Routine, simple, kids in structure however boundaries and fun times.

Summer holidays. Growing spiritually, mentally – enhancing life, power, understanding, enhance, master, creation. The family has their summer holidays.

13th September 2010

I am a little frustrated with some aspects now. Mainly to do with "Oh…are you sure you're, okay?" Admittedly, I am shattered and he has been a bit of a plonker since returning from holiday. What do you do? I am just trying to get on with things and yes, I am short fused! My temper is not good! Anyhow – such is life, and we are carrying on! It's my birthday week. So, I must snap into a better mood! A little like a dark cloud!

#2 – recognised for his sleeping at school, apparently thyroid.

#1 –ear infections

#3 –allergies

#4 – teething

Me, pregnant!

Husband has slept today... Well, lucky him!

Me: sheets, rooms, washing, paperwork, school runs, car service, phone calls…endless…business must pick up though.

Chapter 19

It's A Girl!

"A baby girl is a blessing. A gift from heaven above. A precious little angel to cherish and love." — Anon

14th October 2010

Baby

Miss

6lbs 12oz

Arrived safely between the school runs – a little early and jaundice, she is actually she?? Must double check?

1st November 2010

She has been here for 2 ½ weeks already! She has brought us amazing joy and relief and what an amazing blessing. Pure joy! Thank you, Lord.

June 2011

A new start again. Fresh air. Sometimes we are a busy family, a lot of great times fun and God's blessings.

He is being full-on business creator and father.

We are in a good place, and I thank God that we are working and praying.

Summer half term.

Have had a busy gallery exhibition

B&B

Dog walks

Running the B&B customers

Taking the boys to school, parties, nursery, football, kids play

Ben dog and Honey Pot, being committed dog owners.

I have great help right now. She comes on Wednesday.

I barely get much time for thinking, reflection; however, what I do know is how lucky I am to have such a committed, dedicated, and loving family.

Customers coming and going in the B&B – I pray we are doing a satisfactory/good/excellent job – to meet people's expectations.

We are continuing to strive towards perfection – however, someone's perfection is not always the same as another one's! So, we are doing what we can to the best of what we can.

The Gallery is going from strength to strength, we must continue to develop, expand, push, enlighten, and work hard. Employed staff, this has created some good contacts and ideas.

I know this is a self-centred reason and I am totally happy and blessed, however, I seem to be constantly striving for more.

By God's grace, I am sure I will be fine.

Back to employed work for KIT days tomorrow. I probably am slightly nervous and must get the boys already for school as well, after half term – ekkk.

13th June 2011

I went to work – it was fine, plugging away; it is good for me to step out of the home zone for a few hours, breathing really.

14th June 2011

A weekend to relax, dreams, sleep, the kids are calm right now, the garden is tweeting, it is also clear.

I am researching chickens and rabbits and maybe guinea pigs today!

17th August 2011

In the Maldives – we were meant to be going together however 'sod's' law has shown his face and it has been decided by him that I go with Number one and Number five.

HE IS STAYING AT HOME…

19th August 2011

It is beautiful, seas, skies, palm trees. That saying, 'Wish you were here' really rings true.

We are filling the days with swimming, feeding, walking, swimming, and more swimming.

My darling son growing, capturing, involving, engrossing, sharing in the new surroundings. My little miss is a little young – however, her blue eyes sparkle.

Sunday Night

Boat to Male today – which is the capital of the Maldives. It was fascinating, interesting, not too deep into powers; however, it was satisfactory, and we managed to find a pair of flip flops that he desired.

A trip to the hospital yesterday – because he 'gashed' his knee. He had six stitches – bless his soul. I think all best that I don't tell 'papa' – do you reckon he might kill me! Hope not!

Meeting new people

Breathing new smells

Dreaming big dreams

Watching new scenery

Absorbing new air

Thinking new thoughts

Have not touched a computer or made a telephone call since departure and this is what the holiday was about. Spending time! Time! Time! Away from the mania, telephone calls, direction, shouting.

Of course, both the children are demanding – such is life!

Island hopping, therapeutic bouncing on the ocean surface, walking around other islands and seeing their island life, boatbuilding, and cinema, school and shopping markets. We went to a five-star hotel, which was no different from here – followed by a BBQ and relaxing time on the beach. A doddle of a day. It was quite choppy on the way back and we raced a storm home. Two days now of relaxing indulgence, massage, eating, watching the children absorb the Indian Ocean and Maldivian atmosphere.

Tuesday

I have just finished reading the novel The Red Tent by Anita Diamant. I read it 13 odd years ago now and it has filled me with inspiration. Midwives do achieve remarkable encounters – true blessings of the underworld, the new creations of our beings – first life! Reassurance to the mother.

I must write this passage, learn it, and pass it on to my merry friends and family encountering new journeys.

Fear not, the time is coming

Fear not, your bones are strong

Fear not, help is nearby

Fear not, Gula is near

Fear not, the baby is at the door

Fear not, (he/she) will live to bring you honour

Fear not, the hands of the midwife are clever

Fear not, the earth is beneath you

Fear not, we have water and salt
Fear not, little mother
Fear not, mother of us all

Achieved dear friend achieved –

The lord has my path unravelled – and in turn,

My dear children. Babes, growth within my own womb.

Tomorrow is our last day on the island of the Maldives. It has been a change of scene and a change of pace – delighting in the passage, the view, the ocean, the movement, palm trees, sand, water, health. I am feeling different, relaxed a little.

16th September 2011

Within the last three weeks, returned to the UK – Manchester airport middle of the night, then travelling to meet my new nephew. Relishing and blooming into motherhood, hard work, feeding, feeding, changing, relentless!

Family wedding– he as a very proud brother – walked his sister up the aisle. Such a proud moment. I even managed to deliver a reading – I was honoured although rather apprehensive! The wedding party was a huge success and such fun – everyone had a magical and special time.

Boys have returned to school – Year 3, Year 2 – starting reception – amazing, the years are flowing fast, which leads me to my birthday – I turned 33 yesterday, unbelievable. I had better get on with being 33.

"I am sorry for not appreciating more, maybe I expect too much."

Chapter 20

Fight and Flight...

"F.E.A.R has two meanings – Forget Everything and Run OR Face Everything and Rise." – Zig Ziglar

21st February 2012

It is a great life, and I am hugely lucky to have my five beautiful children, healthy and happy; a husband who I believe has faith that loves me, a business that I continue to strive and work hard at, and lovely friendly dogs that I walk, feed and stroke. And a loving extended family.

I am a blessed person and I thank God each day for my wonderful and special blessings.

We had a great family holiday in Kenya: relished, enjoyed, and took such pleasure in this family time.

What is important? Family time, generating income.

The Purpose Driven Life – Relent!

I know that God uniquely created me. What areas of my personality, background, and physical appearance am I struggling to accept?

Since I was made to last forever, what is the one thing I should stop doing and the one thing I should start doing today?

1) Stop worrying, especially about what people think of me
2) Stop worrying that I'm not making a success
3) Stop worrying when I'm not being a good mum/wife/friend, etc.

Start

Embracing it all with joy, hope, trust, faith, love… Get on with it all, least said soon mended.

START…loving ME. Researching the promised and potential for the future.

What has happened to me recently that I now realised was a test from God, what are the greatest matters God has trusted to me.

"So, we fix our eyes not on what is seen, but what is unseen. For what is seen is temporary, but what is unseen is eternal."
2 Corinthians 4:18

"Life is a temporary assignment.
For everything comes from God alone.
Everything lives by his power,
And everything is for his glory."
Romans 11:36

Where in my daily routine can I become more aware of God's glory?

First thing in the morning, I am usually woken by the children early, loudly and I could embrace it more. This is what God intended.

Walking the dogs, enjoying the peace and tranquillity of the new day, refreshing and alive.

Breakfast – we thank God each day for the food we eat, we pray, take time, and think of the peoples less fortunate.

Driving, working, walking, cleaning, gardening, singing, talking, cooking, watching TV, emailing.

God's grace is with me everywhere and always. If it is what he intended, then I will let him guide me through the necessary and unnecessary.

"The Lord takes pleasure in his people." Psalm 149:44

3rd February 2012

"Friendship with God is reserved for those who reverence him." Psalm 24:14a

What can I do to remind myself to think about God and talk to him more often throughout the day?

Through all the tasks that I do – talk to him – think of him – guidance.

"Draw close to God and God will draw close to you" – JC 4:8a

What practical choices will I make today to grow closer to God?

Practical

Where should I live?

Is it time to switch careers?

What is the best course of action for me?

Decisions shape experiences

Making smart practical choices, God decided it?

I am as close to God as I choose to be...

I REQUIRE GUIDANCE RIGHT NOW.

The Friend

Let us be grateful and worship God in a way that pleases him

Truth – worship in truth reveal

Authentic – genuine

Honest real love

The biggest distraction in worship is you. Your interests and your worries about what others think about you...

Ascetics – solitude and simplicity

Actives – confronting evil, battling injustices, making the world a better place.

Caregivers – loving others – meeting their needs

Enthusiasts – celebration – Adoration/studying.

Naturalists – great outdoors

Senses – appreciate the beautiful. Sight/taste/smell/touch

Traditionalists – rituals, liturgies, symbols

"Love God with all your mind."

Which is more pleasing to God right now – my public worship or my private worship? What will I do about this?

"For God has said, 'I will never leave you: I will never abandon you.'" Hebrews 13:5

How can I stay focussed on God's presence, especially when he feels distant?

I will continue to trust in the lord – especially when he feels distant – because now I must have faith, that this is the reason it must be.

Something is not going to plan...

Food, friends, family, health, and happy situations – there are circumstances not pleasant

Separation/silence

Love, trust, obey, worship. I have been really worried over the last few days regarding: finances, directions, achievements, and what is expected from me.

WHAT IS EXPECTED FROM ME?

What I should be doing, achieving, etc.? I have moved the office under the coach house and really, I believe it will happen.

The lord will bring success or not – however, I hope – I will have trust and faith in him that all will be fine. Deliver, regulate, be reliable. I cannot stomach big change or uncertainty!

Letting it happen – with God's focus pinnacle.

The kids have been unwell, the financial year April. April is changing, the money pot is depleting. He is being himself...

KEEP ME STRONG, PLEASE!

Good and loving

All-powerful

Details of life

In control

Plan for my life

Save me

The entire law is summed up in a single command – love your neighbour as yourself.

Honestly, are relationships my priority? How can I ensure that they are?

- I aim to have positive relationships with everyone.
- I find it difficult sometimes to make people happy. Pray!

A place to belong
HOME

10th March 2012

"Share each other's troubles and problems and in this way obey the law of Christ." (Galatians 6:2) NLT

What one step can I take today to connect with another believer at a more genuine heart-to-heart level?

Invite for coffee

Speak the truth

Be frank, open, and positive

Be honest

Thank the lord – ask questions.

"Obey the commandments."

That's why God calls peacemakers his children.

Relationships are always worth restoring.

"Do everything possible on your part to live in peace with everybody." Romans 12:18

Who do I need to restore a broken relationship with today?

Lent is over

Easter has happened

Spring has sprung

Birds are singing

Blue skies

Buds emerging

Boys playing

My little miss is learning

Home is clearing

I feel strong

I feel alive
I feel ready
I feel enlightened
I feel complete
I feel ready to embrace
Positive
Personal
Present

13ᵗʰ August 2012

Just been in London yesterday –
Closing of the Olympics
The Gallery 'Children's Exhibition'
Workshops – people coming and going
The Bed & Breakfast is full and busy
#1 is learning, growing
#2 is explaining, exciting
#3 is challenging, experiencing
#4is involving, character
#5 is walking, chatting, movement
He just had his birthday
Took children to Ireland for a couple of days
Interesting, exciting
Went to the zoo
Took them on an airplane
Dog walking
Running
Chickens
Jake and Deliha – new cats
JC –has a new girlfriend – we will see!
Involvement
God has grace

12ᵗʰ September 2012

Life of Bed & Breakfast owners
Five wee ones

Nearly my 34th birthday

Mother of a beautiful daughter – wearing dungarees with a pink butterfly on them

Twin black cats

Golden retriever Glory

Cycling kids to school

Back garden changes and growth.

New routines

September breeze

Summer runs.

Son #2 reading, sure he is dyslexic

Son #1 maths homework (help!)

Research dinosaurs and circuses

The summer holidays have just rushed by in a flash. I really enjoyed and relished in the children's days unravelling.

There was limited routine, however, of course, but still some structure to their days; the mealtimes mainly.

Just being outside, breathing, stretching, moving – day trips off to the coast, to Train Land seeing friends, Chocolate Factory, lots of cycling, lots of playing, exploring, seeing friends, running around – adventure really, enjoying being their mum.

Cycling them to school this morning, engaging, not to put too much pressure on their wee souls – stretching their legs. Getting the heart rate up. Good for me to spend time with them learning the rules of the road – seeing how others get to school, work, me, and my babies.

Watched creation – Darwin – what will I achieve – any greatness. The Origin of Species.

Working hard outside – the tractor, the rakes, the spade, and the children watching. Me listening, it's all happening. No rain for a few hours.

Woodland walk.

Contact details

Networking ways and means.

Achievements.

17th September 2012

I am in a good place right now.

    I love my husband

I love my children

I enjoy the business

I adore my animals

My health is good

I respect and honour friends and their wishes and directions

I love my extended family

I am a lucky girl and God is by my side. I really thank you.

It is harvest time.

All good things around us are sent from heaven above! Then thank the Lord for all his love!

I adore cycling the kids to school; such a quality time with them – my wee boys – turning into great men – one day. I have high hopes for them. I truly, truly do pray that they achieve great things, and they might just turn around and say cheers Mum. Just love really.

I like working, raising capital – it is scary sometimes though.

26th October 2012

We are in Corfu. I have never been to Corfu before – however, it appears fresh, Mediterranean palatial ocean views, calm sea, sand, blue skies and reliable, sensible temperatures.

I have experienced a rollercoaster of a ride in the last few weeks with #2. And, after much deliberating last half term, over the holidays and reflection on how he is as a child –it was schooling decision crunch time. He is going to get encapsulated into the Steiner system. Steiner schools – huge decisions, research, and time! It must be a good choice – the most complicated and large as a grown-up parent!

This I believe will then change my focus on #3, who I know is willing, generous-minded, and just a great wee lad despite all his medical problems.

#4 is a such character – a cheek, and involver! He likes very much to be part of everything, steady and is enjoying pre-school and all its involvements.

I do feel like I am failing as a mother.

Of course, I always have the business. Making sure that is a success. It is not always easy.

We need to work on the next stage. Need to complete the property and get deeds separated and rented out ASAP to work out the value and next step.

FAITH,

The beach is good
The people are friendly
The climate is refreshing
The flora is edible
The drinks are flowing
We are blessed!

27th October 2012

There is a thunderstorm outside – rain, rain go away come again another day.
Let's hope it's not going to rain the entire holiday!
Discussions re properties and renovations, rental, and negotiations.
And about the barn – suggestion planning permissions.
Three individual properties.
The kids relentlessly scream and shout and fight now. It has turned into one of
those quality holidays of rain rain rain; fight fight fight – these boys – I am
making light of it. Enjoying my boys and my girl!

19th December 2012

Prague with my greatest girlfriend; it was enlightening, peaceful, a break,
enriching, creative, inspiring.
Wrapping presents and poorly children. Great combination.

27th December 2012

Quintessentially British. Two beautiful swans standing elegantly and peacefully
on the side table. Ben went for a swim. I contemplated life. The progression, the
flooding, the lakes, the river, the improvements.
What does 2013 have in store? Well, let's go with it. Let's make the most of
making it work. Going with the freedom of accomplishment.
Shooting rain.
Dining room table.
Silver, glam, salt, pepper, vinos.

31st December 2012

It has come to an end – it has been a wonderful year, if a little unsettled and
stressful from time to time.

This time last year, I was in Kenya, sailing, walking, breathing in the sun's rays, stunning.

It is beautiful here in the UK, surrounded by friends and family.

Christmas has been hectic if a little shattering. The kids have had a lovely time, if a touch spoiling, giving, and receiving; my children.

My mind is like the M25 or Heathrow Airport – so much going on…

5th January 2013

Happy New Year

The seaside – coast with my babies – seascapes, fishermen, boats, pirates!

15th January 2013

The snow has arrived. Yippee, I say!

It's cold – big decisions with the safety of the kids.

Had a wobble over the weekend – the expectation

Snow – blanket – heavy

Kids – excited – cold – snowmen

Work – UK Power Networks

Him – shameless, self centred, needing.

Me – open, frustrated, happy, and emotional – not really, simply focused, driven, anxious, hopeful, and faithful, working.

Chapter 21

Rocks and Hard Places...

"Still round the corner there may wait, a new road or a secret gate." —J.R.R. Tolkien

20th January 2013

The weather has brought the country to a standstill.

NO heating in the B&B side. Trying to contact necessary bases! However, excuses and more excuses.

Fortunately, the new staff have started with the Gallery facility and a new cleaning team.

I was taken aside last week with the joys of raising my children and possibly being a negligent mother! Simply soul-destroying. The health world called me regarding a pulled elbow. Oh, goodness, the rollercoaster ride of existence! What I know now! It's opposed to what I knew before. The school run to Cambridge has turned into a logistical crazy nightmare.

Fights

Destruction

Alpha brother

22nd January 2013

Think I really could start writing a book.

Right now, 2013 has descended – what an absolute pickle.

Really, really...

- Car is causing problems – new car, new finance – new problems...
- Heating in the guest B&B side has packed in – oh, joys, it is cold, cold, cold. I have been running around like a blue-arsed fly to try and fix the problem... ELECTRICIAN CAME AND SWITCHED A SWITCH!!
- New staff starting in the Gallery – their car has also packed up.
- New cleaner cannot get anywhere due to the snow.
- Traffic jams endlessly on the school run.
- Guests would prefer turkey dinosaurs and smiley faces... The requirements of B&B guests.
- Showing people around the gallery, its freezing cold.
- Salespeople lurking in the kitchen.
- Builders are busy being around everywhere; helping to fix windows, fix locks, re-arrange things.
- Calming the boys to sleep, blissful ignorance!
- Please don't shower it's freezing – cold! cold!
- Even headed to B&Q to get firewood for the wood burner. Goodness me, it's endless.

I have my cycle! The moons I guess are aligning.

What can I do? I feel like I'm between a rock and a hard place.

Tuesday

Lost my sense of self

Lost my sense of being happy

Lost my patience with him

Questioning love, direction, patience, understanding,

Acknowledgement

Confusion

Upset

Exhausted

Is there something missing or is it simply defiance?

HELP HELP HELP – I CANNOT DO THIS!

The grass may be greener; it may not be...

It will still need watering, sunlight, and mowing – it all depends on perspective and attitude. And it's for me to do God's will.

Live and just get on with the things I can and accept the things I cannot change.

12ᵗʰ February 2013

What does the church bring? Comfort and care.

We do try our best with things. Again I have had a week of it! I should just simply relish and enjoy the simplicity of life and my existence.

It's been #2 son's half term this week. Joys! He spends most time looking for eggs – creation, and shells of animals. His passion is being outside and just exploring, creation, life, and death; along with facing the elements, torrential rain, hailstones, blizzards, snow, frosts, strong winds. Sun is shining today though.

Took the tribe to London on another adventure.

We saw a piece of the moon, a globe with different tidal moves, volcano ash and lava, and the experience of being in the Japanese earthquake. #2 son is nuts on Medusa, the planets, space, dinosaur bones, the big whale, questions etc., oh, it was great! We even saw the Sunflowers in the National Gallery by Van Gogh, the Lions in Trafalgar Square and Nelson's column.

We had lunch at the Rainforest Café and simple mummy time with the boys. Tube, red bus double-decker, M&M store.

Oh how I simply adore trips with the lads.

BUT...I got into trouble with the local school though, due to the fact that I took #1 son and #3son out of school in term time for the London trip.

Slapped wrist for that! Maybe I might get it right by the time the youngest two are at school. Can't make any promises though hey!!

The main interrogation was: do I think school, especially primary school is important to their educational life?

Absolutely, of course I do! Life is important for them though, just living. Seeing things, experiencing things, time, motion, and culture.

So, what do I do? Blame me...

  ‼ Yes I was terrible taking them out of school.

  ‼ Yes I am selfish for my family.

  ‼ Yes I was insensitive towards the teachers and their structure.

It's Lent time again. Lent. Choices, directions focusing the Lord at the centre of my wellbeing, existence.

Thursday WIBN. It's interesting and I must act. It's great making connections, involvements, awareness, analysis. Capacity for entrepreneurship and progression going forward.

Sunday, 3ʳᵈ March 2013

All the threes today. I feel very much stuck in three years now and somehow just won't accelerate into three. Maybe at some point, I will.

We gathered collectively for Grandpa's memorial service yesterday. It was special to reunite as a family and I felt oddly at peace when I left.

Sunday funday – hey. Day of Peace – relax family day. United together. My special family...

30ᵗʰ March 2013

Today is one of those days; I simply got out of bed on the wrong side. My patience is minimal, and function is 100% fighting, arguing kiddies, bickering about nothing, sugar, cereal, kitchen paper, milk, mud sprawled everywhere, chocolate.

Is the Easter bunny coming?

What about sitting and reflecting on the resurrection of what Christ has done for us to save our souls!

Cheeky monkeys, explain!

Unblocked the loos, cleaned bathrooms, mopped up the dog wee, fed children…

Walked dogs, fed cats organised B&B guests, and fry-ups still…

I'm exhausted and finding a moment to pee for myself is just non-existent!

30/3/13 makes 10 or 117?

Any clues! Any more clues?

Number playing – always good for a ticking brain. A few things have got to me…

I must stop and reflect what's good / bad for me! Understand all emotions… its relentless! Movements can be challenging and exhausting.

Good Monday – Easter Monday

Ok – Clocks have gone forward. We get an hour less sleep. Not that that makes simply any difference in this home!!

Ah well. Supper last night was delicious. I cooked up a storm if I do say so myself and the kids all went crazy on a lot of chocolate and I had a beautiful grounding Holy Communion at the Cathedral. Sometimes I wonder if it goes in one ear and out the other!

8th April 2013

I took all kids and myself off to Duxford today. The doors opened at 10am and we were there waiting! Went on a Concorde, I thought how narrow it was.

World War One/World War Two, aviation, American bones. Amazing no/yes/don't touch/come on. Amazing place. Return homework, work, and work. Margaret Thatcher died today at 87 years old. Amazing RIP.

Sort out my emotions staffing /guilt/or just a reflection of appreciation! A job is a job.

So, I had a busy day. Being a mum and with distractions. I feel very much graced with God's presence and direction, pace, and control right now, which is refreshing. Timings seem to be channelled by him! The power/spirit.

13th April 2013

What is a vice?

21ˢᵗ April 2013

Opened the photography exhibition on Friday, super turn out – what a spread, fingers crossed for spreading the positive word.

Inspirational art – small business, B&B

Annoyingly website has been hacked, etc.! Oh, well. Fix it & move forward.

27ᵗʰ April 2013

My daily habits are continuous. It is plenty to juggle and I am trying to be organised!

Last week was filled with meetings, AGMs, movement, enlightenment, children, little lady's first big bed, first morning at pre-school. Amazing! Truly fascinating. Movement, maintenance, and running B&B. Art Gallery! Amazing, getting there.

Money, money, money. In and out. Need it in! Need to make it work!

27ᵗʰ July 2013

I now have a new nephew, still nameless. However he is long and beautiful I am totally delighted.

Summer holidays descend. Let the chaos begin!

Bonus days: running in the rain, good moods, wet days, free thinking.

B&B constant. Cool!

One more step along the world I go

Keep me travelling with me you! The way I should!

31ˢᵗ July 2013

End of another month. July has flown past.

Cracks are beginning to feel like they are showing. More about focus – deliverance, passion, diversity, analyses! Well trucking along really.

Love the kids. The holidays, no stresses with getting the kids anywhere, with everything on time! Phew. Relief. No analyses! No judgement. Wish we could continue like that. Not sure whether society believes in the existence.

B&B ticking, gallery taking off! Well I hope. Believe free!

Understanding, must make notes! Be assertive! Be a doer! Manage!

It is a juggling act. Involvement, direction…

25th August 2013

It has got the point where I have decided to home school the eldest two. It's exciting I am really looking forward to it.

I have spoken to a lot of people and am having good support, the networks are essential.

JC is really not well – he is bleeding! What do I do! Support xxx

Canada Trip – Part One

Arrived by the lake. Ste Agathe des Mont's, peaceful, calm, hear the water trickling into the stream. Nothing, other than simple peace.

We left home at 10.30 yesterday morning, travelled to Heathrow, juggled the traffic and powered with the thoughts of are the children going to be ok? Of course they are! Why wouldn't they be?

I have left a list for everyone to be organised in our absence. There will always be one or two mishaps, but as long as the kids are alive and the house is still standing when we get back, then I'm sure all will be grand, no disasters! Please!

Flight took about eight hours. Flew through immigration, fun films uninterrupted by kids playing and prodding, asking, involving. It was sleepy, calm, tranquil.

Arrived at the hotel and simply made sweet, passionate, spine-tingling love, knowing no interruption from children or guests, self-involvement togetherness! Calm, powered, passionate. It was quality and the reason, well, one of the reasons we are alone together.

Depot for the RV, lots of waiting around while paperwork was filled, and a walk around the vehicle.

Arrive Ste Agathe Along with a very large Walmart, which was fab to get some bits and pieces. Phew, lakeside parked. Relaxed. Ate a great meal and got more food for the week.

Ready for sleep it is only early 7.30 Canadian time. We are trying to stay awake. It's tricky considering the time difference. Sleep beckons, so does just processing and reflection.

Canada Trip – Part Two

Walked around the lake and even passed the old college. Breaking mist and dawn, witnessing She Agathe des Mont's waking up – truly blissful. It was a good reflection, patience, listening, time. Truly great. The sun began to shine; we played cards, ate food, and decided to take a dip in the lake, it was refreshing and made me feel alive, such medicine for the soul and enzymes of the body.

Canada Trip – Part Three

September 15th, my birthday. I have been here for 35 years.

I have finally relaxed a little, enjoying time.

We travelled from Montreal to Toronto. It was a long drive and along the 401, followed by a walk down Wasaya Beach; the longest freshwater beach in the world. It was cold; however, we tucked up warm and viewed some adrenaline junkie and hardcore windsurfers. Why not when the wind is in your perfect home location? I just loved the patterns on the sand and getting some cobwebs blown out; especially after a 6-hour journey (this was a few days ago now). We arrived in the town of Collingwood – unsure why the wind took us there – however; we enjoyed our time, went for a walk down the high street and viewed some stunning art galleries. Lovely. We watched a couple of movies and ate/drank/talked and spent time together.

Headed to our friend's wedding, in the middle of nowhere (Holland Centre); however tonight in Algonquin we quite possibly would be more in the middle of nowhere. We arrived somehow, with the help of the angels at Hamilton Creek farm – pure perfection. It was empowering and glorious. Interesting to see the fish hatchery, the school, main walks, where the teenagers hangout, oh, yes, and then the cycle race and the arboretum – all in the space of that morning.

We decided to drive north and then east as opposed to the south then east – new road trip, new day, new strength, we stopped for birthday lunch at Huntsville and got a few supplies for the next few days – supplies included a camera.

Arrived in Algonquin Park a little too late for the Arts Centre. Paid up with parks permit, in the rain, watched a movie, ate, drank, cheers and went for a walk in the rain and saw some yurts – very interesting concept – may have to, will… Invest.

The angels of faithfulness – it was forgiveness and understanding, both very true right now as all I needed to do was forgive those who bring me turmoil and have reasoning and understanding. Good qualities, well, we try! It has been a large digestion and learning curve with the amount going on especially at home. You get found out very quickly if work is not completed or done!

20th November 2013

Goodness, almost two months since I last wrote – time is flying. Well, not just that – I am just so engrossed in life that I just barely get a moment to stop, reflect, think, take time – it's been a rollercoaster ride of emotions. I would be happier if I could delegate more. However, it comes with its own complications I strive hard to make.

3rd December 2013

Christmas is underway. I love buying Christmas presents for people. I so love the giving season.
So, our lifestyle has changed dramatically with the home schooling – the kids are much more relaxed and enjoying their childhood.
I absolutely adore being a wife, I love him very much. Could not imagine life without him, he does continue to insult me, however I guess I will remain humble and cherish him whatever may come.
The kids outside playing football together before school. Him cooking breakfast.
I wonder what today might bring – joy, happiness, peace, tranquillity, enjoyment, pleasure, alone, calm, determination, passage, telling, focus, giving, analysing, accomplishing.
I am dealing with the general highs and lows of running a business. We are focussed, positive, and true and we are on track.
Starting business coaching again. It gives me accountability. Crushing the gremlins...

10th December 2013

When suffering blindness
Sublime statement
Turn your heart towards home

15th December 2013

WE RESERVE THE RIGHT TO REMOVE ANYONE FROM OUR PROPERTY WHEN THEY ABUSE OUR HOSPITALITY.

15th December 2013

I promised I would write a little more and thank goodness I am. Making it part of the daily habit? Mmmm…Don't quite think so, weekly might be achievable though…

It is the run down to Christmas. I am loving the kids, the evolution of them, their lives, me trying to manage, take hold – it's true quality. I am one blessed mummy – so true!

Work is keeping me super busy. Kids are a joy – however they are an immense distraction. Have to let the week pan out. I thought I was organised. I just seem to be endlessly cooking, cleaning, walking, washing, explaining, discussing, moving, oh yes – more cleaning, more cooking.

Oh – watched the X Factor – cheese and wine in hand. Ohhhh a mummy moment. Have been doing lots of painting the walls, making the sitting room warm. My aim is to chill and watch the world go by!

Phew doorbell has gone, 22.38 pm, guests have finally arrived. It's late, late, ah, well, dreams keep happening.

24th December 2013

It is Christmas Eve 2013 – an incredible year of fun, laughter, and blessings. My children, my family, are my everything, so pure and important right now.

Simply. Great tiding to life. Prosperous into the NY. I keep feeling we need placid time – to think, reflect and make the most of everything. Be calm, be kind.

28th December 2013

I am so full of Gremlin right now and not quite in the knowledge or know how of how it has completely engrossed me.

Life – It's a roller-coaster ride!

Peace, path, placidity, time, reflection.

I was in a really great place a few days ago. I really was, positive that 2013 was nearly finished. It has been a trying, but also successful year. I really hope and pray to be learning from this one.

The power of patience, the loss of a loved one, the heart ache of not achieving. Where do we go from there?

Oh yes. The gallery, good, bad, positive, negative, customers, no customers, believe, non-belief, strength, weakness, success, failure, good, bad.

Runaway, stay, focus, happiness, time, reflection.

Space, space, space…

Children

Husband

Family

Tomorrow! Always tomorrow.

Only a day away...

31ˢᵗ December 2013

I am happy that this year is nearly closing. I know it will still be the same tomorrow. However sometimes it's good to wash the slate clean and start afresh.

- Make a difference.
- Happy delivery.
- Aim to go forward.

We all have different paths. I have classically been known for dwelling on negative feelings. I am a happy positive person. People can be incredibly nasty and I think right now through those challenges I must just try to overcome them. It is interesting. Sometimes I wish I could wave a magic wand and make it all much clearer, more positive. I need to have better directions and firmer guides in my own achievements. I will be more organised and select my delegation skills in making it clearer for people to be understanding in our company and home! It's a challenge. Being all in one thing.

Yippee for family time. Yippee for positive work environment and yippee for starting afresh.

Meditation, focus, surround myself with goodness, hope, happiness and classical focus.

Family are my priority however being happy is also!

List for 1ˢᵗ Jan 2014

- Bleed radiators
- Feed animals
- Home and family rules preparation
- Playroom sort out and toys
- Change sheets twin room and ground floor
- Check holiday home
- Take payment for all bookings 2014 so far
- Find the hole punch...

- Kids to write thank you letters
- Plan for 2014 plus date and targets
- Home schooling plan
- Empty all the rubbish
- Dog poo!
- List gallery plans with builders
- Washing pile
- Clear out the washroom
- Tapping
- List daily habits
- Do a future self!

4th January 2014

It's the New Year! Phew!
Research moon path patterns in sync with women
Set up of blood plasma
Full moon
Blood
Emotions in check
Menstruation
Understanding of that?
Influences/icons
Michelle Obama – 50
Catherine of Cambridge – mother
Oldest woman dying
Women in Afghanistan

29th January 2014

Breathe through it today. Let it happen...
Put it in God's hands, allow patience.
I feel like an iceberg at the moment. Just the tip and there is so much underneath
I just cannot comprehend! Life is so hard…
I can do it. Work it. Juggle it, it's all consuming.
Help! Ah!
Lord please provide me with patience, grace, calmness, quality, respect, understanding, clarity. Breathe, breathe!

3rd March 2014

March already and I've managed to get my Monday morning run in before 7am – the daylight is breaking earlier. The birds are tweeting and life is just happening.

9th March 2014

My wallet, phone, and #4 have all vanished. Found him knee deep in the builder's paint!
Getting ready for large clay shooting day 300 people.
Guests in – running well – smooth operation!
BUSY BUSY BUSY!!!

10th March 2014

The Famous Five are outside playing happily – have decided to record the happy giggles and the talk and discussion and the birds tweeting, happily

20th May 2014

My eldest, double figures! A 10-year-old in the home. Where have those years gone?
New word of the year – mindful!
It's everywhere – it's a craze.
Birds singing – cuckoo!
Sun shining
The business continues to focus, and service, direction.
So many people who still today suffer
- Persecution
- Ridicule
- Abuse
- A young Christian woman in Sudan stoned to death result of her Christian faith and belief. So sad.

1st June 2014

Jesus said, "When the comforter has come, the spirit of truth, he shall testify of me!"

Protection against fears and dangers of this world.
The true meaning of Christ – our Lord.
Amen.

5th June 2014

Do you think of yourself as a creative person?

- Making
- Imagine
- Designing
- Open to possibility
- Risk-taking
- Original thoughts
- Creative things
- Buildings

23rd December 2014

Stop venting all your particulars at me!!
It is Christmas time and I'm in it for giving and sharing – especially with my wonderful and special children, Gods gracious gifts.
I do and do and do and give and give and give!

12th January 2015

SWAT – re getting a job.
10 minutes – just for me to breathe please!
Self-sufficient
School
Look after yourself Juliet!
Business –
Must update CV
Staff training needs booking – don't forget!
Talk to a lady about job 3

15th January 2015

Patience and endurance is what is needed
Tasks God has called you to do – God will help you find them.

Ministry gift days – in May.
Stationary, toiletries, knitted things for babies.

23ʳᵈ January 2015

Lunch is serious business – one minute presentation. Eeek!

31ˢᵗ January 2015

Yoga weekend
Cannot wait!
Exciting times.
Workshop
Stress the body stimulants – when our bodies get stressed, flight, fight, and freeze.
Hunters and gatherers – generate a response.
Snake, heron, tiger?
Lifestyle.
-Often introduce stimulants to keep us going.
-Lifestyle judgments.
-Habit – got into.
-Adrenaline gets produced. Exciting in low level stressed state not open; we are in a relaxed state.
-Digestion – digestive system
-Dehydration
-Alcohol used to relax
-Peaks and troughs
-Blood sugar levels – adrenaline
-Blood sugar levels peak and trough. Greater range.
-Sugar is another stimulant to keep us going.

Hydration – start to hydrate your body and release that stress state, deeper levels of stress on the body.
80% water, we are like gardens – we need nutrients, sunlight!
Oils – essential fatty acids omega 3&6
Fish oils
Chia seeds
Grains – swollen

Soup and stew EFAs
Hemp oil/linseed oil – cold pressed oils

1st February 2015

Yoga weekend.
A lot going on in my head – amazing with the cranial-sacral.
Hold back the river
Circle time circle time – listen

Chapter 22

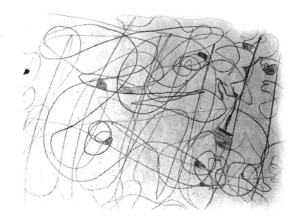

Do as You're Told....

"When writing the story of your life, don't let anyone else hold the pen." – Rebel Thriver

4ᵗʰ March 2015

It is the 4ᵗʰ of March today, where has the time gone?

Flown by, as one would say. I have tried hard to stay sane, to concentrate, to experience, be committed.

I have just attended a teen's translated course today. Very insightful. Gave plenty of excellent and informative information on how to be a good parent. Where to go – and mostly understand listening. Listen! Tres important.

Feeling refreshed and in London today. I am quite relieved to have a day away from the challenges of the home environment and dealing with his grumpiness.

How long can you let it go on like this? I have been thinking about a new life, a new existence, new paths, impossible when you are busy with the day-to-day grind.

I would like to get more into my writing and artwork. Maybe have an art exhibition? That would be a target.

Maybe I do need distance and space from him? Working out why I love him? Who actually is him? Why is he telling me such nasty, nasty things? If that makes him feel better then I guess I will continue to take all the rubbish. It is exhausting though so tiring and draining and everyone is beginning to notice.

Of course, I don't want a divorce. Just some space, separation, appreciation for who I am – would anyone appreciate or value me! Who knows?

Was in Notting Hill today, memories came flooding back to me of a time in which I had just returned from Hawaii. I was a different girl back then. Quite free, open, drank a lot, worked hard, and played hard. I had only me to be responsible for. Times change. Change fast.

It is an old boyfriend's birthday today. He is turning 40 years old. I wonder what kind of day he is going to experience. That relationship had its ups and downs and inconsistencies; that's why we are not together now. The planets simply didn't align.

I do love being a mother; my days are filled with their demands, challenges, rewards, accomplishments.

Each day, I thank God for bringing them into my life. The true blessings of God are children and family. I hope that they of course will make the correct decisions for their paths ahead.

29th March 2015

This weekend has been hard. I have asked him for a separation. I feel devastated, but hugely relieved. It's hard, super hard, he came back last night, and we cried, really cried.

It's hard! The way truth and light will be of peace, calm, and a great future. Please allow time of separation for this to happen. Surrounded though by angels of companion and sharing.

Strength/courage vital!

Lord, please give me the strength and determination for a positive change for the future, for my lovely children and for my health and well-being. All you have delivered with your patience and grace I hugely thank you.

Peace, calm and future focus. Thank you.

18th July – Saturday

Yoga Retreat

The yoga retreat is a positive experience. I am happy being alone, and not having to contend with the children right now. Selfishly or not, I am at peace and opening areas that require opening. Happiness within. I am pleased to be allowed to be free and break loose on the opening.

The heart is a place – it's been buried recently, confused. But now, it's touching freedom. It does allow the emotions to be intensely open.

Yoga Monday – 20th July

I went for a lovely run for about an hour. Then a yoga meditation; focussing on breathing and clearing toxins – watching and feeling the sunshine, excited about the future.

It was a good meditation. Feeling – forgiveness – sharing the love with all. Here and over the world.

20th July 2015 (Actually 19th July)

So, I had my new beginning party last night. Full of wonderful celebrations and friends and family support!

This is the day that the Lord has made. We will recognise and be glad about it! So much has happened over the last year. It's difficult to even start with how I am feeling and just everything that has, and is, going on.

I am a strong, courageous, independent, intelligent, calm, peaceful, and resourceful person. May this book allow me to realise this? I prayed for being cleansed today – God knows my thoughts regarding this; It's time to allow these to be positive – forgive them and allow them to be free to have a happy life. It is time to be inspired by the Holy Spirit in other ways and means. Allow my heart to be free and happy. Breathe and just be! I am hopeful and excited for the future. Thank you, dear Lord.

Not weighing our merits but pardoning our offences. Keep hearts and minds in the knowledge and love of God.

Whatever life throws – we can cope. Life, death, the universe, everything. Have no fear for tomorrow. Jesus is with us – you and me. Amen

21st July 2015

Currently it's a rollercoaster ride of emotions, but I do have an abundance of love around me and surrounding myself with people who care. It's not easy – the ups and downs of living life. It's quite full-on – the summer holidays now!

God, please guide me in your way. What is the best way to move forward the essence of self-knowledge, acceptance, and respect? Allow the happiness to move forward and be happy. Be true to self – who knows my certainty – other than being positive, personal, and present.

27th July 2015

I have made the decisions and taken these actions to provide a secure, calm, peaceful, rational, protective environment for the children and myself. I am loved and trust this is the correct path and direction.

It's been an extremely strange week.

29th July 2015

Going through the motions – I'm here
Auntie Juliet has a niece!

31st July 2015

Affirmation. I am in a stronger place, a good place. Feel much better today.

I filed for divorce yesterday. I feel secure. My life is my responsibility. He is in God's hands. No blame. That's the situation right now. I must take care of me and the kids.

Your thoughts have power – to win over them, you must submit to Christ and control what you allow your mind to dwell on.

Take captive every thought – 2 Corinthians 10:5 NIV

1st August 2015

Once in a blue moon –

He says has slept with someone else and how guilty he feels.

I feel sick.

Would never do that to you.

Goodbye.

God –

Grant me the serenity

To accept the things, I cannot change

Courage to change the things I can

And the wisdom to know the difference.

2nd August 2015

It's extremely rough now. I'm trying desperately hard to rescue me. Let go of this blue moon period. I am feeling much more positive than I did a few months ago – however, it is like waves – rollercoaster rides, the tide changing, nothing constant – until I find some comfort in just allowing myself to be! To be free – allow freedom to take hold and allow my wings to grow freely into the new and bright future.

My heart feels torn, cut, wounded. It's incredibly hard to stay focussed sometimes – especially with everything going on.

This week – Thursday it was. I filed for divorce – cleanse my soul in the newness of life. I cannot look back on what happened – allow the future – take – eat – do it in remembrance of God.

It is now time to truly allow myself and the children to be free of his addictions, his temper.

I must clear the slate – work on the future. Allow me to be. Be strong. Be faithful. Have heart.

I willingly give and graciously receive.

I am surrounded by great friends and family. I allow myself to be firm with decisions and concrete in my allowances.

What, my brother has taken his own life?

Chapter 23

energy is eternal delight (William Blake)

Clouds

"I've looked at love from both sides now. From give and take, and still somehow, it's love's illusions I recall. I really don't know love at all." – Joni Mitchell

8th December 1979 – 1st August 2015

I will hugely miss him – the comfort of just knowing where he is. The truth in his voice and in his heart. The willingness of his soul. He is at peace now. He is calm and in knowing that he is in a happier place. Now – dwelling – dwelling. He was in mental anguish.

Ecclesiastes 3:1

There is a time for everything and a season for every activity under the heavens.

A time to be born and a time to die.

A time to plant and a time to uproot.

A time to kill and a time to heal.

A time to tear down and a time to laugh.

A time to weep and a time to laugh.

A time to mourn and a time to dance.

A time to scatter stones and a time to gather them.

A time to embrace and a time to refrain from embracing.

A time to keep and a time to throw away.

A time to fear and a time to mind.

A time to be silent and a time to speak.

A time to love and a time to hate.

A time for war and a time for peace.

Now, sadly I have had to put Ben dog to rest. So, so hard.

When I thought it couldn't get any harder. He is free now – free from spirit. He has had a wonderful life. My special, special Ben.

5th August 2015

It's so so so hard. I cannot even begin to comprehend it all right now! My heart is hurting so much; firstly the whole situation with him and allowing him to just move on and then with JC taking his own life. I cannot believe that he is now no longer with us! And then my darling faithful friend Ben dog has now passed away – he is gone, gone free. My blessed friend

? How long is it going to hurt?

? How am I going to find the strength to move on?

? Please answer my prayers, dear Lord.

? I feel so very stuck!

7ᵗʰ August 2015

I have departed a marriage

Lost a brother

Put my dog to sleep.

All within the last week. I do feel very overwhelmed by the entire situation. Life is life and it must go on. We must embrace and enjoy what's on offer. I must not be afraid –I must leave the past behind and focus on my five responsibilities. My angels, my complete angels.

It has happened and he isn't here anymore – he was my brother. My lovely little brother – it's so hard.

He's gone – gone forever – he needed out.

I need to focus on my five treasures – my perfect handful – they are alive, well, living, breathing, and being – alive. Let them live.

8ᵗʰ August 2015

On auntie duties – I have the most adorable little dot here beside me – sleeping. It's exhausting and relentless! Bless them! She will be awake before they know it again – she is peaceful, asleep and it's all about gaining strength.

I have mixed emotions – highs and lows – not much in between now. It's all about talking it through – allowing it to be and happen – it's hard, super hard. Each step along with the world I go – from the old I travel to anew – keep me travelling along with you.

20ᵗʰ August 2015

With JC.

Be still JC for the glory of the Lord is with you. I cannot believe you are lying in front of me. Passed away, to your new life. You left behind such memories. You are finally at peace, that's all I can pray for. I will miss you so much. I will miss your passing by – coming and going – your cig smells even. You needed to free yourself. I tried so hard to make life okay for you and honestly, life is hard. I wish I could share my dilemmas with you. I am sure you will just giggle at me really from above.

I try hard to do well and be good and I know through everything you wanted to be happy, trusted, and loved.

You are gone far away, as a dragonfly the kids say. You are with Ben dog. We will scatter your ashes together by the trees. You have left behind an immense hole. Larger than you can ever imagine…

You have taught me though that dying is okay.

It quite possibly could have been the hardest few weeks of my life to date – crazy but true. I am in awe of my true and core friendship and family.

6th September 2015

Summer has fallen this year.

Firstly, it is time to divorce, it's time to be reasoned and free – allow the future to be in God's hands and allow his path and guidance to be my true journey.

Sadly, and more vitally at this point, my brother decided to take his own life. What an amazing heartache he has left behind. How many souls he touched? It's complicated to even express how I feel as he has departed now and nothing, simply nothing, is going to bring him back. He decided to move on.

Then my beloved Ben dog has departed this life, he was, and is an amazing friend, loyal, faithful. Time has gone…

17th September 2015

An abundance has happened this last year, being 36 and turning 37 was hugely emotional. I let loose in the evening and was extraordinarily teary. Not sure where it came from. I have wonderfully special friends – if only I knew what to do next to allow the journey to unravel and unravel. Remember you can't reach what's in front of you until you let go of what's behind you.

Deep pray silence 10 minutes

Allow flowing.

Feel the gut.

22nd September 2015

Finding your hidden treasurer,

Delightful and gentle little book.

Holiday became a treat.

Stop being who you were – and be who you are.

The benefit of silent prayer.

28th September 2015

I pray today for those struggling to find work that the right job comes along when the time is right.

I thank you for my encounters with different people that lead me to different pleasurable imaginations.

I thank you for my health and the abundance that surrounds me.

I thank you for my amazing family and friends that they bring much strength, comfort, and direction.

I pray for those in strife, that are unloved, uncared for, that you protect them with your care. Shelter, food, whatever they may need.

I pray that you grant me serenity, courage, direction – to be a faithful and giving person. To share and spread your love around.

That I might find the peace, grace, and guidance, your will be done. Amen.

8th October 2015

Damsels in Success

Success strategy – do what brings you joy. We fill ourselves up first.

1) Pray and meditate
2) Work or running with the days
3) Swimming
4) Being at home and kids, calm and peaceful
5) Tucking up in bed at a reasonable hour and turning on iPlayer
6) Glass of wine surrounded by all my children and siblings

21st November 2015

It's another Saturday and the first Saturday in a very long time that I do not rush them off around the county for football.

The kids are hard work and full on physical – it's all about fighting.

I am looking forward to going to the St Andrews Ball tonight – will be lovely to meet some new people – and allow myself to be Juliet for the night – whoever Juliet may be now.

28th November 2015

Took the kids to Christmas Fair, Pizza Hut, and panto to see Jack and the Beanstalk, it was all super. Lots of creative minds together. I hope the kids were inspired. They didn't get to sleep until after midnight! The younger ones are rather poorly; hopefully they will get on the mend.

Lord, please grant me the serenity to do your goodwill today, Amen.

13ᵗʰ December 2015

I thank the Lord I have made it to Morocco, it all takes considerable planning, but we did it. The sun is shining, the water is still, the people friendly, the sand is perfect and the type you can walk on for miles. The airplane ride was about four hours.

14ᵗʰ December 2015

How hard is it to let go? Simple affirmations – opening or closing your soul to the one – who cares at the end of the day. Do even the parents – do they, do they? Or are we all insular beasts – roaming for our own peace and satisfaction? I don't know – what I do know is that it's essential to do your best – and to do good to all people – hard and judgemental it maybe from time to time.

I dreamt about him last night – that it was all a joke. Then the belief and realisation hit, that he is dead. Gone. I can never share with him again. Alone hanging – well, 24 hours – he must have been incredibly sad, sad, the suicide – it's heart-breaking. I get scared that he had been so low – so sad in his heart – desperate – then again – I respect and can only respect that was his decision and choice and become certain in knowing that's where he felt he found his peace, calmness in being able to achieve his outcome.

15ᵗʰ December 2015

Surfing yesterday was super fun with the kids, then to top that off, we went quad biking; amazing times for them and for me to see them so happy.

The beach is expansive and full of wildlife. I even think I saw flamingos flying in formation.

Again, I am working on the letting go cycle, it is hard and I'm not sure of what I'm letting go of. I am competitive with myself. Life is sure not a competition – sometimes I think maybe like JC, what is the point?

I cannot believe to think how Mummy and Daddy are coping with the devastation. It really must be hard. I love my children so much and I don't think I could stomach losing one of them.

Thinking of stories. The quad bike, the people in the dunes, the different lives lived, the encounters, the camels, the achievements, the seagulls, the boats, the swimming pool, the noises, the children – exuberant, the children, fighting, despair, desperation, aloe?

16ᵗʰ December 2015

Morocco here is very peaceful, and it appears that women all have their independence to a degree. Islam is the lead religion, but it's not too in your face, which is nice. The people of course want your business, but also, they are not in your face. It's refreshing. The kids in general are being good – calm – excitable.
Good to walk on the beach.
Good to walk on a beach that's good to walk on.
Good to watch the sunrise and the sunset.
Good to take time to pray.
Good to relax with the kids and be still with not much challenge.
Good to be with the kids out of routine – but keeping to primary care needs.
Good to eat healthily and be happy.
Good to run on the beach each morning.
Good to go surfing in the ocean.
Thank you, Lord, for the enabling. It's refreshing. I know only a week – a week of battery charging, a week of change, a week of knowing who we are together, and a week away from the marriage. A week of letting go.

17ᵗʰ December 2015

Hamman last night and it was an amazing sensation. Warmth, scrub, smells water pouring. Meditation, peace, calm – it was blissful and a moment of relaxation and tranquillity.
We watched the sunset on the beach. Completion of yet another day on planet earth.
Women have a soul and need to express themselves in their soulful ways; they must develop and blossom in ways that are sensitive to them without molestation from others.
Don't be afraid to investigate the worst. It only guarantees the increase of soul power through fresh insights and opportunities for re-visioning one's life and self-anew.
Break the old patterns of ignorance.

Follow instincts, see what you see, call up psychic muscle, dismantle the destructive energy. Assert yourself in an even more powerful manner.

18th December 2015

Letting go, meeting the dark side. It's to enable the future. That's what they say, or what is taught. Goodness, it's hard. I know for now I have made the right choice. It is good and we are all happy together – if a little stressed from time to time, generally due to the children being excited and me just needing peace.
Allow a great day to happen – the children, the sun, sea, surf, reading, and breathing – took them around the market yesterday and out for supper.

19th December 2015

Last day in Morocco, it's calm and tranquil.
I am letting go steadily and I'm patiently accepting that this is the time for it all. It's super hard – that is my saying this holiday – well, it's just a process. Friendships have been tricky and maybe I simply open too much of my soul for people – who knows – but what I do know is that intuition is key – and I'm going to start protecting my heart and soul from its dangers – to lead a happy life now – full of enjoyment.
I was flipping in the ocean yesterday. Beyond the surf break. Feeling the moment and motion of the ocean.

31st December 2015

Peace, direction, sense, alignment, clarity, direction, focus, path, driven, compassionate, dedicated, truthful, honest, clear, mindful, accepting, breathe, ability, freedom, alone, peaceful, calm, movement, allowed, open-minded.

1st January 2016

Happy New Year 2016 has begun and what a pure joy, that is fantastic.
I have worked through a lot in the last year and now it's beginning to unravel let go and breathe for the future me. It is exciting and I am truly grateful for my family, siblings, friends, children, contacts, health, God, surroundings, environment.
I am ready to let go of other's negativity surrounding my psyche and allow myself to become and know the good, willing, hardworking, open-minded, accepting, compassionate, caring, hopefully, loving person I am.

The future is bright, along with my children and my determination, I will continue to reign, evaluate, reflect, and learn. But move forward with a new positive direction.

Exciting times, sharing times, being times, aligning times, happy truth.

3rd January 2016

Who knows what this year is going to bring? I know that I will be resilient. I will work hard at just covering my costs, debts in life but also be mindful that I am here to be a mother, to be happy, to remain kind-hearted to simply just be me – and of course accepting of me.

4th January 2016

Monday – first Monday of the New Year. Had a good sleep, good meditation, good run, good yoga, good prayer time, good delegation to cleaning team and now ready to accomplish good and extraordinary things today. It's been a journey and I'm really to embark on the next.

The kids spent the day with their dad yesterday. I managed to go to church, even go to the movies.

Then I cooked a roast dinner, sorted the sitting/playroom – tidied the house, walked, animals and de-nitted the children.

5th January 2016

Back to work yesterday, well, doing business bits and pieces. I do get fearful of the future and uncertainty especially with regards to finances.

8th January 2016

Firstly, a week into the New Year and I am still thriving and striving. I managed to get the children back to school safely, happy, and healthy. Even worked out the clubs they wanted to do!

14th January 2016

Creative writing course. Received lovely praise from the group, find it therapeutic and exciting right now.

I treasure and enjoy my structure now; I do get lonely from time to time but I'm beginning to gain more confidence and structure into being me!

A human being, not a human doing.

Be a doer not a stewer.

15th January 2016

It's cold outside, winter is here
Lots of fires need burning.
Warming the home.
I am happy with the children.
I made pancakes for them this morning.
The children are loved, educated, let them grow and understand their responsibilities.
You are stable, remain on that path and keep humble.
You are only alone if you want to be alone. The time and person will be right – there is no urgency.
You cope with what God knows that you can handle – give it all to him if you feel that you cannot.
You are loved, love yourself. Love your children and love your friends and family.
JC has died now; he is gone. You did everything that you possibly could on this planet. He is in God's hands now, protected, released, and free. You loved him, respected him. He was your brother, now respect his decision in his departure – sin – no, he is free; it's not that he didn't want to die. He just didn't know how to live anymore.
Protect yourself now, you are doing a good job and when people cross your path that you disagree with or struggle with – breathe, accept, pray. But remember, you have a choice. You don't surround yourself with harmful people.
Live in today.

Saturday, 16th January 2016

Be happy and accept yourself for you here and now exactly how you are because:
If you seek wealth – you will worry about every pound.
If you seek health – you will worry about every blemish or bump.
If you seek popularity – you will obsess over every conflict.
If you seek safety – you'll jump at every crack of the twig.
Focussing on God's kingdom giving you everything you need.
Please dear Lord,

Peace, calm, concentration, space, spirit, endurance, perseverance, knowledge, wisdom, understanding, vision, acceptance.
Thank you.

19ᵗʰ January 2016

As you become more spiritually healthy, you'll become more emotionally healthy, and when that happens, you are more apt to find your needs being met. Give each other space.

20ᵗʰ January 2016

I had creative writing yesterday. Mummy goes to school, which is good for me. Especially opening the creative brain. Watched school football match; he did super well, proud of him, a real triumph. He is a great sharer, lovely smile, and brilliant sportsman.
I am feeling different energy and alignment now, which I pray is positive: church, faith, friends, writing, quiet space, reflection, hope, direction, courage, it all helps!

25ᵗʰ January 2016

The tongue is a small part of the body, but it makes great beasts.
Further, please refrain from my careless speech and put a guard on my tongue today and every day.
"A word fitly spoken is like apples of gold in a setting of silver." Proverbs 25:11
26ᵗʰ

26ᵗʰ January 2016

Often, I get asked how you do it. Well, I don't know, although I do have faith, a belief in God. In the knowing and reassurance that I am fine and all will be fine. I ask God and rely on him for his assurance. It's a tricky one. But the value of life, acceptance, charity, humility, they all play a big part. I have to let go, especially of past relationships, whether good or bad. Happiness and security in the knowledge that all will be as it's meant to be. This eases the load of pressure, anxiety, and fear.
"Let us run with endurance the race God has set before us." Hebrews 12:1

28th January 2016

Prayer is the bridge between panic and peace.

I wish you all a good prayer day.

Thank you for my home,

My ability to keep going

For doing yoga

For being able to read

For focus

For my children

For the privilege

For being loved and being able to love

For being able to write

For being able to share

For my family, immediate and extended

For my head, my ears, my tongue

For listening, speaking, talking

For being able to walk, run, swim, cycle, catch, throw

For being understanding, compassionate, deep thinking, external and sharing, caring, cook, clean, work

To provide

Thank you for all the above.

1st February 2016

Always pray, do not give up. Recognising the plans for our lives.

Affirmations:

I will lead a peaceful, calm, and happy life.

I will work through the trials and tribulations.

I will relate positive messages throughout my space and energy.

I will be the best mother I can be.

I will allow my children to work hard and be independent.

I will continue to work hard and allow the flow of energy to help with this.

I will not allow negative people to drag me down but allow their negativity to create a change and a different perspective of acceptance.

I will live each day to my most full.

2nd February 2016

Candlemas – be true. Allow the light to shine.

Have hope, faith, and the source.

Happiness within and enjoy the flow.

Take courage to face the day.

Enjoy the elements.

Let go of the unnecessary.

Find time, joy, hope, and love.

Be, be, be.

4th February 2016

Got up early for a run, and took the kids to London. Did some creative writing yesterday, painted kid's room and the downstairs bathroom. Went swimming. Noodles for teatime.

It takes courage.

Seek a heart of understanding.

Help me slow down.

Search for insight and understanding for hidden treasure.

"Please cleanse me of sin and cleanse me daily."

God's word is the strongest detergent to get into the deepest recesses of thoughts, imaginations, and motives.

Yes, I separated from the love of my youthful life. The father of my children and what I believed to be my soul mate. I am now free from his ways, his force, his love, his enticement. I am free to find my happiness and source and be free!

Lost my brother to suicide, he had mental health issues all his adult life; I feel he has been released, but it's very hard to accept that I will never see or speak with him again.

Lost my golden child Ben dog to old age. He was my rock, my life; he needed to sleep and move on. I miss him each day. He was a very loyal, faithful, and dedicated companion.

My go-to response? Quiet prayer, reflection, running, a glass of wine, yoga, sleep, talking.

6th February 2016

I am feeling good and positive about the future. I am delighted that January breezed through with not too many rollercoasters! Only really the bathroom floor falling into the utility room, which is grand because it's all under construction anyway!

I am enjoying things and feel blessed. Although I do get anxious from time to time, a lot of it is living in the present moment.

I am afraid of rejection, jealousy, abandonment, not being good enough, or being acceptable enough.

I was reminded today that I should not even speak with other people.

I am afraid of the uncertain, but I guess we all are to a degree and fear that I will never be able to open to anyone ever again. The relationship touch and ecstasy feeling of love, penetration, devotion, letting go I guess I am afraid as this is what got me into this divorce pickle.

8th February 2016

Spirit of self-control and patience.
"He guides the humble in what is right." Psalm

10th February 2016

Be where you are meant to be.
Do what you are meant to do.
Thrive how you are meant to thrive.
Accept what you are meant to accept.
Breathe what you are meant to breathe.
Have hope, faith, courage, and love.

11th February 2016

It's all transitional.
Life, abundance, hope, perception.

13th February 2016

Thank you for enabling situations to unblock and free themselves.

15th February 2016

Transgression – I believe it is the decree nisi day.

23rd February 2016

Seeking reconciliation. I am doing good. The half-term was busy. Full on, I was menstrual, and we had new things that we started. We are okay; we are doing well as a unit.

1st March 2016

The first of March already – where have the days, weeks, months gone? So, I feel ready to embark on a great journey. I'm on a great journey.

Today, let's pray for patience, bravery with people who make me feel inferior. Love them and don't believe their put-downs.

My inner monkey/devil – always saying I'm not good enough.

Feb was a good month – I am practising daily yoga, still running, and swimming. Trying to keep the business on the straight and narrow and trying to keep the children calm, grounded, faithful, strong and independent – all in the knowing that they are loved.

2nd March 2016

When God works in someone's life, there can be a degree turnaround – almost immediately.

Please help me understand the acceptance of the end of my marriage. Please provide shelter and understanding for him and he finds peace, tranquillity in his own heart and that one day he frees his own heart and realises what he did to hurt me and the children. Thank you though for the sacrament of marriage and thank you for granting me the opportunity for compassion, marriage, and union times. Please give me the current mindfulness, positive energy to work out what is going to happen next.

Please also give me the patience, guidance, understanding to be the best mum I can be.

1) Be aware who is of influencing your teenager.
2) Get to know their friends.

3rd March 2016

Stay true to your ideas

Learn to say no

Don't confuse distraction for an opportunity.

Trust your gut.

Don't worry about speaking up.

Know what you don't know.

Don't be afraid to ask for help.

Good people are not always the right people.

You're more of a fighter than you think.

Stay focussed.

"Sometimes you just get practical."

9th March 2016

Took kids off to Brighton for Mother's Day weekend. I booked a hotel with a swimming pool and on the seafront. So, we walked to Brighton pier and watched the sunset and the kids played in all the arcade bits and pieces and ate yummy freshly made donuts.

15th March 2016

"Train up a child in the way he should go." Proverbs 22:6

So, I'm getting ready for the children to finish this Easter term and then get organised for travelling to America. I'm excited if a little nervous. Just getting the children on a long-haul flight, renting a car, etc. I know it will all be fine just quite hard work. If the kids are well behaved, we will be fine.

Then wrapping up the business and delegating plenty when I'm away. I know it will all be grand; it's just making sure I leave specific and detailed instructions – everyone knows what they are doing.

Also, leaving the animals.

Yesterday was a beautiful March spring day, glorious sunshine yet cold crisp air. I managed to get to the bank, post office, shop, swimming, choir, home for baking, boys to football, school run, cleaned home, and then church group; it was an interesting full discussion.

Thank God – followed by a peaceful sleep.

25th March 2016

Travelling to California. I love the feeling I have when travelling through the peaceful parts –it makes my heart feel still and humble.

Back to the holiday – Birmingham, Amsterdam, Portland, San Francisco, travel, motion, taxis, rental cars, bridges, blue skies, mountain views, talking, travelling, airport security, people, lots of people, accents.

Like – the change, the mountains, valleys, views, sun, movement, museum, planets, aquarium, time with kids, exploration, finding, bang, allowing running, ballroom, elements.

The only thing I don't like it when the kids fight and hurt one another.

Easter Sunday – Christ Is Risen

Booked hotel in LA, booked a hotel in LV.

The blue skies and my body feels great here – warm, happy, the movement is good, the flow is good. The skies are beautiful, the temperature is beautiful.

California. Lots of greenery, steep, steep hills, lots of people. Lots of healthy-looking people, especially here in Mill Valley. Affluent, peaceful, tranquil.

The houses look spacious, and the communities feel connected. The kids have just slotted into a social butterfly state. I feel content being here. I'm excited about flowing into the road trip…

31st March 2016, Amazing Grace

Anytime you fail or falter, you can "approach the throne of grace with confidence and receive God's mercy and forgiveness." Hebrews 4:16 NIV

I feel privileged to be able to take the children on a trip. We went to Universal Studios and immersed ourselves in the fantastic day. It did lay over me, happiness, and content pleasure.

We saw Water World, Jurassic Park, a tour of the park, special effects, Simpsons. We were enthralled. It was expensive, take a deep breath and put it into the pot! – Worth it. I have no clue, but the kids will hopefully relish and enjoy the moment forever.

Santa Monica – drawn to it – safely content with the beach, sea air, people running, skating, doing amazing tricks at the park. We had a good feed in a surfing restaurant and then a walk on the pier and then around the arcade – and caught the moment of the last sunset. Amazing day, back for a dip in the hot tub.

1st April 2016

Long drive from LA to LV. Amazing though and we did it. Here watching, absorbing…

Las Vegas.

2nd April 2016

Sincere heart.

I am experiencing some wonderfully different emotions – it's quite complicated to explain, but we are getting there – sometimes I blame myself about him and I feel scared that he must have been in much pain – did I contribute to that pain or ease that pain? It's complicated to even express.

Long drive to the Grand Canyon today from Las Vegas. We have had quite an experience. Walking around, adventure, looking, possibly a new school for the kids, Rainforest Café 7/11 souvenirs, swimming, hot tub.

3rd April 2016

Today, I sat with my darling eldest child and watched the sunrise over the Grand Canyon. What a magical experience. Wonder if he will remember this moment? It's okay to be angry.

It's okay to cry.

Acceptance.

4th April 2016

"He gives strength to the weary. Those who hope in the lord. Renew their strength." Isaiah 41:29

I do from time to time feel broken hearted, but today I feel immensely grateful – grateful for the holiday and what I have – I am blessed.

I conquered 12 hours driving myself with five kids in the car!

We drove through Arizona, Nevada, and California. For an amazing new life, a new beginning, success, destination, journey, achievement, good and bad.

Success, destination

Sunrise

Sunset

Palm trees

Blue skies

Dotted clouds

20th April 2016

Time has been all-consuming since returning home – Granny celebrating Queen's birthday.

Visiting the Jungle Book cinema.

Digger land

Hormones.

Money pay-out for the divorce.

Cleaning, mopping, kids' clothes, guests' work.

Gallery, exhibition.

Darling youngest son in hospital – tired, me, doctors, blood tests, etc.

Freedom, flow, acceptance

Be me. Who am I? Me and I. Be Juliet, authentic, believe

Knowledgeable, chatty, engaging, free flow – honest.

22nd April 2016

God used ordinary people to carry out his extraordinary plan.

What should I be doing? I can make a difference.

23rd April 2016

I am having a confliction. Maybe it's the house, maybe it's the time.

Chapter 24

END OF
AN
ERA

Allow the music
to flow ....

Hope. Renew. Soar.

"Have enough courage to trust one more time and always one more time." – Maya Angelou

27th April 2016

I feel strange. I cannot believe it's already the 27th of April, that's amazing, nearly five months into this year. And I am officially divorced now. I'm free.

I am Juliet

I am 37

I am a female entrepreneur

I am a businesswoman

I am fit, healthy, and able

I am strong, determined, focussed

I am a mother

I am a daughter

I am a sister

I am a niece

I am a dog, cat owner

I am an animal lover

I am a friend

I am unique

I am in control of my behaviour

I am happy

I am good

I am a great enthusiast

I am a yoga, meditator, listener

I am a carer

I am a doctor, nurse, therapist

I am a cook, cleaner, dishwasher-upper!

I am a traveller

I am an explorer

I am an adventurer

I am a Christian

I am a follower of God with him in my heart

I am sailing into an uncertain future, but I am surrounded by the faithfulness of God.

I am waiting to see what God will do.

I trust God with my future

I trust God with my children

I trust God I will make the right decisions

I trust God that I am in his presence

I trust God for wonderful surroundings

I trust God for focus, determination, and character

I trust God for the journey

I trust God that I will do what's best for me and the family

I trust God for all my directions, patience, hope, love, clarity, wisdom, freedom, choices.

29th April 2016

I have arrived at the Grand Pupp Karvloytory Hotel. It's almost like I have dreamt of this place.

2nd May 2016

"Let your light shine before others." Matthew 5:13-16

I have experienced a wonderful, if crazy out of my comfort zone few days. I am honestly pleased I have come. It's been an adventure of emotions, a real journey. My life is certainly not bland! Prague – full of stag parties encouraging 7am drinking, not something I can pull off! A trip on a coach to Casbad following through Czech countryside and a big-time ride to the Grand Hotel Pupp, stunning, relief, comfortable, and contained.

Swim and spa treatment – indulgence at its finest. The gather cloth collection and a rendezvous at Hotel Quinseda presidential suite for a champagne reception, introduction, and absorbance.

Trip to welcome drinks, buffet, dancing, delightful company, introductions, and food indulgence, dancing, movement.

Returned for a long walk, being left with my mind. Thoughts, issues surfaced, talked, and enjoyed the moments of looking, reflecting.

Changing for the gala dinner – creation, dress, sparkly tiara, more introductions, stunning dresses, conversation, supper, first-class, dancing, joy – danced the evening away.

I am beginning to feel again, open the heart, same emotions: destruction, self-doubt, not worthy, although free, reflection, future dedication.

Tired feet

Sleep

Wake up. Yoga, stretch, focus, meditation.

Faith

Trust

Love

Walked to the beautiful church service

Listened in German and stunning choir

Took the bread and rejoiced to the sharing of God's message

In-depth and deep conversation, chat, and welcomeness.

Openness

Chat, meeting, talk, talk

Girlie chat, good for me

Walked, talked, sipped champagne

Free – yeah – have devotion, dedication

Peace, peace, peace.

The Animal Kingdom Ball

4th May 2016

Returned from a lovely weekend.

Tired, afraid, certain, who knows?

Keep on keeping on

Protect that heart

Walk with Jesus by your side

5th May 2016

I was emotional and exhausted yesterday. Drained and overwhelmed, my heart hurt…Cry, tired, cry, tired. I was just pooped.

9th May 2016

Overcoming temptation.

1) Prepare yourself – aware in your mind
2) Brace for impact – detect Satan

10th May 2016

"Encourage one another daily." Hebrews 3:13

Sunday, 15th May 2016

I can say with confidence I rise on the wings of the dawn, if I settle on the far side of the sea, even there your hand will guide me; your right hand will hold me fast. Psalm 139:9

17th May 2016

I have Hawaiian friends here and we have been chatting, reminiscing on times in Hawaii. The fun, spiritual, carefree, surfing times – spent being, doing, sharing! What an immense joy and adventure that was. Sharing in the spirits of the island lives.

We went to Cambridge to go punting, a perfectly glorious day for it; followed by a trip to Aldeburgh for fish and chips.

Really awesome quality times.

19th May 2016

- I pray for when I am angry or getting angry.
- I pray for making the right decisions and judgments.
- I pray for patience, knowledge, wisdom, and the right words to share.
- I pray for my friends and their paths.
- I pray for my family, may they all find peace, comfort, and tranquillity.
- I pray for my children that they search their souls and enjoy adventures of learning, growth, and encouragement.
- I pray for all the ladies at the refuge or that are going through a troubled time in their relationships.
- I pray for clarity, patience, knowledge, understanding, sharing, confidence, ability, and movement to write and develop my story and me as a person, ability for moving forward for an abundant life.

21st May 2016

It's all good though and I'm graciously blessed by finding comfort and peace with Jesus by my side. How would he want me to react, live, be? I am at peace and cannot be completely and always high on emotion.

I enjoyed my dinner last night; it was lovely to be able to sit down outside in the presence of sunshine, sunset, children and conversation. Adult chat, interesting rites of passage and movement – friendship and no expectations – what a relief!

26th May 2016

What are the trivial things that waste my time, consume my energy?
Take care of things and make a change.

27th May 2016

I had a great bike ride yesterday, across the valley where we sat in the meadow and drank wine and ate crisps – talked and watched the swallows dancing in the sky. It was true quality. I walked the dogs this morning over to collect my bike. They were good.

I didn't sleep the best last night. It doesn't help to have a very active 5-year-old in bed. I sense life though and I'm happy.

Did the hoovering, some quiet meditation, yoga, pizza for breakfast. School bus and they are off. I've booked for this massage today and all day it's kids' sports day. I think I will be in and out.

31st May 2016

Getting prayers answered. Abide.
Dear God,
Deepest hopes, prayers, and dreams

- I have the deepest hope that I live a successful, kind, generous, calm, abundant, giving and caring life, guided by you. I have hope that I find success and calmness, each day of my life. I can share with people, animals, and myself.
- I hope that my family lives a happy life filled with joy and patience; I hope that my friends all have happy journeys.
- I hope that I make the right choices and decisions.
- I hope that I find comfort, reliance, security, faith, love, and nurturing with a new partner – that I am loved generously, taken care of, provided for.
- I hope that we can share good stories and enjoyable trips, sharing in the unique creation.
- I hope that if I am meant to be a mother to more children than I'm allowed the patience, tools and love to be able to care in your will.
- I pray for a world of peace, beauty, sharing, no conflict, fairness.

- I pray for being able to let go of the past – abiding in God's name that my prayers are answered when God is ready.

God's reply:
You are right; it's when I am ready. There is a journey ahead of you and allow my spirit to be with you in each day, a moment of your life. Jesus is walking next to you, holding your hand, your way, he had happy moments, sad moments, stoney moments and these are all normal. It's how you react and choose to get on with it in the knowing.
"With man, this is impossible, but not with God, all things are possible with God." Matthew 19:26
Remember, all things are possible when you walk in my word.
Take courage and faith, Juliet – Jesus is lord.

- Your family have their journey – be with them and share when you can.
- Equally your friends – be happy in their presence.
- Surround yourself with positivity and happiness, joy, and grow your armour – to fight the fight. Remember everyone has their paths. Be good, be humble, where you can – share my word, you are blessed; you are secure and have shelter. Let go of the negative past and welcome creativity and production. All is possible.

1st June 2016

- How to deal with children when they are angry at each other?
- How to be able to find more time to give generously?
- How to speak to people who are negative about me and the business?
- How to let go off the bad stuff?

Channelling the right energy in the right places.
Stop spreading rumours.
Feed the hungry.
Help those in trouble.
Attitudes and actions.

4th June 2016

You have a purpose.

I need purpose and direction and I go to God.

> There is never a right time to be in the wrong place with the wrong person.
>
> Don't go there.

Aware of lust.

Sex is a path, not a destination.

Prayer and discipline – best weapons.

Text a friend to ask if they need prayer.

American circus

Drink a little too much

Helicopter flying

Sunshine

Cathedral service

Swimming

Kids camping

Ceremony for sports awards

Flying helicopters and sleeping 10 hours!

9th June 2016

I feel quite off track today and I don't mind. I'm not getting stressed about it.

Life is still turning and focussing, working, washing and allowing.

I am avidly loving and moving with life.

Watching kids play cricket.

Getting nails done with my sisters.

Obtaining two new cats to the family.

Helping children with their lives.

Being able to share food and drink with friends.

Opening my home to guests, who are equally happy and sad.

Being able to communicate with friends, old and new.

Feel a love spark of interaction and self-giving.

Sharing my spirit and soul with the world.

Being able to run in the countryside with the dogs.

Being able to plan for the week ahead without me being here in the business.

Tuesday, 21ˢᵗ June 2016

Learning to love – follow the way of love.

God, thank you that you are love and that you love me. Help me love others the way Jesus showed us so that the whole world will know I am your child.

Today I pray for love:

The sun's energy.

The birds that sing.

The women that clean.

The people that work unhappily.

The people struggling.

The people who are sad.

The people who are lonely.

The people who can't open accept.

I pray for my siblings' stability.

I pray for my friends both achieving and those struggling.

I pray for the old people Age UK Suffolk.

I pray for those struggling in business.

I pray for people with injuries, hurt, vulnerable.

I pray for my compliant and different children. That I may serve each one of their purposes and be the mother that God intended me to be.

End discrimination.

There is none in God's eyes.

We are all equal.

"Whoever believes in him shall not perish but have eternal life." John 3:16

"For God does not show favouritism." Romans 2:11

Today, I pray for God to meet everyone's needs. For the wonderful, beautiful, stunning ocean, the waves, the soft water, the glistening seashore. I thank God for the blue sky, green trees, lush landscape, and abundance of plants, wildlife. I thank God for the amazing food and drink. I thank God for the less fortunate than us. I wish for peace, tranquillity, humility, space, calm, openness, for the next step.

For letting go.

For my soul's peace.

For granting understanding, patience, wisdom, hope.

7th July 2016

I know I am on the right path.

Thank you, Lord, for showing me.

Taking time to breathe and flow.

Bless everyone around me.

Fill them with your peace and grace.

Delay – the protective hand of our heavenly father.

Burn the bridges to your old lifestyle.

3rd August 2016

An amazing creature, committed, compassionate, sharing person. A touchable, trainable, teachable, believable business and with hope, enhancement, belief, dedication.

Be powerful in empowering others to share in the abundance of wildlife, nature, water, trees, to be able to change anxiety, stress, and fear into positive. We are enhancing creations.

Where I am: trees, water, cabin, plants, animals, hope, care, cosy, feeling content, hard work, peaceful, creation, life-changing, stable, happy, clean, comfortable, delicious, simple, TV, escape, music, singing, learning, medicine of change, power, healing, steady.

- A loving partner, a companion that's able to take care financially, spiritually, carefully.
- Romantic
- Children and space
- Work and business
- Security and love.

Thank you, Lord, for listening to my asks, desires, prayers, hopes.

5th August 2016

Thank you for allowing me to progress.

The confrontation.

Alone I stand with confrontation.

Developed from stillness of quiet.

The wrong and right – who is it for me to decide?

Other than letting go of the inner turmoil.

Of self-destruction and doubt.

Who knows and feels such pity and dread and the exchange for freedom, liberation?

I'm hurt and low, accept letting go, change. The ride has got tough and rough, and the pride feels determined and beaten.

Although I must remain strong, developed, focussed, ready to fight and challenge each day with its changing emotions, directions, and passing.

Happiness is what?

The life, the abundance, the freedom of accepting self and being content, with the airs, graces, hurts, upset, disappointment, disenfranchise and the devastating loss of closeness? The heart crushed and destroyed – although emerging from time to time? The peace in finding grace, love, trust, hope, forgiveness, and tranquillity? The ability to sleep guilt-free and with no fear?

The letting go of the past self and allowing the new to emerge, let it be. Allow the goodness, the righteousness to embody all the days of your life.

It's been quite amazing the last week.

Off to the IOW tomorrow. A journey – experience – life is just happening, unravelling, engrossing, and embedding in.

I pray for perseverance – I pray for those going through difficult times – and Lord, please allow them, greet them, and enable them to have the strength to give up.

Lord, I pray for all parents, carers, guardians, grandparents this week – and ask your Lord to enable, give, and preserve their wisdom as they face the task, responsibility of raising children.

Lord, I pray for toxic relationships this week for those experiencing a hard, struggle, trying situation within their relationships – and that you grant them time and patience and peace for some needed consideration.

Today, 10th August 2016

Don't be afraid.

I thank you for the spark

I thank you for the change

I thank you for the grounding

I thank you for space

I thank you for the time

I thank you for the patience
I thank you for the breath
I thank you for the food
I thank you for the bread of life
I thank you for the words
I thank you for the encouragement
I thank you for the friendship
I thank you for the people
I thank you for the hugs
I thank you for the conversations
I thank you for the feeling
I thank you for the law of attraction
I thank you for the clothes
I thank you for the decisions
"Can two walk together unless they are agreed?"

Sunday 13th August 2016

- Self-control
- Mastery
- Understanding
- Preventing evil in myself
- Honouring people
- Respecting people
- Discipline
- Getting a grip

Desires

Spending

Anger

Dear Lord, guide me on how to flow with this day and this coming week. I feel the enlightenment, the change of tack and path. Ready to rewrite my life and let the adventure begin again. I know that I'm on the path of righteousness – I am just asking for your guidance in how best to proceed; right from wrong, desires, frustrations.

The simple overwhelming exhaustion. I was tired last night.

Freedom from fear

The pleasure of thought and study you give to the truth you hear will be the measure of virtue and knowledge that comes back to you.

It will transform you.

Grow spiritually

Build better relationships

Get past worry

Break a bad habit

Get healing from emotional wounds.

The seeds get strong – small ideas like the mustard seed have amazing potential to grow to immense strength.

Five things

Growth of a seed

Planting it – nurturing it

Grows while sleeping or waking

Harvest comes and creates and gives an abundance

– Reminds me of ideas

1) Remember Satan never takes a day off
2) Identify the sin you're most prone to
3) Keep your spiritual tank full
4) Walk in God's strength, not your own.

16th August 2016

I accept that I am me.

I will speak my truth always.

I will allow myself to be certain of situations and keep within my self-control and admiration.

I will be proud of who I am, what I have achieved, where I am going.

I will seek understanding in situations.

I will be honest with myself, my children, family, and friends.

I will speak the truth to all around me and most importantly myself.

I am enabling, granting the healing process to take place.

I will try and be the best I can, continually be improving.

17th August 2016

A new soul is compatible in the acceptance of where it is meant to be.
For connection, feeling, spark, touch.

18th August 2016

New relationship
New friendship
New course
New direction
Strong, determined, positive parent.
Empowering people and places.
I thank you for enabling me to be kissed on the beach at Primrose Hill – under the moonlight.
I thank you for granting me an evening of passion, touch, and exchanging in unique activities between two people.
Thank you for my body being able to function and appreciated and more.
I thank you for getting me home safely, for my kids, all to be comfortable, secure, and happy. I pray, particularly, for my third son's health.
Who knows what the future must hold...?
"Be transformed by the renewing of your mind." Romans 12:2
Who knows what the future holds?
Belief, true acceptance
Thank you for allowing me to feel
Thank you for allowing me to kiss
Thank you for allowing me to hold
Thank you for allowing me to open
Thank you for allowing me to converse
Thank you for allowing me to share
Lord, let me see the way to escape
You offer when I'm tempted.
Give me the strength to accept your help I can stay faithful to you.
I know this is your desire for me and thank you that you are at work in me.
What's my temptation? Is it this new chap?
Great blessings.

Tuesday, 23rd August 2016

"As we have the opportunity, let us do good to all people."
   Galatians 6:10 NIV

So, resonate

A new him in my life and pray that I find new hope and direction of encouragement and support and comfort, even a hug. I pray that we come to some understanding and some assurance and peace. Thank you, Lord, for changing tack. It honestly means an immense amount in my heart.

Watch and pray you do not fall into temptation.

Go for it

Enjoy life

Live life

Always be guided by the spirit. God will keep me on track.

Plant the seed and watch it grow

Allow it to be

Steady in progression

Flow free

Freedom of acceptance

Let it all go all– let it breathe

Try not to over think and thank God for the good feelings.

Invite the clarity

Open/stretch

Heaviness and relaxation

Grace

Balance to come to you

No force

Stillness

New start of the year.

Change patterns – change habits

Tap into subtle

Yin practice dedicates 30 days.

Look at why I have the habits I have.

Invite a spirit of contemplation behind these decisions I'm making.

Breathe differently

Open the mind – curiosity about what's going on in your life – what choices, what habits, supporting you – make some changes – light, knowing, and clarity.

Thoughts to let go and habits to let go
Let anger go
Gather new contributor attributes.

29th August 2016

Today, I pray for:
My children and their dreams and passions.
My new relationship, the feelings that I have
The healing of what the heart feels.
The healing of the body.
The love and acceptance of the physical body.
Open the eyes and heart, Lord, I can see you.
I pray for a step son that he has a happy life.
I pray for my friends going through their troubled times.
I pray for my parents and siblings.
I pray for people moving into their new homes.
I pray for peace and progression.
I pray for a placid and calm future.
I pray for his job and direction and hope.
I pray for all my past relationships and thank you.
I pray for all the people who are feeling ill/sick/health bad.
I pray for the lovely weather – abundant sunshine, refreshing rain.

5th September 2016

Thankful for my time on the Isle of Wight.
For the people in the Isle of Wight in trouble.
For all those sailing in the races.
For my new connection – his patience, peace, and acceptance of me.
I pray that a job is finding him soon and we can spend time together.
I pray for new friendships, relationships, exploration, peace, excitement, desire, passion, and peace for us both.
I pray for the business and guests and their tranquillity.
I pray for patience, direction, clarity, and feeling.
Amen

Tuesday, 6th September 2016

Open the day with God's mercies and blessings.

End the day with God's protection and safeguard.

Today:

Thank you for the feelings with him.

For smiling.

For movement.

For finances.

For food.

For making choices.

For talking.

For my space.

For freedom.

For staff.

For my business.

For allowing letting go.

For protection.

For security.

For warmth.

For my family.

8th September 2016

G – give what you can to people who need it.

I – independent sharing.

V – very important to share and share-alike.

I – in everything. Give thanks.

N – now go share the good news.

G – go and be a Fisherwoman of life.

9th September 2016

The explanation.

Be in awe.

A – awesome beauty

W – wonderful light

E – exhilaration feeling

11th September 2016

Anniversary of September 11 attack

S – shining
I – iridescent
L – living, living
V – vulnerable
E – ending, endurance, endeavour, embrace
R – robust, resilient, repellent, radiance
L – loving, living, lively
I – individual, indifferent
N – not known, negligent, negotiate, never, a new beginning
I – irregular, in sync
N – new embrace
G – growing, gradient, gradual, great unknown.

As I embark on this new relationship, I feel the fear but all the excitement. I have the peace and acceptance – that we live now. It's good to plan, expect, control, life is for living right now.
Celebrate life.
I thank you, God, for my life. My 37, nearly 38, years of being here. It's unique, fabulous, different, changing, loving, accepting.
I have hidden your word in my heart.
Nothing can separate me from the love of God.
Never give up

- Feeling
- Thinking
- Believing

Vision
To live a clear, happy, abundant, healthy, fruitful, steady, free, liberated, supported, courageous life.
Be a wonderful mother.
To build a house, next to a lake and the sea.
Have a productive business.
Support, friends, family, community.

I thank you today for –
Last week
Trip to London
Walk around the V and A
Friends
Family
Birthday
Business
Open-mindedness
Strength
Sunshine
Animals
Plants
Bees
Walking
Glistening
Sparkles
Determination
Freedom
Hope, faith, life encouragement
Belief
Acceptance of self, yoga, breathing, schedule.

26th September 2016

I put all my trust in God. What is happening now is happening for a reason and it's in God's plan.

Let God grant his peace – I am in his hands – let's not read deeply into things – other than allow the peace to grant us stability, freedom, liberation, hope, happiness, calmness.

Thank you for the football, the beautiful wedding, the clay shoot, the transgression, the change in direction– the development and creation of a new relationship – the start, me unravelling, the animals, the harvest, the autumn change.

Clothe me in your protection.

Clothe me in your presence.

Clothe me in your righteousness.

29th September 2016

1) Always show appreciation.
2) Put others first – serve wholeheartedly.
3) Serve others gladly.
4) Forgive it, resolve it, and move beyond it.
5) Make time for the people that/who matter.

October 2016

Lord, I thank you for:
Friendship
Sailing
The sea
People
Landscape
Running
Health
Food
Freedom
My children
My new relationship
My parents
Wisdom
Connection
Meditation
Prayer
Pride
Family
Yoga
Peace
Conversation
Wine
Water
Passing time
Comfortable
Intercourse
Kissing

Cuddles
Belief
Movement
Discussion
Future
Plane
Business
Concentration
Wise words from our God

Why the change?
Because there is another path to pursue of joy and happiness.

Why him?
Because it's time to enjoy different adventures, aspects, and paths of the journey, exploration, friendships, aliveness.

Why the children?
Because you are a mother and that's what God intended, money buys to help you accomplish great things, achieve, explore, and journey, and theme for groundedness, helpfulness and female spirit.

Why hospitality?
Because you are good at sharing and housing, providing, enabling, protecting, sharing, compassion, kindness, acceptance.

Why are people nasty?
Because it's a realisation of the devil, keeping protected, allowing God in to serve, being alive, and realising that there are imperfections and important to accept, move on, breathe, everyone is on their paths, directions.

Important for their negativity not to swell and impact my life.
My eating habits, fears, anxiety, self-doubt, suicide, death, mental health, domestic abuse.

You have been given what you can handle to live a life of joy, understanding, relationships, and compassion. Being kind and good and grounded in spirit to keep the channels open.

The moon – the communal movement and of the tides.
The ocean – the right distance.

- I thank you for letting go of my diaries to get them written up.
- I thank you for my future.
- I thank you for my past
- I thank you for that beautiful view of the Solent, the ocean and being able to run there.
- I thank you for direction, challenges, what happens is great.
- I thank you for my parents, for their love, support, concern.
- I respect the direction I put my trust in the lord, let's create, make, support, and trust, faith, and love – for an abundant successful future.

11ᵗʰ October 2016

Learning to reorganise when we are restless, irritable, and discontent.
Safe in surrender and dependency on God.
Feel that
Breathe that
Allow it
Free it
Believe into
Balance it
Take charge of it
Hold in
Be content
Be allowing
Hold God

What is God telling me this morning?
To pray for those suffering.
To be thankful and appreciate what I have.
To love my children and support and encourage them.
To allow the spirit to move through me.
To have hope, trust, and faith in the new relationship.
To have the grace to share with those.
To send wishes to him and his journey and his new job.

To remain grounded and focussed on business.

To clear out the clutter and to not neglect my friends.

To share with friends, family, the hope, feelings, and direction.

To walk the dogs and breathe the air and appreciate the surroundings.

Each morning is filled with the father, son, and Holy Spirit. To free and allow patience in everything I do.

Amen.

14th October 2016

- stop rushing
- breathe each moment
- I have a beautiful daughter, it's her 6th Birthday.
- I thank you for your love, family, and hope
- I thank you for peace, understanding, acceptance, belief, truth, following grace in abundance, courage.

15th October 2016

I pray for today – being able to wake up, do, create, and more.

I pray for not taking simple movements and actions for granted.

I pray that they boys have a good time in London.

I pray that goals are scored in his football game

I hope we find a common bond of compatibility and that we flourish in nurturing, understanding, compassion, desire, friendship, mutual respect, faith, ultimate trust and hope!

Hope, hope for a great future.

- That the London boat party will be a success.
- That my friends and family have a special and wonderful time.
- That we get there safely, securely, and patiently.

That I am confident in speaking and provide humility and direction of God's presence!

What last year especially taught me is that you never know what's around the corner, even with the best plans and organisations.

Stay true to truth and surround ourselves with positive, inspirational, and motivational people – all will be okay.

Enjoy the life, the plan – wee reminders of music, art, creation, change, smile, it's like a big brother giving me some reassurance and adding a spark…

He leads me by still water. The lord is my shepherd.

I have been meaning to stop by the graveyard for a while. Now here I am at the church gates. Today I stopped. I was given the time today.

I am not really used to be given time to stop, reflect, slow down, absorb.

Life slows down in graveyards. The clouds are still flowing overhead; the sun peeks out from time to time. The birds chat away together in the trees, a lonely butterfly flies past, the trees are green, the insects crawling – distant movement and humming of a crash – airplanes, telephone calls. Yet, it is still. All is still.

I thought about what to bring. I found a lonely flight dart in the car.

Bless your life,
Let it be an extension of your state of being giving new life to your life
Bless your past,
that it turns into wisdom
Bless your future,
That it may be filled with opportunity and adventure
Bless the challenges in your life,
May they initiate you into greatness
Bless the divine in you,
the power within you.

Juliet x

Photograph Credit: Helena G Anderson

If you, or someone you know, have been affected by subjects mentioned in Growing Wings, my hope is that you realise you are not alone and that it is possible to create your own masterpiece.

However it is vitally important to reach out to your support network or professional services for help. Below are some of the charities and places of refuge that helped me, and in all honesty put me back on track as I would not be here today without them.

Refuge

Supports women, children and men experiencing domestic violence
Helpline: 0808 2000 247 www.refuge.co.uk

Women's aid

A grassroots federation working together to provide life-saving services
www.womensaid.org.uk

Samaritans

A unique charity dedicated to reduce feelings of isolation and disconnection that can lead to suicide
Helpline: 116 123 www.samaritans.org

Mind

Mental health charity providing advice and support to empower anyone experiencing mental health problems
www.mind.org.uk

Winston's Wish

Supports bereaved children, young people, their families and the professionals who support them
Helpline: 08088 020 021 www.winstonswish.org

Relate

Offers counselling services for every type of relationship
www.relate.org.uk

Rethink

Help people severely affected by mental health to improve their lives
Helpline: 0808 801 0525 www.rethink.org